MEXICO'S DEMOCRACY AT WORK

Political and Economic Dynamics

edited by
Russell Crandall
Guadalupe Paz
Riordan Roett

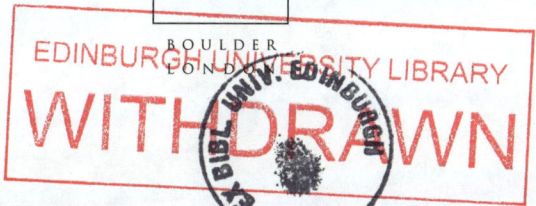

LYNNE
RIENNER
PUBLISHERS

BOULDER
LONDON

Published in the United States of America in 2005 by
Lynne Rienner Publishers, Inc.
1800 30th Street, Boulder, Colorado 80301
www.rienner.com

and in the United Kingdom by
Lynne Rienner Publishers, Inc.
3 Henrietta Street, Covent Garden, London WC2E 8LU

Library of Congress Cataloging-in-Publication Data
Mexico's democracy at work : political and economic dynamics / edited by
Russell Crandall, Guadalupe Paz, and Riordan Roett.
     p.   cm.
   Includes bibliographical references and index.
   ISBN 1-58826-300-2 (hardcover : alk. paper) — ISBN 1-58826-325-8
(pbk. : alk. paper)   1. Mexico—Politics and government—1988–
2. Mexico—Economic policy.   3. Mexico—Foreign economic relations.
I. Crandall, Russell, 1971–   II. Paz, Guadalupe, 1970–   III. Roett, Riordan,
1938–
F1236.M4865 2004
972.08'35—dc22

                                                            2004009270

British Cataloguing in Publication Data
A Cataloguing in Publication record for this book
is available from the British Library.

Printed and bound in the United States of America

        The paper used in this publication meets the requirements
  (∞) of the American National Standard for Permanence of
        Paper for Printed Library Materials Z39.48-1992.

   5   4   3   2   1

Contents

Acknowledgments   vii

1   Introduction: The Challenges of Democratic
    Change in Mexico   1
    Russell Crandall

Part 1: Confronting Political Challenges

2   From Electoral Authoritarianism to Democratic
    Consolidation   9
    Andreas Schedler

3   Mexico's Changing Social and Political Landscape   39
    Federico Reyes-Heroles

Part 2: The Challenges of Economic Transformation

4   Mexico's Domestic Economy: Policy Options
    and Choices   61
    Russell Crandall

v

5   The Fox Administration and the Politics of
     Economic Transition   89
     Manuel Pastor and Carol Wise

6   Mexico's Economic Transformation Under NAFTA   119
     Gary Gereffi and Martha A. Martínez

Part 3: Foreign Policy Dynamics

7   Mexico and the Western Hemisphere   153
     Riordan Roett

8   Mexico's Economic Ties with Europe:
     Business as Unusual?   173
     Javier Santiso

Part 4: Conclusion

9   Making Mexico's Democracy Work Effectively   191
     Guadalupe Paz

List of Acronyms   197
Bibliography   201
The Contributors   219
Index   221
About the Book   232

Acknowledgments

We would like to thank the various individuals who assisted in the completion of this volume. To the contributing authors we owe a debt of gratitude for the time invested and the patience required of them during the publication process. We would also like to acknowledge Mari Jensen for her help with the editing process. To the reviewers of the manuscript we are indebted for their insightful input, which proved invaluable as we prepared the final version. A special thanks goes to Lynne Rienner, Lisa Tulchin, and the superb publishing team at Lynne Rienner Publishers. And, finally, we would like to express our deepest gratitude to the William and Flora Hewlett Foundation for its generous support over the years; this and eight other volumes have been the product of the Hewlett Foundation's support to the SAIS Western Hemisphere/Latin American Studies Program.

—*Russell Crandall, Guadalupe Paz, and Riordan Roett*

I

Introduction:
The Challenges of Democratic
Change in Mexico

Russell Crandall

In 1994, Mexico was simultaneously experiencing social, economic, and political crises: the indigenous uprising in the southern state of Chiapas, the economic effects from the December 1994 devaluation of the peso, and several high-profile political scandals within the ruling Institutional Revolutionary Party (Partido Revolucionario Institucional, or PRI). More recently, however, Mexico has witnessed a peaceful transition of power from one-party rule—a transition accompanied by macroeconomic stability—and limited, yet important, improvements in addressing the country's many social problems.

This rapid and radical transformation from an "emerging market" in critical condition in the mid-1990s to a more economically stable, democratic country might have suggested in 2000, when optimism ran high, that Mexico had finally embarked on a path toward what Francis Fukuyama calls the "end of history," where the most pressing political, social, and economic issues have been resolved.[1] Yet a central theme of *Mexico's Democracy at Work* is that the country is still far from the end of history. Rather, although the political and economic reforms carried out over the past several years are noteworthy and impressive, Mexico remains confronted by a seemingly endless list of issues that the country desperately needs to address effectively if it is to fully institutionalize its political, economic, and social progress.

What is readily apparent after additional scrutiny is that behind Mexico's genuine success story lies a set of unresolved challenges. Take, for example, the case of the North American Free Trade Agreement (NAFTA), the avenue through which Mexican exports to the United States have sky-rocketed. Since NAFTA's inception in 1994, the explosion of bilateral trade has been predicated on an increasingly precarious maquiladora (export-oriented manufacturing businesses) sector in northern Mexico that is facing fierce competition from Asian manufacturers. The Mexican export sector was also severely damaged by the post–September 11, 2001, economic downturn in the United States, demonstrating that macroeconomic stabilization has not guaranteed that Mexico's economic strategies are without risk.

The difficulties with NAFTA were reinforced on January 1, 2003, when the United States and Mexico completely eliminated tariffs on a number of tradable items. Although the significance of these tariff reductions was hardly noticed in the United States, the move was met with significant media coverage and civil protest in Mexico. In particular, Mexican farmers feared that the elimination of trade restrictions on a number of agricultural items would unleash a flood of U.S. imports into Mexico, virtually wiping out Mexican producers in the process. Although contrary to some of the goals set forth by the Mexican government in the 1990s, little was done to prepare the Mexican agricultural sector for this day of reckoning. This example illustrates that Mexico's admirable reform path—in this case, NAFTA—has not always been accompanied by the necessary public policies that would better allow Mexico to more effectively manage NAFTA in the future.

As the contributors to this volume show, for a majority of Mexicans to see benefits from the liberalization process, Mexico needs to reinforce its reform path with aggressive and effective policies in more than just the economic realm. The chapters in this volume make it clear that Mexico's challenges are as much political and social as economic. More specifically, the authors are concerned that, with the democratic transition now in the consolidation stage, Mexican political institutions might not be up to the task of addressing the many still-unresolved challenges of the upcoming years and decades.

Many pressing issues were necessarily overlooked while the political system was undergoing major reforms in the 1990s, and as Mexico entered the twenty-first century the country was, understandably, singularly focused on the historic elections in 2000 that ushered in the first non-PRI president in Mexico's modern political history. Yet overall, as several authors in this volume demonstrate, gains made by Mexico's political authorities during the 1990s can be seen as remarkable in their own right.

At the start of the new millennium, Mexico can be characterized as managing the paradox of success. Through the country's achievements on the broad political and economic issues—for example, the hotly contested midterm congressional elections in July 2003—Mexico has the luxury (and obligation) to start focusing on the matters that have previously taken a backseat to macroeconomic stabilization: stable employment, income distribution, tax collection, demographics, investments in education and other sorts of human capital, immigration accords with the United States, to name several key concerns. These issues certainly warranted great attention and were never completely off the policy radar screen; however, it is only now that they increasingly are becoming policy priorities. By paying attention to the so-called micro issues, this volume hopes to shed light on the most pressing challenges confronting the country both today and tomorrow.

In a sense, this new Mexico is many "Mexicos." It is certainly global; it certainly means a country inextricably linked to NAFTA and economic integration with the United States, the Mexico of democracy, and the Mexico of increased participation and growing assertiveness in international affairs. As Riordan Roett makes clear in Chapter 7, after decades of suspicion of outsiders and a "don't ask, don't tell" policy regarding international issues, Mexico is expanding its international role. The country's new foreign policy maturity even includes experimenting with openly disagreeing with the United States on key global issues, as revealed when officials in Mexico City publicly debated siding against the United States during United Nations Security Council deliberations over Iraq in 2002–2003. The Fox administration has pressured the United States to reform its immigration policy in order to accommodate the nearly 25 percent of the Mexican adult workforce that is employed in the United States, four to five million of whom reside there illegally.[2] In addition, Mexico has partnered with the United States to create a more secure border.[3]

At the same time, however, this is the Mexico whose capital city has one of the world's highest kidnapping rates. Additionally, the nation suffers from an alarming level of poverty, a poor investment in infrastructure and education, and a profound lack of public security in some parts of the country. Mexico has enjoyed an explosion of foreign investment intent on taking advantage of the country's propitious geographic and economic relationship with the United States, but is largely unprepared to assist its farmers with the inevitable increased competition brought about by trade liberalization.

This volume provides a snapshot of the challenges of democratic change in Mexico. In addition to chronicling the evolution of the country's recent political and economic transformations, this book takes the important, yet often difficult, step of suggesting Mexico's direction in upcoming years. What is readily clear is that, despite what NAFTA, low inflation and macroeconomic stability, and "amigo diplomacy"[4] with the United States suggest, Mexico's political and economic development will continue to be difficult and, unfortunately, rife with frustrations and setbacks.

Manuel Pastor and Carol Wise write in Chapter 5 that part of the difficulty rests in the nature of Mexico's path of political liberalization that led to the democratic transfer of national power in 2000. Unlike the more dramatic political transitions that occurred in Argentina and Brazil in the mid-1980s, for example, Mexico's transition was a gradual unraveling of a one-party state. Andreas Schedler's term for this process (see Chapter 2), one that ended 71 years of electoral authoritarianism in Mexico, is democratization by elections. Pastor, Wise, and Schedler believe that the paradoxical result of such a gradual democratization process is that Mexico's political and economic institutions are not fully equipped to handle the challenges of continuing reform in democratic, politically liberalized economic systems.

Gary Gereffi and Martha Martínez reinforce that point in Chapter 6 when they argue that Mexico's impressive liberalization of the economy beginning in 1985—and, more specifically, the export-oriented strategies—masked several "missed opportunities"; overlooking those opportunities made Mexico's economy more vulnerable to external and internal shocks. Paralleling Gereffi and Martínez, in Chapter 8 Javier Santiso addresses Mexico's "great transformation" into a North American economy and how that poses formidable obstacles—and opportunities—for Mexico's economic relationship with the European Union.

Although cautionary, this volume's message should not be viewed as pessimistic; rather, Mexico is firmly situated in phase two of its political and economic reform path. Yet, unlike the dramatic phase one of democratization at the national level and an unprecedented restructuring of its economy during the 1980s and 1990s, phase two is a lower-profile, long-term process. Indeed, in many respects phase two represents efforts to move reform from the "macro" to the "micro," both economically and politically. Federico Reyes-Heroles (Chapter 3) sees this second phase as a social and political revolution of sorts. Mexico's twenty-first-century demographics and social problems will place tremendous pressure on the country's still-fragile democratic institutions and relatively untested economic strategies.

Only when the second phase is completed—most likely decades from now—will Mexico enter into the end of history, when the country's economic, political, and social debates will resemble Australia and Denmark more than Brazil and Guatemala. Membership in this exclusive club is not guaranteed, however; in fact, Mexico could easily remain in phase two indefinitely. What is clear is that Mexico needs to confront its current position as aggressively as it did democratization and economic liberalization over the past decade. This volume does not pretend to cover every aspect of Mexico's contemporary political, economic, and social fabric. Instead, the book attempts to set the appropriate framework within which to continue to analyze Mexico's future paths.

Notes

1. See Francis Fukuyama, "The End of History?" *The National Interest* 16 (Summer 1989): 3–18; Forrest Colburn, *Latin America at the End of Politics* (Princeton, NJ: Princeton University Press, 2002); and Russell Crandall, "Revolution on Hold?" *SAIS Review* 13, no. 1 (Winter–Spring 2003): 273–277.

2. Earl H. Fry, "North American Economic Integration: Policy Options," *Policy Papers on the Americas*, July 2003, vol. 14, study 8, pp. 4–5.

3. Ibid., pp. 8, 14.

4. Richard Wolffe, "The Harsh Realities of 'Amigo Diplomacy,'" *Financial Times,* September 7, 2001, p. 19.

PART I

Confronting Political Challenges

2

From Electoral Authoritarianism to Democratic Consolidation

Andreas Schedler

During the last quarter of the twentieth century, Mexico accomplished a peaceful transition from authoritarian, hegemonic party rule to democratic interparty competition. The literature tends to treat the country's protracted process of democratization as an exceptional case, one that comparative experiences offer little guidance in understanding. This chapter, in contrast, reconceptualizes the Mexican transition as a prototypical process of democratization by elections. Postrevolutionary Mexico, it argues, belonged to a kind of political regime, electoral authoritarianism, that was widespread in the past, and is spreading again in the present. Such electoral autocracies hold regular elections under conditions of relative pluralism while limiting the uncertainty of electoral outcomes by authoritarian means, such as electoral fraud, corruption, and coercion. As the chapter lays out, such ambivalent regimes tend to erode through processes of democratization by elections, in which the struggle for votes (electoral competition) goes hand in hand with the struggle over institutions (electoral reform).

In Mexico, the virtuous circle of competition and reform led to an incremental, yet profound, transformation of the political arena. After decades of hegemonic one-party rule, the regime of the "institutionalized revolution" ended up revolutionizing itself. This chapter traces the main contours of Mexico's dynamics of electoral change from the 1970s until the watershed election of 2000, in which the ruling Institutional Revolutionary Party (Partido Revolucionario Institucional, PRI) finally lost the presidency. The alternation of power in the year 2000, the chapter further argues, symbolizes the end of the country's protracted transition to democratic interparty competition. But the change in power did more than that. It signaled a further momentous achievement of Mexican democratization—the simultaneous closure of democratic consolidation.[1]

Mexican Exceptionalism

At the presidential election held on July 2, 2000, Mexican citizens converged to vote out of power the longest-reigning political party in the world, the PRI. Under various labels, it had monopolized the country's presidency during most of the twentieth century. In 1929, in the aftermath of the civil wars of 1910–1920, the party was founded to put an end to armed strife between regional warlords and rival revolutionary factions. Without a doubt, in its 71 years of continuous rule, the party did accomplish its basic mission. The PRI brought Mexico social peace and political stability to a degree widely admired throughout Latin America. At the same time, it sustained an authoritarian regime that looked as exceptional as its longevity.

Scholars have been creative in coining terms to classify the unclassifiable. Most commonly they have described the postrevolutionary regime as a civilian, inclusive, corporatist, and hyperpresidential authoritarian regime held together by a pragmatic, patronage-based state party. Postrevolutionary Mexico kept looking like a strange animal in the menagerie of political regimes, even with the widespread acceptance of Giovanni Sartori's concept of a *hegemonic party system*.[2] As a generic category developed just for the two cases of Mexico and Poland (even if, in principle, it is open to wider application), the idea of one-party hegemony has done little to insert Mexico into the comparative debate. Quite the contrary, the idea reaffirmed the country's exceptional status.

Mexico's semiliberal authoritarianism *with adjectives* seemed to be perpetually out of sync with the Latin American pendulum moving from democracy to authoritarianism and back.[3] In the 1960s and 1970s, during the harsh times of *bureaucratic authoritarianism*,[4] the country appeared as an island of civil liberties and stable civilian rule. In contrast, during the 1980s and early 1990s, as the *third wave*[5] of democratization carried most of Latin America to the shores of democracy, Mexico appeared to be a bastion of nondemocratic rule.

Ironically, the country of the institutional revolution had joined the third wave early on, enacting significant liberalizing reform in 1977. Yet Mexico's protracted transition dragged on for two decades of electoral reform, postelectoral conflicts, and intense electoral competition before reaching its felicitous culmination in the 2000 presidential election.[6] The

2000 election confirmed the country's membership in the community of Latin American democracies, putting a tangible end to Mexico's long-standing political exceptionalism. Today, one may consider contemporary Mexico a normal Latin American democracy. However, its democratic transition looked so different from previous transitions in southern Europe and South America that many observers concluded that comparative experiences offered little insight into regime change in Mexico. In their view, the country's transition was as exceptional as the regime it brought to an end. The radical particularities of its sui generis transition to democracy seemed to render any recourse to the comparative literature problematic.[7]

Without a doubt, regime change in Mexico displayed some peculiar traits. Driven by a series of electoral reforms starting in 1977, the country went through the unusual experience of regime change without government change (the latter finally taking place in 2000). Under the deceptive surface of constitutional continuity as well as continuity in government, Mexico carried out a silent revolution in its electoral infrastructure, party system, legislative politics, and federal relations. Clearly, when compared with early third-wave transitions in southern Europe and South America, the Mexican process looked like a distinctly postmodern phenomenon, a transition characterized by the absence of events: no collapse, no foundational elections, no big pacts, no constitutional assembly, and (before 2000) no alternation of power.[8]

A small but growing body of literature has started comparing the transformation of Mexican politics with the demise of one-party regimes in other places, such as Taiwan and Senegal.[9] But overall, students of Mexican democratization still tend to conceive their case as a unique beast that escapes the tools of comparative analysis. Granted, the existing comparative literature suffers from a certain "explanatory deficiency" when it comes to making sense of the Mexican transition.[10] However, the country's alleged exceptionalism is less a matter of empirical facts than of theoretical frames. Perceptions of exceptionality always depend on conceptions of regularity. Classifying the Mexican transition as either an outlier or a prototype depends on the answer one gives to the question, What is the Mexican case a case of?

Electoral Authoritarianism

Since the advent of mass elections, parties and politicians have tried to limit electoral uncertainty by institutional design or factual manipulation. Examples abound of political elites struggling to control electoral outcomes through fraud, force, and restrictive legal regulation in Europe, Latin America, and the United States during the nineteenth and early twentieth centuries.[11] In the twentieth century, postrevolutionary Mexico managed to institutionalize a smooth combination of electoral politics and elite control—one which was widely admired and copied (often unsuccessfully) by political elites wishing "to rule perpetually and to rule with consent."[12] Recently, at the culmination of the third wave of global democratization, increasing numbers of authoritarian rulers have rediscovered the charms of staying in power by staging *managed* elections.[13] Especially in sub–Saharan Africa and the successor states of the Soviet Union, autocratic leaders have established restrictive electoral regimes that "cunningly [borrow] some features of democracy in order to substantively avoid it."[14]

The spread of authoritarian elections in the contemporary world has been pushing scholars to devise new conceptual tools for analyzing the new forms of authoritarianism hiding behind electoral façades. Students of democratization have always been aware of the democratic deficiencies that plague many new third-wave democracies. But over time, an increasing number of scholars have come to recognize that in many countries the deficiencies are too profound to maintain those cases in the category of *diminished subtypes of democracy*.[15] In order to avoid the pitfalls of conceptual stretching, one must take the authoritarian features of such countries seriously. Classifying them as diminished subtypes of authoritarianism seems to be more convincing in both analytic and normative terms.[16]

How can one recognize an electoral autocracy? Electoral autocracies reproduce and legitimate themselves by holding periodic elections that show some measure of pluralism but fall short of minimum standards for democracy. In such regimes, rather than being embedded in the "surrounding freedoms"[17] essential to liberal democracy, multiparty elections are constrained by a variety of authoritarian controls. There may be manifold violations of the norms of liberal democracy. Mexico had nearly all of them in place: limitations of civil and political liberties, political restrictions on party and candidate registration, discriminatory rules of representation, as well as electoral fraud, corruption, and coercion, coupled with an uneven playing field wherein the incumbent enjoyed close-to-monopolistic access to media and campaign resources.[18]

The manipulative elections that authoritarian regimes convoke are neither mere embellishments of power nor effective routes to power. They fall into the gray area of institutional ambivalence that lies between the poles of full authoritarian control and full democratic uncertainty. These elections are more than acclamatory rituals, but less than open competitive contests. Thus, authoritarian regimes with elections—electoral autocracies—lie on a continuum between authoritarianism without elections and electoral democracy, although the borders between categories are often fuzzy.[19] Electoral democracies fulfill the procedural minimum for political democracy but contain certain structural defects that prohibit classifying them as full liberal democracies. To establish the precise point where political elections cross the threshold of democratic minimum conditions becomes a notoriously complex and contested task.[20] Contemporary borderline cases at the nebulous frontier between electoral democracy and electoral authoritarianism include, for example, Venezuela, Albania, and Mozambique. Mexico was floating in that indeterminate and intrinsically controversial category during the early 1990s.

The Nested Game

Electoral authoritarianism is a distinctive kind of political regime that is driven by a distinctive logic of transformation. The institutional foundations that sustain the regime—political elections—also provide the institutional bases for subverting it. Many things can happen to an electoral autocracy: it may collapse, stagnate, retrogress, or democratize. Whatever its fate, elections are likely to shape it in a decisive way. Yet, under electoral authoritarianism, electoral contests do not unfold as simply competition for votes. They unfold as *nested games*,[21] in which the struggle for votes (electoral competition) goes hand in hand with the struggle for institutional change (electoral reform).

Authoritarian elections make no one happy. Neither the authoritarian incumbents nor their democratic opponents can accept them as an equilibrium solution that corresponds to their long-term interests. Authoritarian incumbents mistrust managed elections to the extent that they open up a window of uncertainty, whereas their democratic opponents reject such manipulated elections to the extent that they preclude democratic uncertainty. The same as with formal institutions in other spheres of modern life, electoral institutions are legitimate only if their substantive outcomes are indeterminate. Procedural legitimacy presupposes substantive uncertainty.[22] In controlled elections, however, winners and losers are known beforehand. Electoral autocrats do not aim at institutionalizing uncertainty, they strive at institutionalizing electoral certainty. Although democracy is a system in which parties lose elections, electoral authoritarianism is a system in which *opposition* parties lose elections. When managed elections get out of hand and start delivering "unacceptable" results, ruling parties are tempted to tighten up authoritarian controls.[23]

Electoral manipulation thus creates a "structure-induced disequilibrium" that creates conflicting pressures for change.[24] Nondemocratic elections push political actors toward authoritarian regression at the same time they pull them toward full democratization. Parties accept the given rules of the electoral game as a temporary compromise only: a truce contingent on current correlations of power. Due to their contested and contingent nature, authoritarian elections do not unfold as simple games but as nested games, in which "the game in the principal arena is nested inside a bigger game where the rules of the game themselves are variable."[25] The "contingent consent" of both ruling and opposition parties—their acceptance of electoral rules until further notice—leads them to play within the given rules at the same time that they struggle over those same rules.[26] As parties measure their forces in the electoral arena, they battle over the basic rules that shape the electoral arena. Because the game of electoral competition is embedded within the meta-game of electoral reform, the struggle over rules is not extraneous to, but is an integral part of, the struggle over votes.[27]

The political dynamics triggered by the organization of ambivalent elections contrast markedly with the political process opened up by the convocation of democratic elections. The early third-wave transitions from military rule to democracy that took place in southern Europe and South America in the 1970s and 1980s were based on foundational pacts and foundational elections. After a contentious period of institutional choice, founding elections were held using "reasonably fair rules" that were either imposed on or negotiated by the outgoing regime.[28] Contending parties first set up new electoral rules and then moved on to play the game. Institutional design and electoral competition were sequential activities.

In processes of democratization by elections, the sequence of events is different. When the curtain of the first electoral contest falls, the "drama of democratization" is far from over.[29] Elections held under the shadow of manipulation are not the final step of regime change but merely the point of departure. Rather than inaugurating a new regime, they represent focal points of a cyclical "test of forces and of legitimacy."[30]

Virtuous Circles

The nested conflicts over votes and rules can lead to several possible outcomes. Democratization is only one of them. Abortion, retrocession, and stagnation are alternative possibilities. If incumbents control the military (or think they control the military), they may try to shut down the electoral arena, aborting the process. Or, if the majority of citizens, the ultimate arbiters of the game, acquiesce to the ruling party and its practices of electoral manipulation, electoral authoritarianism may settle down as a stagnant, but stable, solution.[31] In addition, rather than propelling democratization, electoral authoritarianism's self-reinforcing two-level dynamic may drive the inverse process, eroding what aspects of democracy exist; incumbents in a democratic or semidemocratic regime may start subverting the electoral process to cement their hold on power. Such activities can set in motion a regressive spiral of decreasing electoral integrity and increasing electoral dominance of the ruling party.[32]

Still, even if democratic progress is not inevitable, the inner logic of the game pulls it away from authoritarianism. As in cases of political liberalization, processes of limited democratization have an intrinsic potential for getting out of hand. And as in the case of extra-electoral guarantees, electoral controls may erode rather than lock in unfair advantages forever. To the extent that opposition parties succeed in accumulating strength in the electoral arena, they improve their chances of extracting institutional reforms from the ruling party. And vice versa: to the extent that they succeed in improving the conditions of electoral competition and electoral governance at the meta-game level, they improve their chances of capturing votes and seats at the game level. Electoral success furthers electoral reform, which again furthers electoral success. Rather than establishing a self-enforcing equilibrium, ambivalent elections thus tend to trigger a "self-subversive" spiral that undermines both the institutional and electoral bases of authoritarian rule.[33]

Cycles of Competition

In Mexico, it was precisely "the power of elections,"[34] the virtuous interaction of electoral competition and electoral reform, that led the country out of the labyrinth of electoral authoritarianism. Notoriously, Mexico's postrevolutionary regime, the exemplary embodiment of electoral authoritarianism, showed deep respect for the forms of electoral democracy. Since 1934, presidential elections have been held with clocklike precision every six years, punctuating a dense calendar of regular legislative, gubernatorial, and municipal elections. But democratic forms were void of democratic substance owing to two mutually reinforcing regime features: the absence of minimal democratic guarantees and the weakness of genuine opposition parties. Over decades, the combination of fine-tuned antidemocratic restrictions plus an immeasurable degree of genuine legitimacy turned the PRI regime into a seemingly unbeatable bulwark of authoritarian rule.

As the country's protracted transition to democracy finally began in the early 1980s, opposition parties succeeded in gradually undermining both pillars of the regime: its antidemocratic structures as well as its popular acceptance. Only by setting (and keeping) in motion such a doubly subversive, self-reinforcing spiral could the opposition parties, after nearly two decades of democratic struggle, arrive at the culmination in the year 2000: the first peaceful, democratic alternation of power in Mexico's independent history. As the opposition parties turned into serious competitors, they were able to peel off, in five electoral reforms since 1987, successive layers of authoritarian regime control. The electoral reforms established temporary equilibria that allowed opposition parties to gain strength in successive rounds of electoral competition and then to extract further concessions from the government. Thus, aided by external shocks, such as the economic crises of 1982, 1987, and 1995, plus the Zapatista rebellion in 1994, democratization was fed simultaneously by a gradual transformation of electoral institutions as well as by a gradual transformation of the correlation of forces among political actors.

The following examples illustrate the increase in competitiveness that occurred in Mexico's party system:

- Opposition parties almost never won municipal elections until the early 1980s. By the year 2000, opposition party mayors governed more than half of Mexico's total population.
- Opposition parties did not win any gubernatorial contest until 1989. By mid-2000, they controlled 13 of the 32 federal states, including the capital.
- The first opposition candidate was elected to the Senate in 1988. In the 1997 midterm elections, the PRI lost its two-thirds majority in the Senate, in 2000 its absolute majority.
- Until 1988, the PRI had always commanded a comfortable two-thirds majority in the Chamber of Deputies.
- In 1997, the PRI lost its absolute majority in the lower chamber, making way for the unprecedented experience of a divided government.

The conservative National Action Party's (Partido Acción Nacional, PAN) victory in the 2000 presidential election was the final, triumphant step of a long march from one-party hegemony to multiparty competition.[35]

Cycles of Reform

Impressive institutional changes made possible, and were made possible by, the increasing competitiveness of the party system. Until the early 1990s, the PRI regime was renowned as one of the world's leading manufacturers of electoral fraud. Since the ruling party's founding, vote-rigging had always been used as a notorious mechanism of last resort to prevent the PRI from losing at the polls. Over the decades, though, rather than stealing votes from opposition candidates, electoral alchemy served to inflate turnout and margins of victory. In the early 1980s, however, in the face of increasing interparty competition, the PRI used electoral fraud as a critical resource for maintaining electoral control. After the 1982 external debt crisis, as the conservative PAN started looking and acting like a real threat in municipal elections in northern Mexico, the PRI initially resorted to blatant electoral fraud to halt the opposition advance.

The institutional conditions that permitted the PRI to commit fraud were rather obvious. The organization of elections lay in the hands of the state, and the state lay in the hands of the PRI. There were no checks, balances, or mechanisms of oversight. The party was free to distort the process at will: shave the voter list, stuff ballot boxes, expulse party representatives from polling stations, and even allow the dead to express their rational preference for the official party. It is no exaggeration to say that, today, all this has changed. Over the course of the past 15 years, Mexico effectively reconstituted its electoral institutions. The negotiated electoral reforms enacted in 1987, 1990, 1993, 1994, and 1996 added up to a veritable institutional revolution within the self-designated regime of the institutional revolution. Tables 2.1 through 2.6 offer a structured synthesis (strangely unavailable in the literature to date) of electoral reforms at the federal level from 1973 to 1996.[36]

The list of institutional electoral innovations is long and comprehensive. The new electoral code spreads a dense network of regulation over the electoral process. A partial list of the changes includes

- a new voter registry that ranks among the world's best in terms of coverage and reliability;
- nominal voter lists that contain individual photographs of all eligible voters, who numbered more than 58 million in 2000;
- the new high-tech voter identification card that has become the major means of personal identification in the country;
- polling station officials who are ordinary citizens (they are selected by a two-stage random procedure);

Table 2.1 Electoral Reforms in Mexico, 1973–1996: Access to the Party System

Year	Membership Requirements	Vote Requirements	Registration Authority	Electoral Alliances
1973	65,000 nationwide, 2,000 in two-thirds of federal states		Ministry of the Interior (Secretaría de Gobernación, SEGOB)	
1977	Definitive registry: 65,000 nationwide, 3,000 in half of states, 300 in half of districts	Conditional registry: 1.5% in one of three consecutive federal elections	Federal Electoral Commission	Permissive rules for common candidacies; restrictive coalition rules: party fusion or abnegation
1987		Elimination of conditional registry		
1990		Reestablishment of conditional registry	IFE,[a] General Council; right of appeal before the electoral tribunal	Elimination of common candidacies
1993		Loss of registry after receiving less than 1.5% at two consecutive elections		Coalitions have to present common electoral platforms
1996	Minimum of 0.13% of voter registry, 3,000 in 10 states or 300 in 100 districts; constitutional prohibition of collective membership	Less than 2% at a federal election: loss of registry for at least two elections; elimination of conditional registry		At presidential elections, "total coalitions" required: common logo, platform, statutes, and legislative candidates; partial coalitions only for FPTP[b] senators and deputies

Sources: Comisión Federal Electoral, "Ley federal de organizaciones políticas y procesos electorales" (Mexico City: CFE, 1978); Comisión Federal Electoral, "Código Federal Electoral" (Mexico City: CFE, 1987); Secretaría de Gobernación, "Código Federal de Instituciones y Procedimientos Electorales *comentado*" (Mexico City: SEGOB, 1990); Instituto Federal Electoral, "Código Federal de Instituciones y Procedimientos Electorales y otros ordenamientos electorales" (Mexico City: IFE, 1994); Instituto Federal Electoral, "Código Federal de Instituciones y Procedimientos Electorales y otros ordenamientos electorales" (Mexico City: IFE, 1996); Ricardo Becerra, Pedro Salazar, and José Woldenberg, *La mecánica del cambio político en México: Elecciones, partidos y reformas* (Mexico City: Cal y Arena, 2000); Javier Patiño Camarena, *Derecho electoral mexicano* (Mexico City: Editorial Constitucionalista, 1995); and Andreas Schedler, "A Brief History of Electoral Reforms in Mexico, 1977–1996," Institute for Advanced Studies, Vienna, unpublished typescript, 1997.

Notes: Constitutional recognition of parties in 1977. Constant requirements of registration: declaration of principles, program, and statutes. Constant exclusions: regional, religious, and ethnic parties. 1977: Legalization of Communist Party. Access to local and state elections: restrictive regulations at state level before 1977; 1977: national register grants automatic right to file candidates at subnational elections. 1993: access to presidential candidacies to Mexicans with foreign parents. Since 1973, growing list of legal obligations parties have to comply with under the threat of losing official recognition.

a. Instituto Federal Electoral (Federal Electoral Institute).
b. First Past the Post, or simple majority, system of voting.

Table 2.2   Electoral Reforms in Mexico, 1973–1996: Access to Resources

Year	Media	Public Resources	Private Resources	Financial Accountability
1973	20 free minutes per month per party in radio and television	Party prerogatives: tax and postage exemption		
1977	"Equitable" free access to radio and television	Introduction of public party funding		
1987	15 free minutes per month per party in radio and television	Initial legal regulation of public funding, proportional distribution		
1990	Increase of free air time before elections, "proportional" to parties' electoral strength	Functional differentiation of funding by types of expenditures		
1993	Regulation of access to commercial media time	Prohibition of party support by public agencies other than IFE[a]	Prohibition of donations by businesses, foreigners, international organizations, and religious associations; lax limits to individual and anonymous contributions	Constitutional obligation to account for party resources; financial oversight by IFE General Council commission; tribunal sanctions; generous spending ceilings
1994	180% increase of free air time			
1996	Qualitative and quantitative increase of free air time and more egalitarian access: 30% equal, 70% proportional, prohibition of "third party" advertisement; legal assignment of news monitoring to IFE	600% increase; constitutional regulation of public funding: predominance of public funds, 70% proportional, 30% equal	Prohibition of anonymous donations; ceiling for private funding: 10% of "regular" public financing; ceiling for individual donors: 0.05% of maximum private funding	Refinement of financial accountability, explicit definition of sanctions

Sources: See Table 2.1.

Notes: Voluntary interparty agreements in 1994: IFE monitoring of news coverage; suspension of governmental publicity 20 days before elections; TV debate of presidential candidates. Evolution of spending ceilings: Generous in 1993 and 1994. Authority to set spending ceilings: For legislative elections shift from IFE local juntas to local councils; 1996: IFE General Council sets spending ceilings for all federal elections. 1996 regulation of spending ceilings for coalitions: same limit as major party in coalition.

a. Instituto Federal Electoral (Federal Electoral Institute).

Table 2.3   Electoral Reforms in Mexico, 1973–1996: Rules of Representation

Year	Senate	Chamber of Deputies	Corrective Rules	Federal District
1973	64 members, 2 per federal state, FPTP[a]	Around 300 FPTP deputies; party deputies: 1.5% threshold, 20 maximum per minority party		
1977		300 FPTP, 100 PR,[b] exclusion of major party from PR seats, separate ballots	Seat ceiling: 75% (300 seats)	
1987	Staggered renovation at 3-year intervals	300 FPTP, 200 PR, conditional inclusion of major party into PR seat distribution, unified ballot	Seat ceiling: 70% (350 seats); governability clause: automatic majority for major party; PR districts and PR formula favoring small parties	Elected consultative assembly, 40 FPTP, 26 PR
1990			Governability clause for parties over 35% plus "mobile scale": two additional deputies for each additional vote percentage, overrepresentation of parties between 35% and 60%	Governability clause for parties over 30% plus "mobile scale"
1993	Four members per state, 3 for the major party, one for the second party ("first minority")		Seat ceiling 63% (315 seats), elimination of governability clause; 1.5% threshold of representation	
1994				
1996	Four members per state, 2 plurality, 1 first minority, 1 nationwide PR, 2% threshold, end of staggered renovation in 2000	2% threshold	8% ceiling of overrepresentation (by PR), redistricting by IFE[c]	Direct election of Mexico City mayor (3-year term, then 6-year term), empowerment of Legislative Assembly, direct election of *jefes delegacionales* in 2000

Sources: See Table 2.1.
Notes: a. FPTP: First Past the Post, or simple majority, system of voting.
b. PR: proportional representation.
c. IFE: Instituto Federal Electoral (Federal Electoral Institute).

Table 2.4 Electoral Reforms in Mexico, 1973–1996: Electoral Organization

Year	Voter Registry	Identification Card	Election Materials	Vote Counting and Publication
1973				One week between polling and announcement of final results
1977				
1987				Publication of results outside of polling stations; publication of "preliminary information" at district level within 24 hours
1990	New registry, elimination of discretion, comprehensive system of party oversight	New high security voter identification cards	Voting screens and transparent ballot boxes	Authorization and intended implementation of program of preliminary results (PREP)
1993				Legal establishment of PREP, acceleration of tally at district level
1994	Permanent party access to electronic database, access to nominal list in paper and on tape (random distribution), 38 external audits	New voter identification cards with photographs	Foliated ballots, certified indelible ink, new design of polling stations to guarantee secrecy	
1996	Nominal lists with photographs			

Sources: See Table 2.1.

Note: Admission of national electoral observers in 1993, and of international observers in 1994. Introduction of electoral assistants in 1996.

Table 2.5 Electoral Reforms in Mexico, 1973–1996: Election Management Body

Year	Supreme Electoral Commission	Decentralized Subcommissions	Electoral Bureaucracy	Polling Station Officials
1973	CFE:[a] Secretary of the Interior, 2 PRI legislators, egalitarian representation: 1 per registered party	Hierarchical control of state and district committees by SEGOB[b]	Hierarchical control by SEGOB; at election times, ad hoc bureaucracy assembled from SEGOB, federal states, and municipalities	Appointed by CFE District Committees
1977				
1987	From egalitarian representation to tempered PR:[c] PRI majority			Hierarchical control of president and secretary; random selection of two scrutineers from party proposals
1990	Tempered PR in IFE[d] General Council: 6 PRI and 8 opposition representatives, 6 nonpartisan "electoral magistrates" proposed by president	IFE General Council appoints 6 citizen councilors to each state and district council	IFE President, the Secretary of the Interior, proposes General Director who appoints lower-level officials	Selection by lot of 20% of registered voters
1993		IFE General Council appoints 9 citizen councilors to each state and district council	2/3 of General Council ratify General Secretary and executive directors, all proposed by General Director	Selection by lot of 15% of registered voters, plus second random selection after training
1994	Parties keep their seats (1 per party), but lose their voting rights; 6 "citizen councilors" appointed by 2/3 of Chamber of Deputies	Parties keep their seats (1 per party), but lose their voting rights		
1996	Secretary of the Interior resigns, IFE president and another 8 "electoral councilors" elected by 2/3 of Chamber of Deputies, legislative representatives (1 per legislative party) keep their seats, but lose their voting rights	IFE General Council appoints electoral councilors, IFE Executive Secretary appoints members of executive boards	IFE General Council appoints Executive Secretary and Executive Directors; electoral councilors oversee electoral administration through internal commissions	More precise procedures and criteria of selection

Sources: See Table 2.1.
Notes: a. CFE: Comisión Federal Electoral (Federal Electoral Commission).
b. SEGOB: Secretaría de Gobernación (Ministry of the Interior).
c. PR: proportional representation.
d. IFE: Instituto Federal Electoral (Federal Electoral Institute).

**Table 2.6   Electoral Reforms in Mexico, 1973–1996:
Electoral Dispute Settlement**

Year	Agents of Electoral Justice	Certification of Electoral Results	Jurisdiction of Electoral Tribunal	Electoral Offenses in Penal Law
1973		Electoral college formed by legislators-elect	Supreme Court as appellate court	Court rulings are not binding
1977	CFE[a] and Supreme Court of Justice			
1987	CFE and TRICOEL;[b] Specialized tribunal, 7 magistrates proposed by parties and elected by Chamber of Deputies	Electoral tribunal, overruled by simple majority of electoral college	Administrative control of legality; appellate court against CFE decisions	
1990	TRIFE:[c] judicial body, 5 magis-trates proposed by president and nominated by 2/3 Chamber of Deputies, decen-tralized	Electoral tribunal, overruled by 2/3 of electoral college	Administrative and judicial control of legality, procedural regulation of appeal	Introduction of electoral offenses into penal law
1993		IFE and electoral tribunal for legis-lative, electoral college for presi-dential elections	Constitution defines TRIFE as "supreme authority in electoral matters"	Establishment of special prosecutor for electoral crimes
1994				
1996	TEPJF:[d] integration into judiciary; magistrates proposed by Supreme Court and nominated by 2/3 of Senate (3/4 in 1996), president elected by magistrates	IFE for legislative and electoral tribunal for presidential elections	TEPJF: Jurisdictions extended to state and local elections; definitive rulings; Supreme Court: control of constitutionality of electoral laws at both federal and state level	More extensive definition of offenses, harsher sanctions

Sources: See Table 2.1.
Notes: a. CFE: Comisión Federal Electoral (Federal Electoral Commission).
b. TRICOEL: Tribunal de lo Contencioso Electoral (Tribunal of Electoral Contention).
c. TRIFE: Tribunal Federal Electoral (Federal Electoral Tribunal).
d. TEPJF: Tribunal Electoral del Poder Judicial de la Federación (Electoral Tribunal of the Judicial Power of the Federation).

- ballot boxes that are now made of transparent materials;
- numbered ballots that have forgery-resistant watermarks, visible and invisible fibers, microprinting, and inverted printing; and
- a special attorney who prosecutes electoral offenses defined as vio-lations of the penal code.

Clearly, the three central pillars of the new electoral system have been a new independent election body, the judicialization of conflict resolution, and comprehensive oversight by political parties. First of all, concordant with an international trend, Mexican parties decided to delegate the organization of elections to a permanent and independent election management body. Today the government no longer has any say in the Federal Electoral Institute (Instituto Federal Electoral, IFE), founded in 1990. Since 1996, it has included nine nonpartisan officials, appointed by a consensus of the three major parties in Congress that control the General Council—the IFE's top oversight and management body. After the 1997 midterm elections, these independent councilors lived through some episodes of sharp confrontation with the PRI but have continually enjoyed the full confidence of the major opposition parties.

Electoral reformers have also set up a new system of judicial dispute resolution. Mexico had a long tradition of congressional self-certification, in which members of Congress validated their own electoral victories without any means of legal recourse for the losers. Starting in 1987, electoral reforms have gradually built up an increasingly autonomous and impartial judicial system of electoral dispute settlement. Today, the Electoral Tribunal of the Judicial Power of the Federation (Tribunal Electoral del Poder Judicial de la Federación, TEPJF) has the last say over any electoral conflicts, including local disputes. On the eve of the 2000 federal elections, the tribunal proudly publicized its apparently unbiased record of findings. Yet, its somewhat erratic jurisprudence in crucial controversies has raised the suspicion that magistrates may not always be concerned exclusively with interpreting the law in an impartial manner, but instead sometimes take major decisions with an eye to governmental preferences, as well as to their own public reputation.[37]

Finally, the political parties have institutionalized a panoptic regime of surveillance that allows them to closely monitor the entire electoral process step by step. Their vigilant presence goes far beyond the deployment of representatives on voting day. The parties act as vigorous agents of accountability in the IFE General Council, to which they belong as consultative members, as well as in other organs of the institute. Also, they are legally entitled to oversee (and actively committed to overseeing) each phase of the organization of elections, from voter registration to vote counting.

The Test of Alternation

The transformations of the party system and the institutions of electoral governance constituted two mutually reinforcing trends. Without the demise of one-party hegemony, it would have been hardly possible to establish an autonomous system of election management and dispute settlement, or vice versa. Without dismantling the PRI's monopolistic hold over electoral governance, opposition parties would have hardly been able to accomplish their long march from marginality to competitiveness. Taken together, these two interdependent structural changes added up to a profound change of the political regime. Nevertheless, throughout the 1990s, political actors as well as political observers engaged in intense controversy about the nature of the Mexican regime. Some argued that clean-election reforms had pushed the country over the threshold of electoral democracy by the mid-1990s; others held that there was no way of gauging the real democratic openness of the regime other than by electoral defeat of the incumbent party.[38]

Before the 2000 elections, Mexico looked like a rare case of regime change without an accompanying change of government. The PRI had lost its hegemonic position in the party system as well as its monopolistic control of electoral governance. But it had not been turned out of power; it still occupied the symbolic summit of the state, the presidency. The former authoritarian party had steered the country to the shores of democracy without vacating the presumptive center of the political system. Impressive amounts of empirical evidence could be cited to support the idea that by the mid-1990s Mexico had already crossed the threshold of democracy, in spite of the PRI's continuity in government. But ultimately this estimation rested upon a counterfactual claim. It assumed that the new electoral infrastructure would be able to withstand the "authentic acid test"[39] of democracy—the victory of an opposition candidate in a presidential election. If the proof of the pudding is in the eating, the proof of democracy lies in the alternation of power. Thus, many analysts insisted before 2000 that only the *reality* of alternation of government could provide compelling evidence that the democratic *possibility* of alternation was more than a political illusion. PAN presidential candidate Vicente Fox's victory on July 2, 2000, finally provided that evidence.

The prospective assessment of democratic uncertainty is one thing; the retroactive treatment of democratic alternation is quite another. Even those who demand to see the ruling party defeated before classifying a regime as democratic should take alternation as an empirical indicator that confirms the presence of democracy, rather than just the initiation of democracy. As Adam Przeworski and collaborators have written, when the incumbent party suffers defeat at the polls, the regime should be classified "as democratic for the entire period this party was in power under the same rules."[40] Under that rule of classification, Mexico should be considered democratic since its last democratizing reform in 1996.

Alternation in power in the year 2000 marked the symbolic end of the democratic transition by giving a convincing demonstration of democracy at work. At the same time, it signaled that democratic consolidation had been accomplished, too. Not all democracies are born fragile and not all democratic transitions lead to protracted processes of consolidation. The more inclusive the foundational agreement on the rules of the game, the more stable is the resulting democratic regime.[41] The very architects of democracy are unlikely to purposefully destroy the edifice they themselves helped build. It is commonplace to note that Mexico did not democratize through the celebration of a decisive democratic pact. Instead of taking one big redemptive leap forward, the country proceeded through a series of smaller democratizing steps. Yet, the sequence of preliminary pacts eventually led to the same desired outcome—the forging of a basic institutional consensus among all major political parties. Due to the comprehensiveness and inclusiveness of the final 1996 democratic pact, the country accomplished the consolidation of its democracy at the same time it completed its transition to democracy. Mexico's protracted transition was crowned by instant consolidation.

Still, even if there is solid ground for optimism, democrats would be ill-advised to just sit back and relax. Few things are more subversive of democracy than complacency about democracy. The most appropriate answer to Guiseppe Di Palma's famous question "At what point can democrats relax?" is simple: never![42] Democrats should never lower their guards. As M. S. Gill, president of India's prestigious federal election commission, wisely states, an "essential condition of making democracy secure is never to take it for granted."[43] Thus, tempering my optimistic diagnosis of democratic consolidation, I would like to introduce just a small note of caution about some potential sources of trouble from within the political party system.[44]

The Inversion of Protest

In early 1995, President Zedillo announced his intention to negotiate a definitive electoral reform. Striving to reach a consensus among all major parties, he made it clear that the reform should not be just another temporary truce, to be broken and revised after the next election in response to shifting correlations of power. Zedillo wanted the habit of renegotiating the rules of the game after each round of the game to be abandoned. The president's declared purpose of building durable electoral institutions (rather than provisional signposts) met with quite a bit of skepticism and mockery. But, in fact, the 1996 legal and constitutional changes, approved after 18 months of troubled negotiations, did lay solid institutional foundations for democratic competition.

This is not to say the current legislation is perfect and made for eternity. The political parties are well aware that current laws contain some contradictions, some points of imprecision, and some legal lacunae that further amendments might remedy. The parties share a vague consensus about the desirability of further legal adaptations, even if they have trouble agreeing on the details. For example, current election laws remain silent about so-called precampaigns: the campaign activities that prospective candidates carry out ahead of the official campaign period (which spans somewhat less than six months in the case of presidential elections). Such campaigns are not subject to any legal financial constraints. Neither income restrictions nor spending ceilings apply, although most political actors and political observers agree they should.[45]

What sets current reform proposals apart from previous discussions, however, is their immanent nature. The proposals do not aim at transcending predemocratic institutions, but rather at adjusting democratic ones. Rather than establishing democracy, the proposals seek to reform democracy. The debate centers not around the issue of democracy itself, but around specific adjustments within the democratic system. In this sense, the nested struggle over votes and rules continues in Mexico today. But in the new democratic context, the nature of the struggle has changed profoundly. It is no longer the legitimacy of elections that is at stake but instead the democratic quality of elections. The rationale of institutional reform has shifted from dismantling the authoritarian regime to democratizing democracy.

The consensus that political parties have reached over the basic rules of the game is of paramount importance. Still, it is worrisome to note that the consensus over rules is sporadically threatened by disputes over the application of the rules. Overall, political parties accept and abide by the rules they negotiated in 1996. However, the parties readily distrust the authorities in charge of administering and adjudicating those rules. The object of partisan discontent has shifted from institutions to actors. Parties tend to perceive any remaining shortcomings of either election management or electoral justice as "a problem not of institutions but of the people who staff them."[46] Institutional distrust has given way to personal distrust.

One can explain the recurrent conflicts in the relationship between political parties and election officials as an expression of the "basic instability" inherent in impartial conflict resolution.[47] Even when contending parties have consented to the rules that govern conflict resolution, they may be still tempted to cry foul if they distrust the arbiter or dislike the result. In Mexico, political parties have tapped both sources of contestation. The relationship between competing parties and election officials has been strained by *ex ante* suspicions of partisan sympathies as well as by *ex post* allegations of biased performance.

The successive electoral reforms that have occurred since the mid-1980s very much revolved around appointment procedures for electoral authorities. Who should select the decisionmakers at various levels of electoral governance? The political parties have tended to, at least initially, view with suspicion those election officials who were proposed by their adversaries. The institutional solutions they agreed upon range from mutual disempowerment (in the selection of polling station officials by lot) to reciprocal veto powers (in the consensual selection of top administrative and judicial authorities).[48] As a result, nobody trusted everybody, but everyone had at least someone to trust.

Most prominently, opposition parties deposited full confidence in the top management officials of the IFE, while the PRI ran into harsh conflicts with some electoral councilors it perceived as personal adversaries sympathetic to opposition parties.[49] In contrast, the former hegemonic party has always been full of praise for the institute's administrative personnel, whereas opposition parties considered those people to be holdovers of the old regime who, as such, should be subject to political cleansing and tight oversight. The top national election authority, the federal electoral tribunal, the TEPJF, was not exempt from this pattern of asymmetric trust. Until 2000, the PRI had considered the TEPJF a reliable ally and a bastion of legality. Opposition parties, in contrast, showed much less enthusiasm for a court that seemed to perform well in routine cases but usually sided with the PRI in crucial cases.

In part, the contrasting appreciations of political parties have had to do with the "original sins" of election authorities: the fact that they had been proposed for nomination by one or the other party. But contamination by origin is not the whole story: performance matters, too. Not surprisingly, parties don't like to lose. And even if authorities adopt an impartial frame of mind, their basic approach to legal rule application is likely to have asymmetric effects on political parties. In simple terms, judicial activism is likely to hurt the party in power (the beneficiaries of the status quo), whereas judicial restraint is likely to hurt parties out of power (the beneficiaries of change). To the extent that the IFE General Council pursued an activist course of action, it was bound to provoke the ruling PRI, just as the TEPJF's preaching the necessity of judicial self-restraint was—until the 2000 presidential election—bound to disappoint non-PRI political actors.

Since the 2000 elections, the TEPJF has started to embrace judicial activism and is moving toward a more assertive defense of the democratic

"spirit" of Mexico's electoral law, together with a somewhat looser inter-
pretation of its letter. In the state of Tabasco, the tribunal annulled the
2000 gubernatorial elections, arguing that the PRI had won under conditions of profound inequality in terms of campaign resources and media
exposure. In Yucatán, the tribunal deposed the local election council that
had been nominated by the PRI-dominated state legislature and nominated
a council of its own to prepare gubernatorial elections in early 2001.

Both decisions (or series of decisions) created periods of considerable
tension and uncertainty. They were the first major political crises and tests
of force that Vicente Fox had to confront as president. Happily, none of
them escalated into violent confrontation (save some scuffling at the local
level). Yet, the bold departure of the TEPJF from its previous philosophy
of self-restraint led the PRI to withdraw its trust from the tribunal, bringing the incipient reversal of roles between the PRI and the former opposition parties close to completion. Between 1997 and 2000, the former hegemonic party had already emerged as the major complainant in electoral
matters.[50]

Since 1997, complaints about discriminatory treatment by state and
federal electoral officials have been almost exclusively from the PRI, rather
than its adversaries. Listening to the PRI today sounds much like listening
to opposition complaints of the recent past. For instance, the PRI's recurrent complaint against the PAN or the Party of the Democratic Revolution
(Partido de la Revolución Democrática, PRD) governors tilting the playing
field in state-orchestrated elections ("elecciones de Estado") very much
resembles past opposition accusations against the former ruling party.

Does It Matter?

The former opposition parties' deep distrust toward the PRI-controlled
system of electoral governance was a powerful force propelling and shaping Mexico's transition from electoral fraud to electoral integrity. Now
that the PAN and the PRD approve of the institutional framework for elections, does the PRI's occasional screaming and shouting matter? One
could say no. The party's often dramatized discontent, one may say, is no
more than a rhetorical bubble, a passing expression of pain by a party
struggling to learn how to live with defeat. As a general rule, when parties
lose and outcomes are close, the losers tend to complain. Still, today, as a
clear sign of democratic progress, complainants no longer carry their
protest to the streets. They go to the tribunals and, even if discontented,
end up complying with judicial rulings. Conflicts are mostly local, and

even if passions run high, the dramatic moments of confrontation are soon forgotten, and the parties go back to normal before the dust settles. As political actors learn to lose, they will stop discrediting the electoral institutions they may need the next time around.

Even if there is much to say in favor of such a cool and sober assessment, it underestimates the latent risk of extra-institutional confrontation that is inherent in the delegitimizing rhetoric of distrust, while at the same time it overlooks the potential benefits that may derive from the parties' refusal to make out blank checks of confidence to election authorities. Both contrasting possibilities derive from the institutional powers the TEPJF acquired in the 1996 reform.

It was long held a truism that state electoral regimes lagged significantly behind democratizing trends at the national level. Over the course of the democratic transition, state electoral codes underwent waves of reform in rough accordance with federal law reforms. After a certain time lag, states caught up with federal law, but did so in a somewhat uneven fashion. Some states forged ahead; others lagged behind. Yet overall, state election codes converged toward the democratic baseline established at the federal level.[51] Still, institutional reforms sometimes looked better on paper than in reality. In the late 1990s, especially in the context of continuing PRI dominance, the autonomy of state electoral institutes and tribunals was still precarious and vulnerable to executive encroachment.

Responding to the uneven development of local electoral regimes, the 1996 federal reform introduced a powerful tool to level the electoral playing field across the nation. The reform made allowance for judicial review of local rules and acts of electoral governance. Extending the chain of appeal against local irregularities to federal courts (the TEPJF and the Supreme Court) compelled local actors to conform to *best practices* established at the federal level. In 1996, it was clear that the possibility of judicial review would not bear fruit immediately. It established a "fire alarm" system of oversight that would allow parties to seek redress of local irregularities by resorting to federal courts.[52]

Judicial review of subnational electoral institutions and decisions fulfills the classical function appellate systems are supposed to serve. National court hierarchies are typically established to "break through the web of local interests" in the name of "nationalizing interests."[53] In a democratizing Mexico, it was understood that taking a laissez-faire attitude toward subnational regimes would have amounted to giving local power cliques a free hand to lock in authoritarian enclaves.

Yet, when the federal electoral tribunal is granted final say, not just in federal conflicts but also in any local conflicts in electoral matters, local disputes stop being just local disputes. If they are not resolved to the satisfaction of any party involved, the disputes turn into a federal matter, which implies that the parties' eventual dissatisfaction becomes a federal matter as well. The centralization of conflict resolution involves the centralization of protest. If the national appellate court works fine, and is seen to work fine, its power of review is a big asset; if not, the court's power of review may turn into a big liability. If the review is credible, it deflects and defuses local tensions; if not, it attracts and heightens tensions, local as well as national.

From this perspective, watching the TEPJF and the PRI turn against each other is a matter of concern. The generalization of the former hegemonic party's distrust of federal election authorities upsets the previous "checks and balances" of asymmetric distrust between the PRI and its adversaries. If a major party like the PRI feels election authorities are mistreating it, electoral tribunals may fail to channel and contain critical electoral disputes, and violent extra-institutional protest may resurge again. The risk of actors turning their backs on courts and returning to the streets is particularly high in election standoffs (as occurred in the state of Tabasco in 2000) where the difference in votes between winners and losers lies within the (inevitable) margin of administrative error.

To say that powerful appellate courts like the TEPJF may be magnets of public protest, however, is only part of the story. In normative terms, one might add that such institutions actually *should* be magnets of public criticism. All supreme courts that issue final decisions without further appeal pose serious dilemmas of oversight. The irreversibility of such rulings dramatizes the classical conflict between judicial independence and judicial oversight. Since the norm of independence requires shielding judges from almost any kind of institutional sanctions, there is only one way to reconcile the demands of insulation with the demands of accountability: through public debate.

It is only through *deliberative accountability* in the public sphere that citizens can hold supreme courts accountable for their decisions. In this perspective, alert and critical oversight by citizens, scholars, journalists, and political parties is not only legitimate, it is essential in order to subject a supreme court like the TEPJF to a minimum of public accountability. The temptation to establish "gag rules"[54] that prohibit questioning court rulings in public would be counterproductive. It is the political parties themselves who have to manage the balancing act between respecting judicial independence and criticizing legal judgments.

Conclusion

With the peaceful alternation of power in 2000, Mexico's velvet transition from electoral authoritarianism has reached its culmination. The chapter of transition is closed; the country has turned into a normal Latin American democracy. Needless to say, Mexican democracy is not heaven on earth. Much remains to be done to construct a high-quality democracy. Democratizing democracy is the huge pending task of Mexican policymakers. Even so, as conventional wisdom has it, democracy is not the solution to all problems. It is only an institutional framework for seeking solutions and resolving conflicts in a peaceful way.

Still, the institutionalization of electoral democracy is no small achievement. Actually, it is without precedent in Mexican history and it again places the country in an advantageous position with respect to its Latin American neighbors. Mexico's simultaneous achievement of political and economic stability compares favorably to the tumultuous setbacks countries like Ecuador, Paraguay, Venezuela, and Argentina have been living through in recent times. In other words, now that Mexico has finally reached Latin American "democratic normality," it starts looking exceptional again.

There are solid reasons for optimism then, but even better ones to temper our well-grounded optimism. As stated previously, the best way to keep democracy safe is never to take it for granted. Like Greek architecture, democratic consolidation is at its best when slightly imperfect. Democrats should know that relaxation might be self-defeating, that they are well-advised to stay alert and resist the temptation of complacency, and that they should conceive of consolidation not as a life achievement but an unending Sisyphean task: one pushes the stone, one reaches the top, one relaxes and stretches, and the stone tumbles back again. Yet, there is nothing depressing about the inconclusive nature of democratic consolidation. As the great melancholic Albert Camus put it: "One must imagine Sisyphus happy."[55]

Notes

1. By democratic consolidation I refer to the attainment of a high degree of expected stability of the political regime. Naturally, if we embrace broader conceptions of consolidation, we may reach different conclusions (see note 44).

2. Giovanni Sartori, *Parties and Party Systems: A Framework for Analysis* (Cambridge: Cambridge University Press, 1976), pp. 231–238.

3. Authoritarianism with adjectives echoes "democracy with adjectives." See David Collier and Steven Levitsky, "Democracy with Adjectives: Conceptual Innovation in Comparative Research," *World Politics* 49 (April 1997): 430–451.

4. Guillermo O'Donnell, *Modernization and Bureaucratic Authoritarianism: Studies in South American Politics* (Berkeley: University of California Press, Institute of International Studies, 1979).

5. Samuel P. Huntington, *The Third Wave: Democratization in the Late Twentieth Century* (Norman: University of Oklahoma Press, 1991).

6. For an analysis on protracted transitions, see Todd A. Eisenstadt, "Eddies in the Third Wave: Protracted Transitions and Theories of Democratization," *Democratization* 7, no. 3 (2000): 3–24.

7. See, for example, Ricardo Becerra, Pedro Salazar, and José Woldenberg, *La mecánica del cambio político en México: Elecciones, partidos y reformas* (Mexico City: Cal y Arena, 2000), p. 30; César Cansino, *La Transición Mexicana 1977–2000* (Mexico City: Centro de Estudios de Política Comparada, 2000), p. 281; and Luis Medina Peña, "México: Historia de una democracia difícil," in *Elecciones, alternancia y democracia: España-México, una reflexión comparada,* edited by José Varela Ortega and Luis Medina Peña (Madrid: Biblioteca Nueva, 2000), p. 196 (195–303).

8. For a systematic analysis of the "missing links" of the Mexican transition, see José Antonio Crespo, *Fronteras democráticas en México: Retos, peculiaridades y comparaciones* (Mexico City: Océano, 1999), pp. 191–222. On postmodernity as a "collection of absences," see Zygmunt Bauman, *Intimations of Postmodernity* (London: Routledge, 1992), p. 218.

9. See, for example, Hermann Gilomee and Charles Simkins, eds., *The Awkward Embrace: One-Party Domination and Democracy* (Amsterdam: Harwood Academic Publishers, 1999); Dorothy J. Solinger, "Ending One-Party Dominance: Korea, Taiwan, Mexico," *Journal of Democracy* 12, no. 1 (2001): 30–42; and the "protracted transitions" thematic issue of the journal *Democratization* 7, no. 4 (Autumn 2000).

10. Medina Peña, "México," p. 196.

11. See, for example, J. Morgan Kousser, *The Shaping of Southern Politics: Suffrage Restriction and the Establishment of the One-Party South, 1880–1910* (New Haven, CT: Yale University Press, 1974); Fabrice E. Lehoucq and Ivan Molina, *Stuffing the Ballot Box: Fraud, Electoral Reform, and Democratization in Costa Rica* (Cambridge: Cambridge University Press, 2002); and Carlos Malamud, ed., *Legitimidad, representación y alternancia en España y América Latina: Las reformas electorales (1880–1930)* (Mexico City: Fondo de Cultura Económica, 2000).

12. Adam Przeworski, Michael E. Alvarez, José Antonio Cheibub, and Fernando Limongi, *Democracy and Development: Political Institutions and Well-Being in the World, 1950–1990* (Cambridge: Cambridge University Press, 2000), p. 26.

13. National Democratic Institute (NDI), "Lessons Learned and Challenges Facing International Election Monitoring" (Washington, DC: NDI, 1999).

14. William F. Case, "Can the 'Halfway House' Stand? Semidemocracy and Elite Theory in Three Southeast Asian Countries," *Comparative Politics* 28, no. 4 (1996): 438 (437–465).

15. Collier and Levitsky, "Democracy with Adjectives."

16. For an early warning against authoritarian practices under the cloak of electoral routines, see Terry Lynn Karl, "The Hybrid Regimes of Latin America," *Journal of Democracy* 6, no. 3 (1995): 72–86. For some recent calls to turn scholarly attention to the new forms of authoritarianism, see Larry Diamond, "Elections Without Democracy: Thinking About Hybrid Regimes," *Journal of Democracy* 13, no. 2 (2002): 21–35; Steven Levitsky and Lucan A. Way, "Elections Without Democracy: The Rise of Competitive Authoritarianism," *Journal of Democracy* 13, no. 2 (2002): 51–65; Andreas Schedler, "Elections Without Democracy: The Menu of Manipulation," *Journal of Democracy* 13, no. 2 (2002): 36–50; and Jason M. Brownlee, "Double-Edged Institutions: Electoral Authoritarianism in Egypt and Iran," 97th Annual Meeting of the American Political Science Association (APSA), San Francisco, August 30 through September 2, 2001.

17. Guillermo O'Donnell, "Democracy, Law, and Comparative Politics," *Studies in Comparative International Development* 36, no. 1 (Spring 2001): 13.

18. The list does not include suffrage restrictions. Electoral regimes that exclude broad parts of the adult population from suffrage rights might be qualified as "competitive oligarchies." See Robert A. Dahl, *Polyarchy: Participation and Opposition* (New Haven, CT: Yale University Press, 1971), p. 7. On the broad "menu of electoral manipulation" available to electoral autocrats, see Schedler, "Elections Without Democracy."

19. Larry Diamond, *Developing Democracy: Toward Consolidation* (Baltimore: Johns Hopkins University Press, 1999).

20. See Schedler, "Elections Without Democracy"; and Jørgen Elklit and Palle Svensson, "What Makes Elections Free and Fair?" *Journal of Democracy* 8, no. 3 (1997): 32–46.

21. George Tsebelis, *Nested Games: Rational Choice in Comparative Politics* (Berkeley: University of California Press, 1990).

22. Niklas Luhmann, *Legitimation durch Verfahren* (Frankfurt/Main: Suhrkamp, 1983).

23. On the institutionalization of uncertainty, see Adam Przeworski, "Democracy as a Contingent Outcome of Conflicts," in *Constitutionalism and Democracy,* edited by Jon Elster and Rune Slagstad (Cambridge: Cambridge University Press, 1988), p. 63 (59–80). On the relation between the substantive uncertainty and procedural certainty of democratic elections, see Shaheen Mozaffar and Andreas Schedler, "The Comparative Study of Electoral Governance—Introduction," *International Political Science Review* 23, no. 1 (2002): 5–27. On democracy as a system in which parties lose elections, see Adam Przeworski, *Democracy and the Market: Political and Economic Reform in Eastern Europe and Latin America* (New York: Cambridge University Press, 1991), p. 10.

24. I am paraphrasing Kenneth A. Shepsle and Barry R. Weingast, "Structure-Induced Equilibrium and Legislative Choices," *Public Choice* 37 (1981): 503–519.

25. Tsebelis, *Nested Games,* p. 8.

26. My use of "contingent consent" is ironic, of course. It denotes the opposite of what O'Donnell and Schmitter expressed with the term, namely, consent to

democratic rules regardless of their contingent outcome. Guillermo O'Donnell and Philippe C. Schmitter, *Transitions from Authoritarian Rule: Tentative Conclusions About Uncertain Democracies* (Baltimore: Johns Hopkins University Press, 1986), pp. 59–61.

27. For the present purpose, I treat the concept of *nested games* as equivalent to the idea of "two-level" games. See Robert D. Putnam, "Diplomacy and Domestic Politics: The Logic of Two-Level Games," *International Organization* 42, no. 3 (1988): 427–460. I will refer to electoral competition as the *game* level, and to electoral reform as the *meta-game* level. See also Andreas Schedler, "The Nested Game of Democratization by Elections," *International Political Science Review* 23, no. 1 (2002): 103–122.

28. O'Donnell and Schmitter, *Transitions from Authoritarian Rule*, p. 58.

29. Laurence Whitehead, "The Drama of Democratization," *Journal of Democracy* 10, no. 4 (1999): 84–98.

30. Bolivar Lamounier, "Authoritarian Brazil Revisited: The Impact of Elections on the *Abertura*," in *Democratizing Brazil: Problems of Transition and Consolidation*, edited by Alfred Stepan (Oxford: Oxford University Press, 1989), p. 69 (43–79).

31. Case, "Can the 'Halfway House' Stand?"

32. Fabrice E. Lehoucq, "Can Parties Police Themselves? Electoral Governance and Democratization," *International Political Science Review* 23, no. 1 (2002): 29–46.

33. Yet not all democratizing countries make small steps toward democracy. Some take huge leaps. As Serbia and Peru showed in 2000, transitions from electoral authoritarianism do not inevitably follow an incremental logic. Some electoral authoritarian regimes erode, others implode. I borrow the idea of "self-subversion" from Albert O. Hirschman, *A Propensity to Self-Subversion* (Cambridge, MA: Harvard University Press, 1995). On the notion of electoral governance, see Mozaffar and Schedler, "The Comparative Study of Electoral Governance."

34. Giuseppe Di Palma, *To Craft Democracies: An Essay on Democratic Transitions* (Berkeley: University of California Press, 1990), p. 85.

35. On the multifaceted, long-term trends of increasing power sharing between government and opposition in the course of Mexico's democratization, see Alonso Lujambio, *El poder compartido: Un ensayo sobre la democratización mexicana* (Mexico City: Océano, 2000). See also Irma Méndez de Hoyos, "Electoral Reform and the Rise of Electoral Competitiveness in Mexico, 1977–1997," Ph.D. dissertation, Colchester: University of Essex, 2000; and Diego Reynoso, "Federalismo y democracia: Las dos dinámicas de la transición mexicana," *Revista Mexicana de Sociología* 63, no. 1 (2002): 3–30; Juan Molinar Horcasitas, *El tiempo de la legitimidad* (Mexico City: Cal y Arena, 1991); Miguel Angel Centeno, *Democracy Within Reason: Technocratic Revolution in Mexico* (University Park: Pennsylvania State University Press, 1994); Alonso Lujambio, *Federalismo y congreso en el cambio político de México* (Mexico City: Instituto de Investigaciones Jurídicas, Universidad Nacional Autónoma de México [UNAM], 1995); Soledad Loaeza, *El Partido Acción Nacional: la larga marcha 1939–1994— Oposición leal y partido de protesta* (Mexico City: Fondo de Cultura Económica,

1999); Vikram K. Chand, *Mexico's Political Awakening* (Notre Dame, IN: University of Notre Dame Press, 2001); Yemile Mizrahi, *From Martyrdom to Power: The Partido Acción Nacional in Mexico* (Notre Dame, IN: University of Notre Dame Press, 2003); and Todd A. Eisenstadt, *Courting Democracy in Mexico: Party Strategies and Electoral Institutions* (Cambridge: Cambridge University Press, 2004).

36. In 1973, the largely cosmetic "political reform" under President Echeverría set the baseline for subsequent democratizing reform. In 1996, President Zedillo's "definitive reform" arguably concluded the long cycle of democratizing reforms since 1977. Since then, parties have advocated some further amendments to the electoral legislation, but to date with little success (see also this chapter's section titled "The Inversion of Protest").

37. See also this chapter's section titled "The Inversion of Protest."

38. Schedler, "The Nested Game."

39. José Antonio Crespo, "Balance electoral de 1997," *Metapolítica* 1, no. 4 (October–December 1997): 660.

40. Przeworski, et al., *Democracy and Development,* p. 24.

41. See Di Palma, *To Craft Democracies,* pp. 109–121.

42. Ibid., p. 141.

43. Manohar Singh Gill, "India: Running the World's Biggest Elections," *Journal of Democracy* 9, no. 1 (January 1998): 167.

44. As stated in endnote 1, I confine the meaning of democratic consolidation to the attainment of a high degree of expected stability of the political regime. Here, I also narrowly confine my view on (hopefully) residual problems of democratic legitimacy to the electoral arena and to political parties. For an analytical reconstruction of broader usages of the concept, see Andreas Schedler, "What Is Democratic Consolidation?" *Journal of Democracy* 9, no. 2 (April 1998): 91–107. For a theoretical synthesis of structural, attitudinal, and behavioral factors that affect processes of democratic consolidation, see Andreas Schedler, "Measuring Democratic Consolidation," *Studies in International and Comparative Development* 36, no. 1 (Spring 2001): 61–87.

45. For discussions of pending reforms, see José Antonio Crespo, "La reforma electoral pendiente," *Política y Gobierno* 7, no. 2 (2000): 445–480; and Mauricio Merino, "El Instituto Federal Electoral por dentro: algunas zonas de incertidumbre," in *El Dos de Julio: Reflexiones Posteriores,* edited by Yolanda Meyenberg Leycegui (Mexico City: FLACSO, IIS/UNAM, and UAM-Iztapalapa, 2001), pp. 39–53.

46. PAN Congressman Fernando Pérez Noriega, cited in Todd A. Eisenstadt, "Off the Streets and into the Courtrooms: Resolving Postelectoral Conflicts in Mexico," in *The Self-Restraining State: Power and Accountability in New Democracies,* edited by Andreas Schedler, Larry Diamond, and Marc F. Plattner (Boulder, CO: Lynne Rienner Publishers, 1999), p. 94.

47. Martin Shapiro, *Courts: A Comparative and Political Analysis* (Chicago: University of Chicago Press, 1981), p. 2.

48. For an overview of the evolution of nomination procedures for the top managers of the Federal Electoral Institute, see Andreas Schedler, "Democracy by Delegation: The Path-Dependent Logic of Electoral Reform in Mexico," paper

presented at the 95th Annual Meeting, American Political Science Association (APSA), Atlanta, September 2–5, 1999.

49. Andreas Schedler, "Incertidumbre institucional e inferencias de imparcialidad: El caso del IFE," *Política y Gobierno* 7, no. 2 (2000): 383–421.

50. See Takeshi Wada, "Economic Restructuring, Political Liberalization, and Shifting Patterns of Popular Protest in Mexico," unpublished paper, Department of Sociology, Columbia University, New York, 2002.

51. For a synthesis until the mid-1990s, see José Antonio Crespo, *Votar en los estados: Análisis comparado de las legislaciones electorales estatales* (Mexico City: CIDE, Friedrich Nauman Foundation, and Miguel Angel Porrúa, 1996); and Ricardo Becerra, Jesús Galindo, Manuel Palma, and José Woldenberg, *Así se vota en la República: Las legislaciones electorales en los estados* (Mexico City: Instituto de Estudios para la Transición Democrática, 1996). See also Méndez, "Electoral Reform."

52. On the distinction between centralized "police patrols" and decentralized "fire alarms," see Matthew D. McCubbins and Thomas Schwartz, "Congressional Oversight Overlooked: Police Patrols Versus Fire Alarms," *American Journal of Political Science* 28, no. 1 (February 1984): 165–179.

53. Shapiro, *Courts,* p. 24.

54. Stephen Holmes, *Passions and Constraint: On the Theory of Liberal Democracy* (Chicago: University of Chicago Press, 1995).

55. Albert Camus, *The Myth of Sisyphus and Other Essays* (New York: Vintage International, 1991 [original 1942]), p. 123.

3

Mexico's Changing Social and Political Landscape

Federico Reyes-Heroles

The year 2010 will mark one century since the beginning of the Mexican Revolution. In 1910, Francisco I. Madero set off a democratic uprising to overthrow the dictator Porfirio Díaz and install democracy. Although Madero successfully ousted Díaz, he failed to unify revolutionaries and conservatives during his short-lived presidency (1911–1913), and the bloody revolutionary struggle continued until 1920. At the time, Mexico was immersed in illiteracy and ignorance—essentially a country of peasants, sparsely populated, with a small middle class.

The twentieth century was, for Mexico, a century of great transformations. The population ceased being primarily rural and became urban. Industry and services gradually displaced the primary sector as the driving force of the economy. The middle classes grew fast. Although the country still faces daunting unmet social needs, no one in the early twentieth century could have imagined the Mexico of today. Mexico ended the twentieth century with a strong export economy closely tied to the United States and a democratic system under construction. What, then, will become of Mexico in the decades to come as we embark on a new century?

Portrayals of Mexico have been too often inclined toward myth and fantasy. The very images fostered by the postrevolutionary Mexican state for more than half a century have contributed significantly to this phenomenon. For example, one speaks of revolutionary Mexico, whereas all the studies of deep-seated values show that the Mexican population is essentially conservative.[1] Until very recently, there was talk of workers and peasants as the majority classes, although for some time now, the services sector has absorbed the lion's share of the labor force. Mexico has simply undergone the changes typical of any country that industrializes and urbanizes; now it is evident that modernization has brought with it a growing sense of realism and pragmatism to the Mexican psyche.

Clearly, at the start of the new century Mexico is at a political and economic crossroads. As Andreas Schedler states in Chapter 2, the political landscape has undergone a silent revolution, and authoritarianism at the national level has been replaced by an increasingly consolidated democratic system. On the economic side, suspicion and even paranoia of the international economic system have now been replaced by policies that reflect a growing consensus on the need for Mexico to integrate with the global economy. What has fueled Mexico's rapidly evolving domestic and international orientation is a kind of social and political revolution within the country.

This chapter elucidates several key interwoven and often conflicting issues that define this historic era in Mexican history: demographic changes and urbanization, changing political values in the context of democratization, and a growing and worrisome dichotomy between the North American Free Trade Agreement (NAFTA)–led development of the north and the intractable poverty in the south. These issues are essential in determining Mexico's political, social, and economic priorities in the decades to come.

Mexico's Demographic Challenges

One can only begin to understand Mexico's challenges ahead by examining the country's demographic dynamics. In the late 1960s and early 1970s, Mexico's population growth rate reached its highest point—3.5 percent—an increase that can be attributed to a considerable decline in infant mortality and a significant increase in life expectancy.[2] In the 1970s and 1980s, Mexico's population profile showed a country consisting primarily of children and young people, and Mexico concluded the twentieth century with 55 percent of its population under 25 years of age.[3]

In response to the alarming population growth rates in the 1960s and 1970s, the government implemented a series of demographic policies that have garnered positive results.[4] The fertility rate—the number of children per couple—declined from 7.3 in 1960 to 2.4 in 2000, and the total rate of population growth decreased to 1.6 percent.[5] Today, for the first time in Mexico's recent history, the supply of primary school services outstrips demand. Yet these developments pose a number of challenges for Mexico's future generations. All projections indicate that the population of Mexico will level off at approximately 130 million by 2040.[6] This means that between 2000 and 2040 Mexico's population will increase by 30 million, and the number of adults is such that the relative weight of young people in the total population will suffer an irreversible decline. Slowly, Mexico is ceasing to be a country of the young and is becoming one of adults and dependent elderly. These demographic changes are key determinants for future political demands.

Also important in terms of Mexico's changing political demands is the fact that new generations of Mexicans have very little to do with postrevolutionary Mexico. One interesting statistic is that of the approximately 22 million families in Mexico, almost one-fifth are sustained exclusively by women.[7] Some sectors of Mexican society have also undergone significant changes. For example, 30 years ago the main political demands grew out of labor unions and peasant organizations, but that is no longer the case. Labor unions have adapted to a new reality of political and economic liberalization in Mexico, and peasant demands for land—a constant for decades—while still present, today occupy a smaller place on the political spectrum.[8] It is not surprising that peasant demands have decreased significantly when one considers that in 1996 only around 22 percent of the Mexican population made a living through farming, and that the number of farming families, which account for an ever-smaller share of the total population, was just five million.[9] This reality is due in great part to the urbanization of Mexico's population.

Migration from rural areas to the cities and the rise of urban and middle-class segments of the population augur an important shift in Mexico's social and development needs. Mexico's cities now account for 75 percent of the population and two-thirds of the country's poor.[10] The peasant population is diminishing by approximately 1 percent annually, which means the country will end the first decade of the twenty-first century with less than 10 percent of the population dependent on farming for a living.[11]

This evolution toward an increasingly urban Mexico will ease the traditional demand from the peasant sector for land, but it will increase the demands typical of city dwellers—those for housing, water and sanitation, education, medical services, pensions, transportation, to name a few—areas in which Mexico already faces significant shortcomings. Fast growing cities and the historical population centers—Mexico City, Guadalajara, and Monterrey—face daunting urban development challenges, and urban population growth has far outstripped both the local and the federal governments' capacities to meet the demand for infrastructure services. In some parts of the Mexico City metropolitan area, for example, population growth exceeds 10 percent annually.[12] No government, whatever its form, can effectively address the needs of its citizens under these circumstances, yet voters are increasingly holding governments accountable for failure to meet these needs. It is no coincidence that support for the Institutional Revolutionary Party (Partido Revolucionario Institucional, PRI)—the party that governed Mexico for more than 70 years (1929–2000)—noticeably deteriorated in areas with high population increases where the PRI governments simply could not satisfy citizen demands.[13]

Even though the population levels are stabilizing because the growth rate continues to decline, the greatest efforts at improving urban infrastructure will have to be made over the next 25 years. It is estimated that the total investment needed to meet Mexico's demand for infrastructure services, both national infrastructure—telecommunications, roads, and energy—and urban infrastructure—housing and water—over the next decade is on the order of $20 billion per year.[14] However, one recent positive development, owing in large part to Mexico's economic liberalization strategy adopted in the mid-1980s, is that urban growth has become increasingly more balanced, with medium cities acting as regional growth poles and employment centers in various parts of Mexico, including the poorest states in the south. As indicated in a World Bank study, this more balanced urban system "implies the emergence of cities large enough to experience substantial agglomeration economies while being more manageable in terms of congestion costs . . . [and] these cities act as catalysts of growth for the regions around them."[15]

Mexico's accelerated industrialization and urban development in the last several decades has also created new challenges on the environmental front. A marked increase in pollution, waste generation, and degradation of natural resources has not only become alarming, but it has disproportionately affected the poor, especially in urban areas. The urgency in addressing Mexico's environmental health is a relatively new challenge that current and future politicians must face. Therefore, the central challenge for Mexico is to develop an urban strategy that is sustainable environmentally, socially, and economically.

Changing Political Values

The urban Mexico that is emerging tends to favor the individualization of political demands. The political shake-up in the last decade of the twentieth century can be attributed in part to the rise of the volatile vote, that is, the tendency of individuals to vote for candidates of different parties from election to election or even within the same election, instead of voting consistently for the candidates of a particular party affiliation. These Mexicans, growing in size as a political entity, are much harder to grasp, insofar as they do not commit their vote to ideologies or to stable doctrinal positions. While many voters continue to identify with a particular party affiliation, the volatile voters will determine, in large measure, the political course of Mexico in the decades to come. What are these Mexicans like?

It is with great ease that one speaks of a prototypical Mexican, a child or grandchild of the Revolution strongly inclined toward change. However, only a minority of less than 20 percent supports radical change, and most Mexicans resist such change.[16] That would explain, at least in part, the extended period the PRI was able to stay in power. Interestingly, perhaps because political discourse for decades relied on revolutionary and postrevolutionary rhetoric, coupled with the existence of a very noisy radical left, the image that Mexico's population is largely leftist does not reflect reality. The radical left—the old Communists and socialists of all stripes organized under the umbrella of the Unified Socialist Party of Mexico (Partido Socialista Unificado de México, PSUM)—garnered only 5 percent of the vote on average during the height of their political success in the 1980s.

The center-left, represented by the Party of the Democratic Revolution (Partido de la Revolución Democrática, PRD)—with Cuauhtémoc Cárdenas as its founding standard-bearer and three-time presidential candidate—reached its high point in the 1994 national elections, garnering approximately 25 percent of the vote. Yet the data on ideological self-identification in the elections of the 1990s and beyond show a clear shift to the center-right. It is not surprising that 37 percent of high-income Mexicans and 36 percent of the middle-income bracket define themselves as sympathizers of the right.[17] What is noteworthy is that 31 percent of the low-income population, which one would expect to be more likely to support the left, favors the right. It is also striking that 34 percent of the population under 30 years of age support the right, and only 28 percent support the left.[18]

The emergence of a mainstream of values identified with the center-right and a growing population of volatile voters who increasingly define electoral outcomes has important political implications. If the current trends in ideological self-definition continue, the political parties that seek to win votes in order to gain access to power will have to situate themselves in the center and center-right in the coming decades. In the 1970s, such a scenario would have been unthinkable. However, as the electorate becomes more pragmatic and volatile, and as voters acquire greater exposure to the various political alternatives (President Fox of the National Action Party [Partido Acción Nacional, PAN] and Mexico City mayor Andrés Manuel López Obrador of the PRD are leading examples of this exposure), it is quite possible that a pragmatic candidate from the center-left could emerge victorious in a not-too-distant presidential election.

Another significant change that will be accentuated in the coming decades will be the strengthened role of regional and local political officials. Political change in Mexico, defined as the systematic alternation of parties in power, began in the periphery (provincial states and cities, at first especially in the north) and then advanced toward the center (in and around Mexico City). The much-touted election of 2000, in which the PRI lost the presidency, was the culmination of this trend, which began in the most populous provincial municipalities in the 1970s, then, in the 1990s, reached the state level with gubernatorial elections. Prior to 2000, the highest-profile victory at the state level was the election of Cuauhtémoc Cárdenas to the governorship of the Federal District (Mexico City) in 1997.

One little-known piece of information that bolsters the idea of political change from the periphery to the center is that, at the municipal level, more than half of the population was already governed by an opposition party (i.e., opposition to the PRI) when Vicente Fox of the PAN won the presidency in 2000.[19] It is no coincidence that the three contenders for the presidency in 2000 were all former governors. Thus, in the coming decades, the demographic and political dynamics point to an increasingly significant role of the mayors (*presidentes municipales*) of the new and growing cities and the governors of the most industrialized states of the country in the national political landscape. The states of Nuevo León and México, which together account for a large percentage of the country's industrial output, are likely to play leading roles, while centralism, which was one of the characteristics of political life in the second half of the twentieth century, will tend to diminish.

Mexico's Social Landscape

As noted before, even as Mexico becomes a more industrialized, urbanized nation, many of its people still live in poverty. Although definitions of poverty and calculations of poverty levels vary, it is reasonable to take as a point of reference the World Bank's estimate that of the approximately 100 million people living in Mexico at the turn of the century, some 45 million are poor, while 10 million of them live in extreme poverty.[20] This means that nearly half of Mexico's population has an income of less than two dollars per day.

The majority of Mexicans living in extreme poverty belong to indigenous communities. In the mid-twentieth century, a large percentage of the population was still considered to belong to one of Mexico's indigenous groups; however, with rural-urban migration the indigenous populations are diminishing rapidly. Even so, in absolute terms, the number of people living in extreme poverty in Mexico today is staggering—it exceeds by far the population of several Central American countries.

The ever-increasing number of people migrating to the cities means that many of the indigenous groups will not see their grandchildren—and in some cases not even their children—live in their communities. Should current trends continue, and there is no reason to imagine they will change, by the year 2040 Mexico's indigenous population will be a very small minority, as indigenous rural-urban migrants integrate into the continuously growing, majority *mestizo* population.[21] The indigenous world in Mexico has come to be composed of veritable islands of misery that resist integration. Peasant life is part of their identity, but also one of the reasons they continue to live in misery. The problem is very complex, and the weight of cultural tradition is undeniable.

Another factor that allows better insight into the phenomenon of extreme misery in Mexico is the population's dispersion. In 2000, about 25 percent of Mexicans lived in communities with a population of fewer than 2,500.[22] Thus, it is materially impossible to bring public services to all the small communities. This explains, in large measure, why electricity, which today reaches 95 percent of Mexicans, does *not* reach an even larger percentage of the small communities. Because of the lack of a critical mass of people, many of these communities are condemned to disappear. It is highly likely that many of them will become ghost towns in the next two decades.

Of increasing importance in the medium and long term is the fact that all social indicators point to a clear division between northern Mexico and southern Mexico. The highest rates of illiteracy, maternal and infant mortality, school dropouts, unemployment, and, of course, the lowest incomes, are concentrated in the southern states.[23] In addition to having the worst poverty indices, the southern states, particularly Oaxaca, Guerrero, Chiapas, Hidalgo, Veracruz, and Puebla, also have the largest percentage of indigenous people. Paradoxically, many of these states have considerable natural wealth.

Within this context, the situation in these states will continue to deteriorate in the coming decades, and, as explained later in this chapter, their citizens will become, to a certain extent, politically radicalized. The radicalization of political demands will likely focus on the debates about the allocation of federal resources and the exploitation of natural resources (such as petroleum). For example, Campeche and Chiapas—two states rich in natural resources—are the leading producers of oil and electric power in Mexico, yet they are characterized as socially backward relative to other parts of Mexico.

For all practical purposes, the south begins a few kilometers from Mexico City in the state of Morelos and is characterized by very low levels of industrialization and scant development of the services sector. The southern states lose the most people to migration to the north, particularly to medium-sized cities. These states also depend the most on agriculture and, to make matters worse, many of their agricultural products are condemned to low prices in the global economy. Three such products, which may be the best known but are not the only ones, are corn, coffee, and sugar. Many of the workers in these activities will have to find new jobs in other areas or sectors. Although in the north industrial linkages and the sudden development of export plants offer a very attractive and promising future, the effects of globalization, and particularly of NAFTA, have been very painful in the south.

Prospects for the Coming Decades

What will be the impact of Mexico's changing sociopolitical landscape in the coming decades? Several scenarios are already emerging: First, the radicalization of political demands as a result of inequality and unmet social needs. Second, the rapid decline of Mexico's agricultural sector in the absence of a reformulation of agricultural development strategies. Third, the continued lag in Mexico's economic development and in the homogenization of political demands as a result of unmet educational needs. Fourth, the rise in importance of citizen organizations in the political arena. Fifth, the "Westernization" of Mexican culture and the emergence of a new type of nationalism. And, finally, Mexico's entry into a stage characterized by the so-called demographic dividend. A brief analysis of these issues will shed light on their importance to Mexico's political and economic future.

The Radicalization of Political Demands

In the coming decades, Mexico may witness the emergence of radical groups that do not accept democratic rules. This would mean the reappearance of guerrilla groups in a setting of widespread marginalization and misery that is unlikely to change in the next few decades. How successful might these groups be? The general indicators show that, overall, the Mexican population rejects violence and increasingly demands that conflicts be solved through the political process and via elections. The uprising of the Zapatista Army for National Liberation (Ejército Zapatista de Liberación Nacional, EZLN) in 1994 in the state of Chiapas is atypical, in that violent means were transformed into political discourse in a matter of days. More recently, there have been other uprisings, such as those of the People's Revolutionary Army (Ejército Popular Revolucionario, EPR) and the Revolutionary Armed Forces of the People (Fuerzas Armadas Revolucionarias del Pueblo, FARP), which have been rejected by the population at large.

Nonetheless, the cumulative lag in Mexico's growth and industrialization in the 1980s and 1990s has sparked the reappearance of groups that do not believe in the path of greater involvement in the global economy. These groups represent segments of the population that have not obtained tangible benefits from the export economy and that, to the contrary, have seen their incomes diminish with the successive economic crises that affected Mexico in the last quarter of the twentieth century. To what extent will these groups radicalize? This depends largely on the pace of growth of the Mexican economy in the coming decades, and, of course, on its capacity to generate new jobs.

To reduce unemployment, Mexico needs to grow at more than 5 percent annually and generate more than one million jobs per year, yet sustained growth at such rates has not been achieved since the late 1980s.[24] At present, only about 600,000 jobs are created annually, and, in order to meet the needs and expectations of its citizens, especially in terms of job creation among the poor, Mexico will have to grow at a rate of approximately 7 percent in the long term.[25] Nonetheless, even assuming that the country experienced sustained growth at such a rate, southern Mexico will still face serious obstacles to becoming part of the global economy given the lag in infrastructure investment in that region, particularly in communications and transportation.

The Decline of Mexico's Agricultural Sector

One of the greatest challenges Mexico faces in the next two decades is the need to modernize and capitalize the agricultural sector. The roots of the problem lie in the past. The postrevolutionary state emerged with the support of various groups, an important one being the peasantry who fought during the Revolution for better land distribution. The initial demand of the peasant revolts headed up by Emiliano Zapata and Pancho Villa in the 1910s was aimed at breaking up the huge estates that flourished during the 30-year dictatorship of Porfirio Díaz. At first, the redistribution of the large haciendas had a pacifying political effect. Nonetheless, the postrevolutionary regime institutionalized land redistribution as a means of securing political control. This led to an absurd situation whereby lands that were not at all suited for farming were distributed to peasants, then passed on to their children and grandchildren.

Mexico's agricultural sector is the subject of another of the great postrevolutionary myths: Mexico has abundant agricultural wealth. Recall that only 14 percent of the national territory is suitable for farming, and almost 40 percent of the economically active population came to depend on this fraction of the territory around the 1930s.[26] As a result, many of the land plots delivered to peasants as *ejidos* (*ejido* dweller, or *ejidatario*, being a legal description of one who has title rights to a government-distributed agricultural property) were completely inadequate for supporting a family, particularly when the fertility rate meant that couples generally had more than five children.

The geometric increase in population and the relative scarcity of agricultural lands led to a severe crisis in the rural development scheme. As an aggravating factor, the system of subsidies and supports was based essentially on corn as the key product consumed domestically. In an effort to alleviate the problem, Mexico undertook an agrarian reform in the mid-1990s that sought to modernize the agricultural sector. This required constitutional amendments that would allow the millions of peasants who possessed agricultural lands to associate, rent, or even sell their properties in order to seek more productive arrangements. However, the agrarian reform, which was key in the medium and long term, never really took hold and the modernization of agriculture simply has not begun.

The investments necessary to make Mexican agriculture competitive in an open economy are not flowing, primarily because legal obstacles still prevail. Even if this changes, the capitalization of Mexican agriculture would require several decades of systematic investment to achieve levels of productivity in line with the demands of the global markets. Nonetheless, this would not mean generating more jobs; to the contrary, it would accentuate workers' expulsion from agriculture because modern agriculture relies more on machines than it does people.

Accordingly, in the coming decades we will inevitably see the explosion of agricultural producers whose products simply have no future. The most dramatic case, of course, is Mexican corn—with some regional exceptions—which has very low yields compared with other producer countries, including the United States. Mexico's role as a producer of cereal grains is not significant at the international scale, and, therefore, many of its current agricultural development strategies should be reformulated. Yet the agricultural producers facing crises will not enjoy automatic support from a population that is increasingly urban and for whom such problems are distant.

The other side of the coin is that if Mexico is able to disentangle the legal obstacles that inhibit investment, the country's agricultural potential could be greater. Mexico, the fourth leading country in biodiversity, has countless microclimates that facilitate the production of fruits and vegetables year-round. While it is true that only 14 percent of the national territory is agricultural, it is also true that, in absolute terms, Mexico is several times larger than some European countries. Furthermore, Mexico's geographic location is very favorable for the export of agricultural products to the U.S., Asian, and European markets, some of which have severe winters. The new production technologies open up any number of opportunities for Mexico in the production of agricultural goods that have a high value-added. The future of some of the southern states, which have alarming poverty today, will be largely dependent on what happens in agriculture, and reform of the agricultural sector will play a key role in preserving political and social stability in southern Mexico.

The Education Variable

One of the most important variables affecting the country's economic development will be the educational levels of Mexicans in the twenty-first century. Mexico ended the twentieth century with an average general level of schooling of less than eight years. It goes without saying that the best levels are, once again, in the north. Nonetheless, perhaps what is most dramatic is that in the last decade of the twentieth century Mexico was able to increase the general level of education by only one year, on average. Should this trend continue, it will take Mexico 40 years to reach the educational levels of those countries that are its partners and competitors. The opportunity cost for Mexico in the coming decades lies in the fact that the unmet educational demand is focused on the last three years of primary education and the three years of secondary education. If Mexico does not make a decided effort in the next 15 years to invest in its human capital, there will be no solution to the general productivity problems currently present. It is thus critical to place in perspective the importance of meeting Mexico's educational needs.

Some studies have shown that political demands undergo a transformation as education levels increase. For example, one study uses traditional authority and bureaucratic authority as coordinates.[27] Traditional authority brings together very fundamental political demands and favors personalized representations. The level of abstraction increases with the general level of education, and political demands are transformed into conceptual lists. These differences are evident when one compares the political demands in Mexico City with those of Chiapas. Mexico City today has the highest level of education in the country. The kind of political demands that arise there are much more elaborate and have to do with issues such as the representation of the rights of minorities and the environment. Such political demands are very similar to those found in developed countries. In contrast, the state of Chiapas today has the educational level that Mexico City had in the 1950s and the political demands arising there are much more elementary.

In the first years of the twenty-first century, Mexico has a highly varied menu of political demands closely linked to those very different educational levels. Homogenization of political demands is still very far off. In northern Mexico, a largely urban region, political races tend to be more sophisticated, catering to a well-informed population. In contrast, the elections in the south rely on more traditional tactics. The degree of integration of the various states of Mexico plays a role in this, along with how citizens get information. Thus, those states in which television has reached the large majority of households can be clearly distinguished from those in which political communication occurs through campaign rallies and gatherings. It will be hard for this differentiation to disappear in the coming decades, as the socioeconomic conditions do not allow for a sudden turnaround. This distinction represents a challenge to the political parties, which need to attend to a clientele that is highly differentiated in terms of educational level and information. Consequently, in the coming decades it is very likely that there will continue to be different forms of popular representation.

The changes experienced in recent years in the federal Chamber of Deputies are perhaps a good indication of where the state legislatures and municipal councils are headed. The changes began with the political reforms of 1977–1979 that introduced proportional representation in Congress.[28] A new generation of university-educated professionals, whose discourse illustrated a level of training far more sophisticated than that of traditional legislative representatives, arrived to the Chamber of Deputies, slowly displacing those without comparable professional credentials. The latter, however, continue to play an essential role in some states with low educational levels. In the coming decades, depending on advances in education, this trend will progress, leading to a very significant change in the profiles of the elites who run the country. Nonetheless, the lag is such that it will take time to see a widespread professionalization of political activists.

The Rising Role of Citizen Organizations

One sector that will become an increasingly prominent political actor in the coming decades is that comprising citizen organizations.[29] In Mexico, in contrast to what happened in the United States and some other countries, the natural tendency of citizens to organize was supplanted for decades by the corporatist structure of the party in power, the PRI. This vertical top-down formula encompassed millions of peasants who were centrally organized and also millions of workers represented in corporatist organizations. Thus, in Mexico, for decades, the corporatist organizations were the necessary intermediaries between the citizens and the state.

Corporatism extended far beyond workers and peasants, as it also came to embrace the incipient middle classes. By law, corporatism extended to the merchants and businessmen, forcing them to belong to organizations that oftentimes did not represent the true interests of the members—to give just one example, Mexico's taxi drivers were for many years affiliated with a federation that in reality was controlled by the PRI. This organizational scheme bound the governing party to grant seats in the Chamber of Deputies and in the Senate to the leaders of these organizations. In the hard-fought and highly questioned election of 1988, the PRI pushed the corporatist apparatus to the hilt so absurdly that it brought about a real rebellion. From that moment on, slowly but systematically, the corporatist structures for peasants, workers, the middle class, and the business sector have been collapsing. The necessary legal reforms have been approved by the Supreme Court.

Thus, citizen organizations have been gradually replacing the old corporatist structure and have begun assuming the traditional role of political pressure groups. Their rise has not been uniform nationwide, partly because the three main national political parties—the PRI, the PAN, and the PRD—were openly distrustful of citizen organizations. For the PRI, the reasons center on the corporatist structure explained above. But it is striking that some leaders of the opposition to the PRI also considered the free association of citizens as risky for party interests. Citizen organizations face important challenges, such as limited budgetary resources, which in turn limits their ability to create jobs, while at the same time many of their problems are exacerbated by legal obstacles, chief among them the strong limits on tax deductibility.

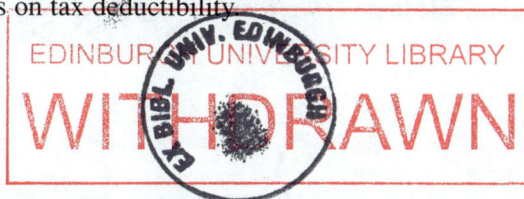

Scant citizen interest in participating actively in a political party or belonging to a trade union has as its corollary the growing desire to belong to citizen organizations. The areas of concern are many: the environment, sports, and the fight against corruption, to name a few. The vast majority of citizen organizations could be described as third-generation, insofar as they are not linked to the political parties and are expressly nonpartisan groupings.

One case that may cast light on the complexity of the new political intermediaries that are cropping up is that of the religious organizations. In the 1990s, with the amendment of the Constitution and the respective statutes, religious organizations were permitted to register and to have a broader public role.[30] As a result, a whole set of small actors, hitherto unknown, surfaced. In Mexico, where Catholicism has long been the predominant religion, comprising about 90 percent of the population, the high-level clergy were always accorded importance. Nonetheless, when religious organizations registered with the authorities, hundreds of different denominations, all affiliated with Catholicism, came out of the woodwork.

The matter of citizen groups is sufficiently complex that the authorities have decided to open a new office in the federal government to keep track of and support citizen organizations. If current trends continue, in the coming decades Mexico's political parties will have few active members and be increasingly dependent on their presence in the media for support. At the same time, a great many social organizations will become the necessary intermediaries with the authorities.

Nationalism and the "Westernization" of Mexican Culture

Another aspect of national cohesion undergoing major change is nationalism. One of the great myths often used to explain Mexico was the alleged existence of strong nationalism, but the facts illustrate a different reality. When the figures are analyzed, it is evident that nationalism in Mexico is much more folkloric than real, and it would appear that a certain realism or pragmatism has been permeating the consciousness of Mexicans over time. For example, opinion polls show that Mexicans admire, first, the United States, followed by Japan and then the European countries.[31] What ever happened to the "big bad wolf" image of the United States?

The data show a less romantic and folkloric but much more modern reading of Mexico. For example, Mexicans prefer to trade with the United States than with their Latin American counterparts, and what Mexicans admire most about the United States is, first, its wealth and, then, its democracy.[32] Is there any reason why this preference for the United States

over Latin America would be reversed in the coming decades? Clearly not. Mexico's trade relations with the rest of the world, especially the United States, have expanded exponentially in the past decade. Throughout the decade from 1930 to 1940, there were some 200 million border crossings between Mexico and the United States. By the end of the 1990s, the rate of crossings per year had risen to approximately 300 million.[33] Many scholars of cultural consumption are concerned because the vast majority of television programs and films shown in Mexico and much of the popular music heard on radio stations comes from the United States. For some, these are signs of the total yielding of the expressions of traditional nationalism. Linguists express similar concerns about the increasingly frequent use of English-language expressions in the daily life of Mexicans, not to mention the growing number of Mexicans who learn English from early childhood.

The medium- and long-term projections indicate that in the next few decades there will be a very significant cultural confluence between the new inhabitants of Mexico and the citizens of the United States.[34] The "Westernization"—and, in particular, the "North Americanization"—of Mexico involves openly imitating the organizational forms of the United States and other nations. The Mexican elite follow with ever-greater detail the proposals coming out of the United States and the European countries and unabashedly propose importing those schemes—an attitude that would have been unthinkable in the mid-1970s, when cultural nationalism pervaded everything. This cultural openness does not, however, imply a total elimination of nationalist sentiment. Careful examination of the conduct of the citizens from the extensive Mexico–U.S. border reveals that despite the intense interaction, there are behaviors that continue to differentiate the two cultures.

In any event, Mexicans are witnessing the disappearance of a nationalism that operated during the stage of economic and cultural statism of earlier times, but that turned out to be inoperative in the face of the process of political and economic liberalization that Mexico embarked on in the 1980s and 1990s. Today, Mexicans could be witnessing the rise of a new type of nationalism, perhaps less tied to the traditional expressions of dress, language, and food, and referring more to other issues such as political and economic rights for Mexican nationals working in the United States. A new form of nationalism may slowly be taking shape as the U.S.–Mexico bilateral relationship continues to mature and deepen—a nationalism that distinguishes Mexico's views on foreign policy and other areas from those of its neighbor to the north, yet never loses sight of the two countries' close partnership.

The Demographic Dividend

Finally, the so-called demographic dividend will have a noticeable impact on Mexican politics. This phenomenon is a unique opportunity in the demographic history of a nation, which involves the decline, to a minimum, of the number of dependents per worker.[35] Mexico is entering a demographic dividend stage estimated to last some 20 years, a period over which its dependent minors will decline significantly in number, without there being a concomitant increase of elderly becoming dependents.

This demographic juncture makes it possible for the country to save on social expenditures, as it has not been able to do hitherto. Several factors contribute to this opportunity. First, as already stated, the proportion of minors is diminishing relative to the economically active population. Second, the growing entry of women into the workforce results in more households with two salaries. And finally, there is a smaller proportion of dependent elderly.

If Mexico takes full advantage of this opportunity, the country's domestic savings rate, which stood at approximately 20 percent of gross domestic product (GDP) in 2000, will increase significantly; therefore, the number of ways of satisfying social demands will also grow.[36] If so, the social tensions will diminish, and the raison d'être for radicalism will diminish. If Mexico does not take advantage of this population juncture to save and grow, however, the country could be facing a terrible situation where, within 25 years, it would have a downtrodden and poor population. In demographers' terms, it would shift from being a country of poor children to a country of poor elderly. Whether productive use will be made of this opportunity will depend largely on the country's democratic institutions, which are slowly sinking roots, and on reducing the number of families in extreme poverty.

Conclusion

Mexico's changing social, political, and economic needs—and the government's ability to effectively address them—will define the context within which the country continues its economic and political evolution. Failure to ameliorate the pressing needs of a fast changing society will hinder Mexico's efforts to, once and for all, leave behind the country's status as a "developing" nation. Macroeconomic stabilization or U.S.-educated technocratic teams cannot accomplish this alone.

As this chapter illustrates, Mexico is at a critical juncture in its development. An armed revolution that began in 1910 launched the country into a century of extraordinary transformations, a protracted social, political, and economic revolution of sorts. As Mexico embarks on a new century, the challenges are many, as are the opportunities. The question is, what kind of revolution will the country undergo in the twenty-first century? The issues addressed in this chapter might provide a sound point of departure in the search for an answer.

Notes

1. See, for example, Alejandro Moreno, *World Values Survey 2000* (Mexico City: Reforma, 2000); Miguel Basáñez and Alejandro Moreno, *World Values Survey 1990–1993* (Mexico City: MORI de México, 1990); and Instituto Mexicano de Opinión Pública (IMOP-Gallup Mexico), *World Values Survey 1981–1984* (Mexico City: IMOP, 1981).

2. Consejo Nacional de la Población (CONAPO), *La situación demográfica de México* (Mexico City: CONAPO, 1999), pp. 11–27; and Instituto Nacional de Estadística, Geografía e Informática (INEGI), "Tasa de crecimiento media annual, 1950–2000," Dinámica de la Población, available online at www.inegi.gob.mx (last accessed March 2004).

3. Ibid.

4. For a study of the demographic policies implemented in Mexico in the twentieth century, see María Eugenia Zavala de Cosío, *Cambios de fecundidad en México y políticas de población* (Mexico City: Fondo de Cultura Económica, 1992).

5. CONAPO, "Tasa global de fecundidad, 1960–2000," Indicadores de salud reproductiva, República Mexicana, Población de México en Cifras, available online at www.conapo.gob.mx (last accessed March 2004).

6. CONAPO, *Proyecciones de la población de México, 2000–2050* (Mexico City: CONAPO, 2002), p. 30.

7. INEGI, "Hogares y su Población por Entidad Federativa y Grupos de Edad del Jefe del Hogar, y su Distribución Según Sexo del Jefe del Hogar," *XII Censo General de Población y Vivienda 2000* (Mexico City: INEGI, 2000). Available online at www.inegi.gob.mx (last accessed March 2004).

8. The corporatist apparatus that endured for decades in Mexico, and which arose from the reconfiguration of the political power structure after the Mexican Revolution, rested on three pillars: the peasant-agrarian sector, labor, and the so-called popular sector (bureaucrats, teachers, and other social groups). These three groups formed their own organizations that granted them access to the party apparatus and provided them with a political voice through collective action. As Mexico's political system liberalized, the role of these groups in the political process weakened considerably.

9. Grupo Financiero Banamex-Accival, *México Social 1996–1998 Estadísticas Seleccionadas* (Mexico City: Banamex, 1998).

10. World Bank, "Mexico Urban Development: A Contribution to a National Urban Strategy," Report No. 22525-ME, Vol. 1: Main Report, July 15, 2002, p. 10.

11. Grupo Financiero Banamex-Accival, *México Social.*

12. Ibid., p. 643.

13. Alonso Lujambio, *El poder compartido* (Mexico City: Editorial Océano, 2000).

14. All dollar amounts are in U.S. dollars, unless otherwise noted. Richard Clifford, "Growth and Competitiveness," in *Mexico—A Comprehensive Development Agenda for the New Era,* edited by Marcelo M. Giugale, Olivier Lafourcade, and Vinh H. Nguyen (Washington, DC: World Bank, 2001), pp. 69, 78.

15. World Bank, "Mexico Urban Development," pp. 10–11.

16. Ronald Inglehart, Miguel Basáñez, and Alejandro Moreno, *Human Values and Beliefs: A Cross-Cultural Sourcebook* (Ann Arbor: University of Michigan Press, 1998).

17. National Poll (Encuesta Nacional), MORI de México, Mexico City, December 1997.

18. Ibid.

19. Instituto Federal Electoral (IFE), Mexico City, online at www.ife.org.mx (last accessed March 2004).

20. World Bank, "Mexico: Country Brief," available online at www.worldbank.org (last accessed March 2004). The World Bank defines "poor" as living on less than $2 per day, and living in "extreme poverty" as surviving on less than $1 per day.

21. The term *mestizo* refers to any person of mixed blood; in Mexico and other Latin American countries, the term broadly denotes a person of combined indigenous and European blood.

22. INEGI, "Porcentaje de población por tamaño de localidad, 1950–2000," in *Estadísticas sociodemográficas,* available online at www.inegi.gob.mx (last accessed March 2004).

23. Grupo Financiero Banamex-Accival, *México Social.*

24. Marcelo M. Giugale, "A Comprehensive Development Agenda for the New Era—Synthesis," in *Mexico—A Comprehensive Development Agenda,* edited by Giugale, Lafourcade, and Nguyen, p. 8.

25. Ibid.

26. Luis Téllez, *La Modernización del Sector Agropecuario y Forestal* (Mexico City: Fondo de Cultura Económica, 1994).

27. Inglehart, Basáñez, and Moreno, *Human Values.*

28. The Chamber of Deputies has a designated number of proportional or "plurinominal" seats. Plurinominal deputies are elected based on the percentage of votes cast for each party. See Jorge Alcocer V., "Recent Electoral Reforms in Mexico: Prospect for a Real Multiparty Democracy," in *The Challenge of Institutional Reform in Mexico,* edited by Riordan Roett (Boulder, CO: Lynne Rienner Publishers, 1995), p. 59.

29. For more on this subject, see Julia A. Millán Bojalil and Antonio Alonso Concheiro, eds., *México 2030, Nuevo siglo, nuevo país* (Mexico City: Fondo de Cultura Económica, 2000).

30. For an overview of the legal reforms on religion in Mexico, including the historical background of church-state relations, see Roberto J. Blancarte, "The 1992 Reforms of Mexican Law on Religion: Prospects of Changing State-Church Relations," in *The Challenge of Institutional Reform,* edited by Roett, pp. 95–113.

31. National Poll (Encuesta Nacional), MORI de México, Mexico City, December 1997.

32. Ibid.

33. CONAPO, "Migración mexicana hacia los Estados Unidos," in Migración internacional, available online at www.conapo.gob.mx (last accessed March 2004).

34. Inglehart, Basáñez, and Moreno, *Human Values.*

35. David E. Bloom, David Canning, and Jaypee Sevilla, *The Demographic Dividend: A New Perspective on the Economic Consequences of Population Change* (Santa Monica, CA: RAND, 2002). Available online at www.rand.org (last accessed March 2004).

36. "Putting 'Missed' Chances Behind," *Financial Times,* December 14, 2000, p. 5.

PART 2

The Challenges of
Economic Transformation

4

Mexico's Domestic Economy: Policy Options and Choices

Russell Crandall

The December 2000 peaceful transfer of the presidency from Ernesto Zedillo to Vicente Fox marked a watershed in Mexican politics. After 71 years of single-party rule by the Institutional Revolutionary Party (Partido Revolucionario Institucional, PRI), governmental power at the national level had finally been transferred to an opposition candidate. For decades to come, political scientists will continue to study that event to find more clues to help understand the lessons learned from that extraordinary moment in Mexico's political history—one that will certainly serve as a model for other countries attempting to make the transition to true democratic governance.

Yet nearing the end of the Fox administration (2000–2006), it is clear that many of the difficult tasks he faced upon assuming the presidency are still unresolved and new ones lie ahead.[1] While honeymoons are by definition ephemeral, today President Fox, from the National Action Party (Partido Acción Nacional, or PAN), can no longer rely upon the cushion of political legitimacy as a political outsider (at least at the national level) that initially insulated him from many of the criticisms piled upon the previous presidents, all of whom were from the PRI. The 2003 midterm elections served as a cold reminder to the Fox administration that politics did not end in Mexico in July 2000. Though no longer the dominant single party, the PRI performed well in the elections, replacing the 500-member federal Chamber of Deputies, gaining 14 seats, and bringing its total to 222 Chamber seats; the PAN lost 56 seats and is left with 151; the Party of the Democratic Revolution (Partido de la Revolución Democrática,

PRD) nearly doubled its Chamber seats to 95.[2] What is evident is that the PRI has no intentions of going the way of the Communist parties of Eastern Europe or the Soviet Union—rather it wants to challenge for national power in a democratic context, and it stands in a good position to do so.

The success of Fox's presidency—and of Mexico's social, political, and economic development—rests heavily on his administration's ability to provide strong and clear political and economic leadership under which sustainable development can take place. As is almost always the case, much of his success will depend on how well Fox manages economic policy, because although "no one lives in the macroeconomy," Mexicans know all too well (from examples such as the economic crises of 1982 and 1994) how difficult life can be in an unstable macroeconomic climate. Thus, a key question about Fox throughout his term of office has been and will continue to be how well he manages the economy, especially the macroeconomic fundamentals. As this chapter indicates, the *macro* and *micro* of economic reform are increasingly inseparable in Mexico; thus Fox's macroeconomic policies will often include many microeconomic details.

Fox's predecessor, Ernesto Zedillo (1994–2000), entered office just as Mexico was beginning to experience a profound economic crisis. Mexico's currency, the peso, plunged almost immediately after his inauguration in December 1994, and by January 1995 the country was stuck in a deep recession. Yet under Zedillo's deft economic stewardship, the Mexican economy quickly rebounded from its 1995 trough. After several years of solid growth, Zedillo left office with the economy growing by 7 percent.

Thus, unlike Zedillo in 1994, Fox assumed the presidency at a propitious time in Mexico's economic history, a moment when many observers believed that the country had, perhaps, finally laid to rest its interminable cycle of economic instability. After almost two decades of repeated attempts at economic reform and liberalization, with some success as well as failures, many hoped that Mexico had finally emerged from its status as an emerging market. The economic climate also enabled candidate Fox to promise growth rates of 7 percent annually.

Yet the reality of Mexico's economic situation is much more precarious and complex than the heady days of the end of the Zedillo administration suggested. Once Fox's administration moved beyond campaign rhetoric, his team learned the hard way that Mexico still has deep structural economic issues that make continuous 7 percent growth rates an almost absurd notion. Indeed, Mexico remains mired in a structural web of economic problems that threatens to hinder the country's future economic performance. The components include a lack of competitiveness throughout Mexican industry that is exacerbated by a stubborn nominal exchange rate and increased competition from Asian and other Latin American producers, an increasing dependence on the growth of jobs in the export industries that straddle the border with the United States, fiscal revenues that remain far below what an industrialized country requires in order to maintain strong institutions and promote social welfare, and out-dated petroleum and energy sectors that need serious reform and whose demise could easily undermine success in other sectors of the economy, especially at the macro level.

Following on the heels of Zedillo's post-peso-crisis stabilization efforts, the Fox administration needs to demonstrate the ability to effectively manage the macroeconomy and to institutionalize prudent management so that the Mexican economy's structural stability can be taken for granted. Fox's government also needs to consolidate the export industries in northern Mexico that have now become the country's economic locomotive. After almost a decade of boom years fueled by the North American Free Trade Agreement (NAFTA) and the 1994 currency devaluation, the maquiladora industry faces severe structural and cyclical competitiveness issues that must be quickly addressed.

In fact, competitiveness is a concern not just for the maquiladora sector—Mexico's economic competitiveness lies at the heart of its efforts to institutionalize its impressive recent economic gains. In today's global economy, stability is not enough. Mexico is not only competing against Honduras, Jamaica, and Ecuador, but also Malaysia, Hungary, Turkey, and China. It is not sufficient that Mexico become a country that avoids debt default, "lost decades," and peso crises. Instead, Mexico must become a nimble, competitive player in the international economy, one that can take advantage of its excellent geographic location (complete with free trade access) next to the world's largest economy.

The paradox that confronts the Fox administration is that economic reform has often proven to be more difficult in a democratic Mexico than it was during the PRI's democratic-only-in-name tenure in office. Fox realizes that any lasting economic reform will entail disrupting entrenched special interests. It will likely also require a continued reassessment of the Mexican nation's understanding of its economy, especially with respect to natural resources. Unlike the previous PRI administrations, the PAN's Fox cannot rely upon the national and local party–state apparatus that worked to ensure support for the PRI's economic policies. Instead, Fox must convince the Mexican people through his own efforts that the nation must make changes. He needs to provide the one thing that many accuse him of lacking: leadership.

That is not an easy task. Quite frankly, the Fox administration might ultimately serve as the "democratic bridge" to a successor government that is more able to implement lasting economic reforms. The legacies of the PRI's provision of economic and social patronage in return for support at the polls remain embedded in the Mexican psyche. While undemocratic, that system provided material benefits to the Mexican populace for decades. There is no reason to believe that Mexicans will cease to have high expectations for what their government can deliver just because it is no longer from the PRI.

Six years is not a long time to break that type of thinking, but Fox's efforts will nonetheless set the stage for further reform and consolidation. Furthermore, being a democracy also means that the Mexican Congress, a legislative body that to date has shown itself eager to embarrass President Fox and prevent him from moving forward with his agenda, will first have to approve most of his reform policies. Like the Bush administration's efforts to line up allies in the war on terrorism, Fox must work hard to establish governing coalitions that will enable him to put his policies into practice.

Ernesto Zedillo left office in 2000 with 70 percent approval ratings; Vicente Fox entered into the presidency with comparable ratings. The biggest difference between the two, however, is that Zedillo had to earn his approval over the course of his presidency, one that stimulated a remarkable recovery from the 1995 recession. Unless Fox's government assumes a more proactive position of leadership and authority that focuses on the key issues of the Mexican economy and is not afraid to anger entrenched constituencies, he could easily leave office with the same low approval ratings that greeted Zedillo during the 1994–1995 peso crisis. One of Fox's most visible campaign slogans was "Ya!" (Enough already!). Consolidating a vision of how to govern in Mexico remains a key challenge for Fox. He will need to jettison the old ways of doing politics in Mexico and emerge as the president who reshaped the country's political and economic parameters. If not, soon enough, Mexicans will be responding to Fox's presidency with new exclamations of "Ya!"

Two Decades of Reform:
Mexico's Path to Economic Liberalization

Mexico's industrialization began in earnest during World War II, as U.S. diversion of its production to war meant that Mexico increasingly had to produce its own industrial products. The industrialization process picked up steam—and gained more ideological underpinnings—when Miguel Alemán (president 1946–1952) actively imposed import tariffs in order to protect domestic industries. Unlike many Asian countries such as South Korea and Taiwan that only protected certain domestic industries and that even then eventually made them compete on the international market, Mexico implemented a model that protected industries across many sectors and intended their output for domestic purposes.[3] Those economic policies came to be known as import-substitution industrialization (ISI) and defined the Mexican economy—for good and bad—until the middle-to-late 1980s.

Mexico's ISI boom years were roughly between 1950 and 1970 when Mexican industries quickly expanded their production, taking advantage of government subsidies, a captive market, and the lack of foreign competition. During those years, real gross domestic product (GDP) per capita almost doubled—as did the population.[4] During the 1970s, the Mexican state also became much more directly involved in the economy, as reflected in the expansion of the number of state-owned enterprises from 84 in 1970 to 845 in 1977.

Under President Luis Echeverría (1970–1976) the Mexican government began to shift its economic policies away from just economic development to include social development.[5] Although a noble effort, it also entailed more public spending, something that was not matched by additional fiscal revenues (a problem that continues to plague Fox's efforts to expand social programs). Mexico's discovery of new oil fields at a time when oil prices were surging helped bridge the gap. In addition, the unprecedented windfalls of petroleum revenue allowed the Mexican government to borrow even more from international capital markets, spurring a remarkable growth in public expenditures.[6]

With interest rates often negative in real terms, Echeverría's strategy seemed foolproof: borrow cheaply, grow the economy, promote social welfare, and use seemingly endless petroleum revenues to service the debt. Mexico had located the proverbial "free lunch" of economics and assumed it was possible to enjoy present consumption through seemingly innocuous foreign debt obligations. The strategy also provided for a rapidly growing population, one that was increasingly questioning the ruling party's legitimacy, especially following the political upheavals surrounding the Olympic Games in Mexico City in 1968. However, the euphoria ended abruptly in 1981: oil prices plunged and the U.S. Federal Reserve embarked on a sustained policy of raising interest rates to finally eviscerate "stagflation" from the U.S. economy.

Because much of Mexico's international debt had been negotiated at variable interest rates, the rate hikes dramatically increased its debt burden, a reality that quickly led to economic chaos. Import-substitution industrial-ization had spurred impressive growth rates for decades; yet by the 1970s, Mexico's ISI experiment had also institutionalized an economic system that was devoid of productivity gains and could not stand up to serious competition. Paranoid about the economic and political giant to the north, Mexico staked its economic future on dynamism in the domestic economy, a strategy that proved to be mostly a failure. In fact, by the end of José López Portillo's presidential term of office (1976–1982) Mexico's "boom" was officially over.[7]

That reality was driven home in 1982 when López Portillo responded to the growing debt crisis by nationalizing the banking system, suspend-ing payments on $80 billion of foreign debt, and devaluing the peso.[8] Although a currency devaluation was virtually unavoidable at that point, the Mexican government's decision to default on its debt severely restricted the country's access to international capital markets.

Reeling from the effects of the devastating economic crisis that en-sued following the 1982 debt default and peso devaluation, Mexico re-mained a mostly closed economy in the mid-1980s. President Miguel de la Madrid (1982–1986) then began to implement the first of what would now be considered neoliberal reforms.[9] His administration focused on the macroeconomic side, attempting to stabilize the exchange rate and keep inflation in check. Economic growth during those years remained anemic, exacerbated by international lenders' reluctance to return to Mexico after the bitter experiences of default earlier in the decade.[10] The lack of foreign capital meant that Mexico needed to keep the current account balance in surplus in order to finance the capital account. The government achieved the surplus through repeated currency devaluations, which in turn sparked domestic inflation. Despite some earnest efforts at stabilization, the 1980s were a bitter decade for Mexico. Yet the underpinnings for stronger eco-nomic performance began in 1988 when the election of the PRI candidate and economic technocrat Carlos Salinas de Gortari signaled the broaden-ing and deepening of what at that point was a still-untested neoliberal path.

The Salinas Years, 1988–1994

Carlos Salinas entered the presidential residency as a radical reformer. With a Harvard University graduate education in orthodox economic poli-cies and experience as a loyal and fierce bureaucrat under de la Madrid, Salinas was committed to setting Mexico on a new economic path. His reforms attempted to bury what he believed were the excesses and distortions of the ISI period, one that was viewed by many technocrats as an anachronism of an early, more ideological period. For Salinas, the end of history had arrived in Mexico.[11] The country's path to salvation no longer rested in knee-jerk, anti-U.S. policies and protected industries but in firmly embracing the global economy, especially that of the United States. The Salinas administration used its patron-client networks—more specifically, the use of political pacts with societal groups—to guarantee support for its policies within critical labor and industry (both rural and urban).[12] With that political insulation in place, the Salinas team aggressively privatized state-owned enterprises, liberalized domestic prices and subsidies, and opened up domestic industry to foreign competition.[13]

Salinas's most significant economic policy was the implementation of NAFTA with the United States and Canada. Signed on January 1, 1994, NAFTA marked the successful institutionalization of the new path of neoliberal reforms that Salinas had embarked upon since his term of office began. Lower trade barriers and bilateral trade between Mexico and the United States had exploded before the implementation of NAFTA: by 1990, Mexico's exports had grown to 14 percent of GDP, double that of a decade earlier, and, as indicated by Gary Gereffi and Martha Martínez in Table 6.3, Chapter 6, between 1995 and 2001 exports as a percentage of GDP averaged more than 30 percent.

With the ruling party's suspicious, nationalistic path becoming a thing of the past, the Salinas administration now based Mexico's economic future on privileged access to the North American market. It was expected that Mexicans would be able to buy a variety of products cheaper, that Mexican industries could take advantage of their propitious geographic and political position, and that the country would forever leave behind its developing country status. Needless to say, many Mexicans did not share Salinas's vision of free trade and integration into the U.S. market. For example, in a tremendous act of symbolism, the Zapatista rebellion was launched on the same day as NAFTA's inception. Yet, the undemocratic nature of Mexico at that point meant that the Salinas government could largely ignore societal opposition to its neoliberal policies.

His strategy seemed to work: growth averaged 2.8 percent during the Salinas years, and inflation fell from 159.2 percent just before his term to 7.1 percent in 1994. Real interest rates fell from 16 percent in 1988 to between 4 and 6 percent in 1994. Underpinning the impressive growth was a stable exchange rate that attracted foreign investment to what was then seen as a modernizing emerging market. Foreign capital poured into Mexico: foreign direct investment (FDI) increased by 58 percent from 1989 to 1993, and portfolio investment increased by some 8,000 percent.

By the mid-1990s, portfolio investment was almost 90 percent of total investment flows, compared with only 11.3 percent in 1989.[14]

With the economy supported by a decision to maintain a strong and stable nominal exchange rate, Mexico experienced a boom in consumption in the early 1990s. With higher inflation than in the United States but the nominal exchange rate remaining relatively unchanged, the peso's appreciation fueled the consumption of imports and worsened the current account balance. Like the earlier view that borrowing at negative real interest rates could make up the fiscal gap in the 1970s, Mexican monetary authorities were convinced that they could indefinitely finance the current account deficit with the seemingly endless supply of impatient international capital knocking down doors trying to get into Mexico. At first, the policy worked fine: Mexico could enjoy low inflation and higher consumption, all the while using foreign capital to finance the budgetary gaps. The policy's ability to promote greater real purchasing power pleased the Mexican middle class. The "crawling peg"—in actuality the nominal exchange stayed quite stable—pleased international investors who wanted to see their profits emerge from Mexico at the same exchange rate at which they came in.

What those same Mexican authorities now know all too well is that hot international capital can leave a country just as quickly as it enters—a true double-edged sword. For Mexico, 1994 was "the year of living dangerously." The Zapatista revolt, the March assassination of PRI presidential candidate Luis Donaldo Colosio, and other political scandals scared off badly needed fresh flows of foreign capital. U.S. Federal Reserve Chairman Alan Greenspan's decision to raise U.S. interest rates also lowered the real rate of return that international investors could hope to realize in Mexico.

We now know that Salinas's "economic miracle" was predicated on a best-case scenario in which the influx of foreign capital had to continue at its ferocious pace.[15] Another pressing problem was the paradox of economic-exchange-rate stability. By keeping the nominal exchange rate stable, international investors flocked to Mexico. Yet any moves to adjust the exchange rate to address the growing current account deficit in 1994 would have been seen as a red flag, further scaring off what had now become vital foreign capital flows. In an election year, government authorities decided against any significant adjustment of the peso and instead hoped that the introduction of more dollar-denominated debt instruments called *tesobonos* would keep international capital interested in Mexico. The issuing of tesobonos skyrocketed in 1994, a growing indication of impending doom that was largely overlooked by domestic and international analysts alike.

In a story that has been well told by now, the tesobonos were not enough to keep Mexico on the best-case scenario path. During the second half of 1994, foreign capital flows dropped by 75 percent. Mexico's central bank authorities spent billions trying to keep the nominal exchange rate stable (again, a strong peso was the linchpin of the macroeconomic plan), and reserves dropped from $30 billion to $6 billion by the end of 1994.[16] It was within that economic environment that Ernesto Zedillo took office in late 1994.

The Zedillo Years, 1994–2000

With domestic and international investors furiously selling pesos at the rate subsidized by the Mexican central bank, on December 20, 1994, the recently installed Zedillo government widened the exchange rate band by 15 percent. In the 48 hours between the announced devaluation and the forced devaluation of the peso, Mexico's foreign reserves dropped by $4 billion.[17] The flow of international capital had blown open the floodgates of the exchange-rate regime—investors sold pesos in droves and the nominal price of the peso almost immediately plunged from three pesos per U.S. dollar to six per dollar (see Figure 4.1).

Figure 4.1   Exchange Rate Between the Peso and the U.S. Dollar and Mexico's Rate of Inflation (rate of inflation is reflected in the consumer price index, CPI), February 1994–February 2002

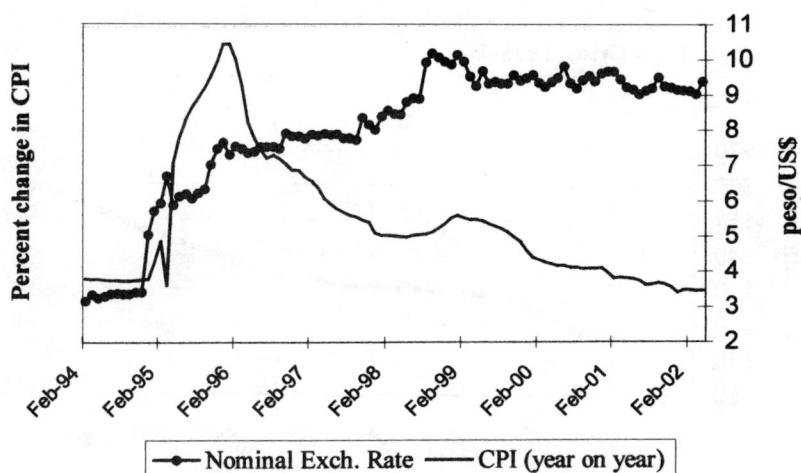

Source: Bank One, Mexican Finance Secretariat (Secretaría de Hacienda y Crédito Público, www.shcp.gob.mx), 2002.

Confronted with formidable foreign debt obligations—a situation exacerbated by the move into dollar-denominated tesobonos—Mexico teetered on the precipice of economic collapse. Default or a forced rescheduling of international debt appeared imminent. Although highly controversial at the time, with the benefit of hindsight it is clear that U.S. President Bill Clinton's $47 billion loan to Mexico staved off an economic catastrophe. Amid fierce scrutiny in the U.S. Congress, the Clinton administration prepared the loan in late February 1995;[18] the funds included contributions from the International Monetary Fund (IMF), the Bank for International Settlements (BIS), and the United States Exchange Stabilization Fund.[19] The financial rescue sent a strong signal to international investors and Mexican residents that the United States was throwing its support behind the new Mexican administration. In financial terms, the tremendous size of the loan allowed Mexico to fill up its foreign reserve coffers and continue to service and reschedule its debt to end the liquidity crunch that the December peso devaluation had provoked (see Figure 4.2).

While the rescue package surely prevented the situation from becoming much worse, Mexico nonetheless plunged into a deep recession. In 1995, GDP dropped by 6 percent and real wages dropped by more than 10 percent. A crime wave swept across the country, especially in Mexico City. The situation was grim. What few inside and outside realized at the time is that, while severe, the economic recession would last only 18 months.

Figure 4.2   Change in Mexico's Foreign Exchange Reserves After the Peso Crisis, 1995–2003

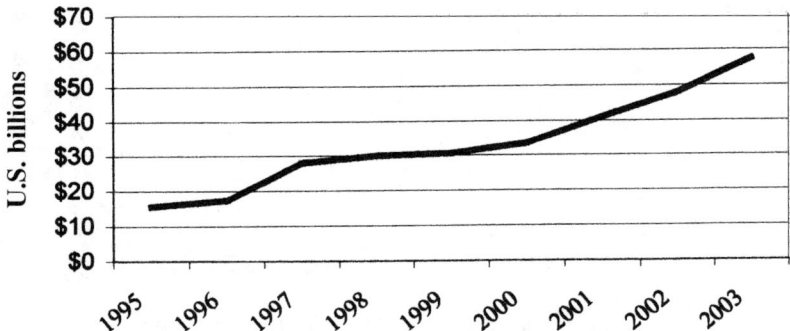

Source: Bank One, Mexican Finance Secretariat (Secretaría de Hacienda y Crédito Público, www.shcp.gob.mx), 2004.

The J-curve in economics theory predicts that countries that devalue their currency will first see a worsening of the current account balance before an improvement. This occurs because, given the fixed price of contracts and other transactions, the country's consumers and producers will not immediately switch their consumption habits to reflect the higher cost of imported goods and services. Thus initially, a country will continue to purchase the same volume of goods at higher prices. Over time, local producers and consumers will switch their consumption to reflect the new prices and the current account balance will normally improve.

In Mexico during 1995, the J-curve barely registered at all. The switch from a bilateral trade deficit to surplus took only a few months.[20] Indeed, trade with the United States—something made more fluid and attractive by NAFTA—was the locomotive that pulled Mexico out of what looked to be its worst nightmare. In 1995 and 1996, the U.S. economy had recovered from its mild recession and was embarking on a period of rapid growth. With post-devaluation Mexican goods now much cheaper in real terms, the U.S. demand for Mexican products soared, lifting the Mexican economy along with it. The Mexican export sector's dynamism during that time solidified the sector's central place in Mexico's economic philosophy during the Zedillo years and continues to do so today.

Even though Mexico's recovery turned out to be quicker than almost all analysts had predicted, the crisis left residual effects in the economy that plagued the Zedillo administration for years. What this example showed is how a macro crisis—the 1994 devaluation—drove a micro crisis, which in this case was the devastating increase in real interest rates and the ensuing credit crunch. Interest rates shot up to more than 100 percent at times in 1995, and, not surprisingly, consumer credit dried up instantly.[21] Debtors that were reeling under the effects of the new debt burden formed groups such as *El Barzón* that emerged to demand that borrowers receive a break in their obligations, something that in turn placed greater pressure on an already fragile banking system. Moreover, debt was virtually impossible to collect as arcane bankruptcy laws made it difficult to collect overdue obligations.[22] The private debt problem began to subside when Mexican monetary authorities eased interest rates after Mexico's macroeconomic situation stabilized and inflation started to drop. But the Zedillo administration was forced to deal with the legacy of the banking crisis for the rest of its tenure.

While much of the banking crisis had its roots in overlending during the consumption boom under Salinas, the postdevaluation interest rate spikes were what exposed the rot within the system.[23] A government-led bailout was almost unavoidable, and it soon became the Zedillo administration's policy. Modeled on the Resolution Trust Corporation that dealt with the U.S. banking crisis in the 1980s, the Savings Protection Banking Fund (Fondo Bancario de Protección al Ahorro, Fobaproa) was the government agency given the task of purchasing the bad loans that were sitting on books of many of the country's largest banks. Fobaproa's efforts began inauspiciously, because it announced the relatively high minimum prices at which it would buy bank debt, a move that discouraged banks from continuing to go after their past-due debt. As a result, banks dumped their liabilities on Fobaproa, as there were no limits to the amount that the agency could guarantee.

By 1998, the agency had acquired around $65 billion in liabilities. Mexico's 11 largest banks made up around half of the total liabilities.[24] The agency took a long time to sell its assets, thus slowing down its revenue flow. Critics also charged that the agency was rescuing wealthy bankers from risky loans that they should have never made in the first place. The case became most controversial when the Zedillo administration went to Congress to request that the cost be absorbed into public debt. After much debate and criticism, the banking crisis cost the Mexican government around 15 percent of its GDP, $65 billion.

Starting with the recovery from the peso crisis and continuing until Fox's December 2000 inauguration, Mexico's economic performance— and its ability to weather external shocks—was nothing short of remarkable. GDP grew by an average of 5.1 percent between 1995 and 2002, and inflation, which had peaked at 52 percent in 1995, was 4.4 percent in 2001. The current account—which, along with the fixed (and overvalued, in real terms) exchange rate, had caused so much damage in 1994— improved significantly. (Although more recently, the current account has become a concern even though it is being financed with more FDI than was previously the case and with less of the volatile portfolio capital that ran for the exits in 1994.) Moreover, a higher domestic savings rate (12 percent of GDP in 1994 and 20 percent in 2000) allowed Mexico to tap internal markets for its borrowing needs to finance the fiscal deficit that in 2000 amounted to a manageable rate—less than 1 percent of GDP.[25] The Zedillo administration's move to a floating-exchange-rate system cured one major headache of the Mexican authorities—devaluation. Alarm bells routinely sounded as the nominal exchange rate stubbornly clung to the rate of 10 pesos per U.S. dollar, which threatened to spark an even greater real appreciation and pressure the current account balance; however, central bank authorities no longer feared a disruptive currency crisis provoked by massive capital flight.

Here, too, Ernesto Zedillo laid the foundation for Mexico's economic growth and stability. It almost seems as though, after getting burned so many times, his economic team was determined to do everything right so that no blame could be attached to it if Mexico were to suffer another catastrophic crisis.[26] Oil revenues are a poignant example. Unlike the oil shocks in the 1970s, when Mexico used windfall revenues to borrow even more money (ultimately precipitating the debt crisis of 1982), Mexico used the 1999–2000 surge in the price of oil to prepay—three years early—$3 billion of debt to the IMF.[27] Conversely, when the price of oil was barely over $10 a barrel in 1997, Mexico's Energy Secretary Luis Téllez cut spending to ensure that Mexico could operate under the new economic reality. Another stark example of Zedillo's macroeconomic success was the dramatic drop in international debt, a burden that in early 1995 looked to overwhelm the Mexican economy. In the mid-1980s, Mexico had a gross federal debt to GDP ratio of 115 percent; in 2001 that ratio was 39 percent, compared with the average ratio for G-7 countries of 80 percent. Equally as impressive, fiscal deficits that hovered around 15 percent of GDP at the heart of the crisis were less than 1 percent by 2002.[28]

Structural Economic Reform:
The Key to Fox's Economic Success

Analysts in the IMF, on Wall Street, or behind the ivy-covered walls of academe have no trouble identifying what a country such as Mexico needs to do in order to promote structural economic reform. The laundry lists of reforms recommended by the Institute for International Economics, a prestigious Washington, D.C., think tank, or the financial firm Merrill Lynch in New York, detail seemingly obvious solutions to what ails countries such as Mexico. Yet all politics is local, and that statement certainly applies to the Mexican case. Here again is the democratic paradox: painful but often necessary reforms will be more difficult to implement in the now more democratic Mexico. Although that poses a challenge for the Fox government, in the long run, economic reforms implemented democratically will be more lasting, as the domestic population will tend to feel invested in the decisions and therefore be more willing to ride out any difficulties.

Although there are countless solutions to Mexico's structural economic problems, there are very few practical ones that can cut through the politically charged atmosphere of a newly democratic country attempting to leave behind decades of patronage and undemocratic governance. To be sure, such a democratic context does not apply only in Mexico. In the United States one sees similar cases, such as the economically counterintuitive, but politically logical, decision to impose steel tariffs in 2002. Thus, just as it is quite rational for a West Virginia steelworker or senator to support tariffs on imported steel, the strong opposition to the Fox administration's economic reform policies should not come as a surprise.

In the Mexican Congress, opposition through 2003 to Fox's reform agenda was spirited and effective. The PRI's success at the July 2003 elections for the lower house of Congress only reinforced the reality that Fox's political opposition is not only organized and determined but also holds its own mandate from voters. What Fox needs—especially now past the midterm elections—are governing coalitions, ones that broaden his legitimacy beyond the strength of his personality and the novelty of being the first non-PRI president in Mexico's history. This will also hold true for his successor. Fox's "lone ranger" governing style has largely failed, as the political and economic pressures in a country as diverse and complex as Mexico are simply too great. Mexico is not the Coca-Cola Corporation he headed in Mexico or even the state of Guanajuato where he was governor in the 1990s.

To effectively govern on the national stage, Fox must broaden his political support by creating ad hoc alliances that coalesce over individual or multiple reform issues. Mexican politicians are inexperienced when it comes to implementing reform with a legislature and executive of different parties, yet recent divisions within the PRI's congressional bloc may facilitate coalition building. December 2003 saw the PRI split over tax reform leading just over half of its 222 legislators in the Chamber of Deputies to vote to replace Elba Esther Gordillo as their leader.[29] Division within the ranks of the PRI may provide a window of opportunity in which to craft alliances, if Fox is willing to take it. Change is never easy in politics—it often means making new enemies—and that is especially true of economic reform. By trying to please everyone, Fox pleases no one. Even worse, he will spend precious political capital in the process.

Macroeconomic Stability Under Fox

After five years of solid growth, Mexico experienced a slowdown in 2001: growth was an anemic minus 0.3 percent, and it only ticked up to 1.3 percent in 2003.[30] Because the U.S. economy moved close to a recession in 2001, the slowdown in Mexico was largely due to a drop in external demand for Mexican goods. Exports of goods and services dropped to 5.1

percent of GDP in 2001, a sharp contrast to the 2000 level of 16.4 percent of GDP. The manufacturing sector also cooled significantly, with its output falling by 2.8 percent in 2001.

While a drop in U.S. demand for Mexican products explains Mexico's downturn in 2001, there are deeper structural and policy issues that will determine Mexico's macroeconomic path during the remaining Fox years. Following the successful macroeconomic stabilization under Zedillo, Fox's goal with regard to the exchange rate should be to make everyone forget about the peso. The peso only comes into the news when it is in trouble. Thus, a peso that is gently managed by Mexico's central bank but still free to adjust according to market forces helps ensure the country will not see a repeat of 1982 or 1994 anytime soon.

Yet in what is a holdover from the last few years of the Zedillo administration, the Fox government still needs to ensure that the relatively stable nominal exchange rate does not, over time, lead to an unsustainable real appreciation of the peso vis-à-vis the U.S. dollar. Coupled with high interest rates in order to keep inflation at impressively low levels, significant amounts of capital fleeing Argentina's protracted economic crisis have found their home in Mexico. Again Mexico is experiencing the paradox of success: strong macroeconomic fundamentals have made it a country that attracts capital that is fleeing more unstable waters. The downside of this situation is that the inflow of capital increases inflationary pressures and keeps the nominal exchange rate stuck, hurting the increasingly important export sector. It should be pointed out, however, that the fortunes of the critical maquiladora sector are more dependent on demand in the United States than on the exchange rate. The nominal exchange rate began to depreciate slightly in 2002 and reached a record low at the close of 2003, yet this advantage for the export sector was provoked by lack of confidence in Fox's ability to promote growth and tax collection after the PAN's July 2003 defeat at the polls.[31] However, by the opening months of 2004 the peso had appreciated once more to levels considered strong by historical standards.[32]

The Fox administration has provided unprecedented price and monetary stability. At the close of 2003, the budget deficit was one-third of what it had been when Fox assumed the presidency, and foreign debt decreased to less than 20 percent of GDP. Annual inflation fell in 2003 to a record low of 4 percent, compared with its high of 180 percent in 1988.[33] In February 2002, Standard & Poor's upgraded the country's long-term sovereign credit rating to BBB– from BB+. This means that Mexico enjoys investment-grade status from all of the major rating agencies, in turn easing access to international bond markets for public and private needs and lowering the cost of borrowing. This is a structural transformation, one that should not be overlooked. Mexican monetary authorities took advantage of the upgrade to prepay external debt. On the downside, the credit upgrade has also attracted more foreign capital, contributing to the peso's strong nominal price. Tight monetary policy also keeps the peso expensive. Yet despite the tight monetary policy, Mexican interest rates continue to come down (see Figure 4.3).

The Maquiladora Sector: New Challenges

The rapid increase in the growth of the maquiladora-based part of the Mexican economy is one indication of its response to seemingly insatiable U.S. demand for goods produced in Mexico.[34] Following the demise of the Bracero Program in the 1940s that allowed Mexican migrant laborers to work legally in the United States, during the mid-1960s the Mexican government established the maquiladora program. The program was designed to allow capital equipment to be imported duty-free when used in maquiladoras or in-bond industries.[35]

Figure 4.3   Convergence of Mexican and U.S. Interest Rates (default comparable rates are the U.S. discount rate and Mexico's 28-day Cetes rate), September 1999–March 2002

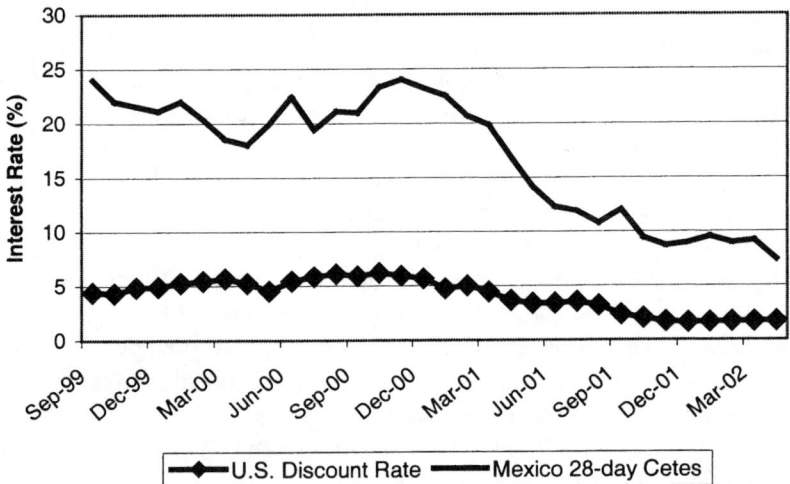

Source: Bank One, Mexican Finance Secretariat (Secretaría de Hacienda y Crédito Público, www.shcp.gob.mx), 2002.

These manufacturing plants now produce about half of Mexico's exports, and the sector grew some 20 percent annually between the inception of NAFTA and the 2001 economic downturn.[36] By 2000 the maquiladora sector provided 1.4 million jobs, compared with 546,000 when NAFTA began in 1994.[37] While the maquiladoras have been an engine of economic growth, unfortunately they are not a panacea for development ills.

One concern is that only about 3 percent of the maquiladoras' inputs is locally produced, a figure that lowers the potential for backward links to other sectors of the manufacturing economy. A much more pressing concern is that of the maquiladoras' role in accentuating regional economic imbalances. NAFTA has induced "a giant sucking sound," not from Mexico to the United States, but rather from southern to northern Mexico. With wages and job prospects significantly lower in the southern part of the country, an internal migration process has been under way for years, but the social and economic effects are just beginning to be known. What is well understood, however, is that the booming maquiladora-driven border cities do not possess adequate infrastructure to provide basic human services to the newly arrived residents. The maquiladora sector also lacks the ability to absorb the over one million potential workers that come of age each year in Mexico.[38]

The social impact of the rapidly changing maquiladora sector is also a key concern. In fact, the way that President Fox responds to the social effects of Mexico's economic and social transformation will help determine the success of his administration. Economic integration with the United States and the maquiladora-dependent nature of Mexico's economy are, for the foreseeable future, irrevocable realities of Mexico's economy and society; how Mexico chooses to deal with that reality is an entirely different issue. In addition to an aggressive plan to humanize the conditions under which Mexico's workers labor to maintain the country's economic growth rate, the Fox administration will need to find ways to promote job creation in nonborder regions. Given Fox's impressive track record for successful efforts of that type while he was governor of Guanajuato, it is likely that his national government will rise to the occasion. Fortunately, there are already signs that some maquiladora-structured manufacturers are moving south. For example, a Japanese cable car company hired 2,500 people in Chiapas, and manufacturing veterans in Guanajuato and Puebla are also gearing up to welcome maquiladoras.[39]

It is also increasingly evident that the Mexican maquiladora sector is losing some of its competitiveness vis-à-vis other countries. A large part of the growing lack of competitiveness stems from the fact that, despite Mexico's privileged location and tariff-free access, the growing real wages in the maquiladora sector are prompting capital to move to more competitive labor markets. Thus, Mexican maquiladoras are closing at an unprecedented pace and moving to countries such as Costa Rica, El Salvador, and even China. In recent years, more than 500 maquiladoras have closed, translating into between 250,000 and 300,000 lost jobs.[40] Of the approximately 144,000 formal jobs lost in 2001, about two-thirds were in the maquiladora sector. In what is a bittersweet paradox, the maquiladoras' economic success has generated higher real wages for maquiladora workers, an unarguable benefit for the workers who enjoy these higher wages; however, that development has also sparked a worrisome transfer of production out of the sector.

More than half (236) of the closed maquiladoras were in the clothing industry, which suggests that these labor-intensive jobs may have shifted to other low-wage countries.[41] Much of Mexico's competition is coming from China, and in 2003 China replaced Mexico as the number one supplier of clothing to the United States.[42] Mexico's average daily wage for maquiladora workers is $8, while Chinese wages are approximately $2 per day.[43] The Mexican labor secretariat stated in mid-2003 that around 300 of the closed manufacturing plants had relocated in China.[44] Mexican growth in exports to the United States has decreased to about 2 percent per year, while China's has increased to around 20 percent per year since 2000.[45] FDI in Mexico averaged $14 billion per year between 1994 and 2002, yet in 2003 FDI contracted by 25.7 percent to $10.7 billion and new investments fell by almost 67 percent.[46] Meanwhile, in 2002 China became the world's largest recipient of FDI.[47]

The Fox administration needs to confront this paradox head on or see the indisputable gains in the maquiladora sector be lost to lower-wage foreign competitors. Mexico will need to move beyond low wages for its comparative advantage in the export sector. Indeed, Mexico must continue to work to move up the food chain in the maquiladora sector by improving job training and skills so that these industries can continue to be competitive even if real wages are rising. Perhaps more problematic are indications that Mexico's competitiveness suffers not only from rising wages but from lack of competitiveness at the institutional level. Difficulty implementing reforms leaves energy and telecommunications costs far above Mexico's competitors, manufacturing is highly taxed to compensate for tax evasion elsewhere, rigid labor laws further increase the price of overall labor costs, and poor infrastructure adds to transportation costs thus lessening Mexico's comparative advantage of proximity to the United States.[48] Institutional barriers that prevent addressing Mexico's disadvantages must be reformed to compensate for the loss of comparative advantage in terms of wages.

Revenue and the Labor Market

In addition to the critical maquiladora sector, a key issue for Mexico's long-term economic well-being remains fiscal revenue. In particular, although domestic savings have increased in recent years, tax revenue remains well short of what will be required to fund Fox's myriad social programs: greater spending on teachers and schools, for example, and an aggressive attack on absolute poverty. For the next several years, almost 85 percent of budget expenses have already been earmarked for specific programs. The Fox administration must find a way to increase tax revenues as a percentage of GDP in order to make good on promised investments in education, infrastructure, and the social sector.[49]

Raising tax revenue has never been an easy chore in Latin America. Profligate governments anywhere oftentimes waste revenue, which in turn makes citizens and corporations hesitant to pay more. Mexico has been no exception, and its tax take is the lowest of the 29 members of the Organization for Economic Cooperation and Development (OECD). Excluding taxes on oil (around 4 percent of GDP), tax revenue stood at 12 percent of GDP in 2003.[50] The current government hopes to increase that figure to around 16 or 17 percent, a tall order, but an essential one. Simplifying the tax system and cracking down on evasion are the two strategies most likely to produce results, combined perhaps with a lower corporate tax rate.[51] Official estimates put tax evasion in Mexico at around 30 percent, so there is plenty of money for the government to target. Another key element is widening the tax base by incorporating the sizable informal economy into the formal economic system.

The legitimacy Fox has because of his reputation as an honest, no-nonsense businessperson should foster greater will to honor the tax code; Mexicans will be less inclined to evade taxes if they know their resources will not line the pockets of corrupt politicians. But Fox still faces the challenge of pushing controversial and always unpopular tax reform through Congress without a clear majority and with only weak backing from his own party. In 2001 the Mexican Congress only partially enacted the Fox administration's comprehensive tax reform package. The reforms included reducing the number of tax brackets, a 10 percent telecommunications tax, luxury taxes, a 20 percent capital gains tax on certain types of equities, and the elimination of tax credits on private salaries.[52]

Other efforts to increase revenue include the New and Clean Account (*Borrón y Cuenta Nueva*[53]) program. This system overlooks taxpayers' past failures to pay taxes as long as they begin declaring their taxes. In 2001 the program has so far resulted in an additional 1.4 million new tax declarations. Mexican authorities also initiated legal proceedings against more than 680 tax dodgers.[54] To date, Fox's biggest failure has been the inability to implement a single rate for the value-added tax (VAT). The Fox administration's draft budget for 2004 included cutting the VAT rate from 15 to 10 percent but applying it to everything. The president, however, has met much congressional resistance. The PRI campaigned in the 2003 midterm elections against applying the VAT to food and medicine and was bitterly divided over a proposal to tax the production of food and medicine.[55] Streamlining the VAT is critical, because Mexico's VAT revenues have hovered around 3 percent, roughly half the rate of many industrialized countries, though in 2003 collection of the VAT increased by over 11 percent due to reforms allowing small businesses to calculate their own taxes.[56] Despite these partial reforms, the slowed economy forced the Mexican government to match the drop in revenue by cutting spending in order to keep the fiscal deficit below 1 percent of GDP.[57]

Along with increasing tax revenue, a key element in Mexico's microeconomic reform process will be dealing with Mexico's corporatist labor legacy.[58] Even after the death in 1997 of union boss Fidel Velázquez, who for 53 years oiled the wheels between the PRI and labor, the Mexican labor system is still plagued by unrealistically high severance packages that discourage managers from hiring and firing, automatic promotions that increase costs without having any connection to productivity, and closed shops that limit labor mobility. These rigidities put a severe strain on the dynamism of the economy, especially in the small- and medium-sized business sector.[59] Although various forms of workers' protection such as social security and the ability to organize should remain fundamental rights of Mexican workers, many observers feel that a strong dose of "modernization" should be administered, especially if Mexico is to compete effectively, not just with countries such as Jamaica and Colombia, but also with Indonesia, Thailand, and South Korea.

While not much of an issue during the country's experiment with ISI, Mexico's now-firm commitment to economic integration will mean greater scrutiny of Mexican firms' record-keeping and business practices. The Enron and Arthur Andersen scandals demonstrated that no country is immune from sloppy or mischievous corporate behavior; yet Mexico will still need to work to bring its standards up to international levels. Liberalization also opened the Mexican economy to greater competition, and this has meant that many relatively uncompetitive small- and medium-sized producers—a traditional pillar of employment in Mexico—have suffered greatly over the past decade.[60]

Sectoral Reform: Petroleum and Electricity

Effective reform of the petroleum and electricity sectors is an issue where attempts at necessary reform run right up against Mexico's current pluralistic political system as well as its political heritage. Oil is no longer the savior to the Mexican economy that it was in previous eras. In fact, oil has often caused as much harm as good, such as when it got Mexico into trouble during the debt-led growth era of the 1970s. Yet oil continues to be a symbol of economic sovereignty and national patrimony for many Mexicans. For that reason, it is not surprising that most politicians are reluctant to address its reform. It is readily apparent that the petroleum sector will face a severe crisis if reforms are not enacted soon. In August 2001, Raúl Muñoz Leos, director of the state-owned petroleum company Pemex, warned that unless private investment was allowed, Mexico's crucial oil exports could drop 66 percent by 2006.[61] Muñoz also warned that without the necessary investment, and if internal spending remained the same as it had for the previous 15 years, Pemex could face institutional collapse within five years.[62] More recent indicators suggest that Pemex has moved away from the expected financial abyss. In September 2003 Pemex announced that it was spending $10.3 billion in exploration and production, an increase of almost 50 percent from the previous year.

Beyond nationalist sentiments, part of the difficulty is that Pemex is squeezed by high taxes, as it is a great source of revenue for the government. Currently 62 percent of Pemex's sales go to the government. In 2001, oil accounted for 24 percent of public revenue, 5.2 percent of GDP. With the Fox administration's firm commitment to keep the fiscal deficit in check, any attempt to lessen the tax burden on the petroleum (and electricity) sector means that the revenue must be made up somewhere else. It has been difficult for the Fox administration to increase fiscal revenues. Yet Pemex's investment needs require that it have a lighter tax burden. It is a vicious cycle: if Pemex does not invest in technology and infrastructure, it will not modernize and grow, and the government will lose its longtime cash cow. On the other hand, lowering Pemex's tax burden will squeeze the fiscal balance at a time when the Fox administration's reform agenda requires every spare peso.

Many analysts have suggested partial or complete privatization of Pemex as a way to cover the gap between investment needs and available capital. President Zedillo attempted partial privatization of Pemex in the late 1990s, but most of those attempts went nowhere. It is likely that President Fox will push for incremental reforms of the petroleum sector in order to keep the sector out of bankruptcy. And, quite frankly, there is little that his administration can do, other than try and try again, if the electorate demands that the government maintain what the people believe is an important symbol of their identity as Mexicans. An important signal of possible progress occurred in 2003 when Pemex invited foreign energy companies to assist in the exploitation of the Burgos natural gas field in northern Mexico.[63]

In upcoming years, demand for natural gas in Mexico will increase 10.3 percent annually, while supply will grow only by 7.3 percent.[64] This is occurring at a time when natural gas is rapidly becoming the principal source of fuel for power plants. In 2002 natural gas was the principal fuel for 16.6 percent of Mexico's power plants; by 2009 the figure is estimated to be closer to 50 percent. Mexico presently gets most of its natural gas as a by-product from its offshore petroleum drilling. Yet Pemex lacks the resources to explore for new gas sites, especially those not associated with oil.[65] Former energy secretary Ernesto Martens estimated that Mexico will need to invest $13.7 billion per year for decades for Pemex to be able to respond to the increased demand for natural gas. Though Mexico is estimated to have natural gas reserves larger than either the United States or Canada, constitutional restriction of private and foreign investment forces Mexico to import around 15 percent of its natural gas at costs over twice as high as domestic prices.[66] Constitutional reform will prove difficult considering that the PRI stands accused of receiving more than $45 million of illegal campaign funds from Pemex's workers union.[67]

To address the energy problem, in 2001 the Fox administration went ahead with an effort to allow private electricity plants to increase their sales of energy to the grid. The government chose this policy in order to circumvent the politically explosive and procedurally difficult process of amending the constitution. Nevertheless, the Mexican Supreme Court ruled that Fox's decision was unconstitutional, a ruling that was supported by many in Congress. The court decision has resulted in the delay of significant inflows of money ($25–$30 billion) into the electricity system, because foreign electricity companies have cancelled their investments. Mexico is now expected to face energy shortages in the future, a reality that might actually wind up making reform of the electricity sector more appealing to the Mexican populace.[68]

Conclusion

Vicente Fox's government faces enormous challenges as it finishes the second half of its six-year term of office. Elected in a popular upsurge of voters' desire for an end to the battle-tested, but increasingly outdated, political system, Fox quickly became all things to all people. In the hope that change had finally arrived in Mexico, Fox was seen as someone who could solve all problems painlessly. And Fox did little to disabuse Mexicans of this notion. Many took Fox at his word when he promised that growth would continue at 7 percent annually or that the conflict in Chiapas would be resolved in "fifteen minutes."

Several years into his term, Mexican voters know better, but this does not mean that Fox will not—or should not—be the reformist president that he has portrayed himself to be. Rather, he must now realize that today in Mexico, effective public policy is in many ways more difficult to implement than ever. The right policies are just the beginning of the political—and often social—battles in this new democracy. Fox must be patient yet persistent, open-minded and willing to work across the political spectrum, but also ruthless in the execution of his policies.

If not, Mexicans will come increasingly to see their president as one who is comfortable eating steaks with U.S. President George W. Bush in Crawford, Texas, but unable to govern an often intractable congress at home. Mexico has made the difficult transformation from one-party rule to a pluralistic democracy. Yet in the liberating and exciting forum of democracy, the Fox administration must not let itself become overwhelmed with politics. It must lead and shape the political agenda so that Mexicans buy into the need for reform. Nothing short of Mexico's political, social, and economic future rests in the balance.

Notes

The author would like to thank Akilah Jenga for her invaluable assistance with his chapter.
1. See Mary Jordan and Kevin Sullivan, "The New Face of Mexico: Vicente Fox's Mexican Revolution," *Harvard International Review* 23, no. 1 (Spring 2001): 24–28; Robert Leiken, "With a Friend Like Fox," *Foreign Affairs* 80, no. 5 (September–October 2001): 91–104; Michael Massing, "Seeing Mexico: Twelve Years, Three Leaders, Three Prisms—How We Keep Missing the Big Picture," *Columbia Journalism Review* 40, no. 2 (July–August 2001): 46–50; Lucy Conger, "Mexico's Long March to Democracy," *Current History* 100, no. 643 (Fall 2001): 58–64; Judith Adler Hellman, "Opting for Fox: Why, and How, Mex-

icans Went for the PAN," *Report on the Americas* 34, no. 2 (September–October 2000): 6–10; "Happy Birthday, Señor Fox," *The Economist,* July 8, 2000, pp. 31–32; Elliott Abrams, "Fox Populi: Thanks to NAFTA and Zedillo, Mexico Finally Holds a Democratic Election," *Weekly Standard* 356, no. 8178 (July 2000): 31–32.

2. Cámara de Diputados, H. Congreso de la Unión, "Composición de la Cámara por Partido," and "Integración LVIII Legislatura," available in the official Chamber of Deputies website: www.cddhcu.gob.mx (last accessed September 2003).

3. For more on Asian versus Latin American developmental models in the 1950s and 1960s, see Riordan Roett and Russell Crandall, "The Global Economic Crisis, Contagion, and Institutions: New Realities in Asia and Latin America," *The International Political Science Review* 20 (July 1999): 3; and José Edgardo Campos and Hiltion Root, *The Key to the Asian Miracle: Making Shared Growth Credible* (Washington, DC: Brookings Institution Press, 1996).

4. "PRIde Before the Fall," *The Economist,* October 26, 2000, Mexico Survey section, pp. 5–7.

5. Jonathan Heath, "The Impact of Mexico's Trade Liberalization: Jobs, Productivity, and Structural Change," in *The Post-NAFTA Political Economy: Mexico and the Western Hemisphere,* edited by Carol Wise (University Park: Pennsylvania State University Press, 1998), pp. 174–175.

6. Sebastian Edwards, *Crisis and Reform in Latin America: From Despair to Hope* (Washington, DC: World Bank, 1995), pp. 18–19.

7. Ibid., pp. 20–21.

8. All dollar amounts are in U.S. dollars, unless otherwise noted. See Heath, "The Impact of Mexico's Trade Liberalization," p. 176.

9. For an overview of the reform process in the 1980s, see Edwards, *Crisis and Reform*, pp. 17–40.

10. Manuel Pastor, "Pesos, Policies, and Predictions: Why the Crisis, Why the Surprise, and Why the Recovery," in *The Post-NAFTA Political Economy,* edited by Wise, p. 122.

11. For an explanation of the "end of history" concept see Francis Fukuyama, "The End of History?" *The National Interest* 16 (Summer 1989): 3–18; Forrest Colburn, *Latin America at the End of Politics* (Princeton, NJ: Princeton University Press, 2002); and Russell Crandall, "Revolution on Hold?" *SAIS Review* 13, no. 1 (Winter–Spring 2003): 273–277.

12. Maria Lorena Cook, Kevin Middlebrook, and Juan Molinar Horcasitas, "The Politics of Economic Restructuring in Mexico: Actors, Sequencing, and Coalition Change," in *The Politics of Economic Restructuring: State-Society Relations and Regime Change in Mexico,* edited by Maria Lorena Cook, Kevin Middlebrook, and Juan Molinar Horcasitas (La Jolla: Center for U.S.–Mexican Studies, University of California–San Diego, 1994), pp. 3–52; Carol Wise and Manuel Pastor, "Mexican Style Neoliberalism: State Policy and Distributional Stress," in *The Post-NAFTA Political Economy,* edited by Wise, p. 44. Also see the entire volume of Wayne A. Cornelius, Ann L. Craig, and Jonathan Fox, eds., *Transforming State-Society Relations in Mexico: The National Solidarity Strategy*

(La Jolla: Center for U.S.–Mexican Studies, University of California–San Diego, 1994).

13. See Laurence Whitehead, "Political Change and Economic Stabilization: The 'Economic Solidarity Pact,'" in *Mexico's Alternative Political Future,* edited by Wayne A. Cornelius, Judith Gentlemen, and Peter H. Smith (La Jolla: Center for U.S.–Mexican Studies, University of California–San Diego, 1989), pp. 181–214.

14. Pastor, "Pesos, Policies, and Predictions," p. 125.

15. Timothy Kessler, "The Mexican Peso Crash: Causes, Consequences, and Comeback," in *Exchange Rate Politics in Latin America,* edited by Carol Wise and Riordan Roett (Washington, DC: Brookings Institution Press, 2000), p. 46.

16. Ibid., pp. 44–45; Rudiger Dornbusch, "The Folly, the Crash, and Beyond: Economic Policies and the Crisis," in *Mexico 1994: Anatomy of an Emerging-Market Crash,* edited by Sebastian Edwards and Moisés Naím (Washington, DC: Carnegie Endowment for Peace Press, 1997), pp. 125–140; Rogelio Ramírez de la O, "The Mexican Peso Crisis and Recession of 1994–1995: Preventable Then, Avoidable in the Future?" in *The Mexican Peso Crisis: International Perspectives,* edited by Riordan Roett (Boulder, CO: Lynne Rienner Publishers, 1996), pp. 11–32.

17. Manuel Pastor, "Pesos, Policies, and Predictions," p. 136.

18. See Jacqueline Mazza, *Don't Disturb the Neighbors: The United States, Democracy, and Mexico* (London: Routledge, 2001).

19. Ngaire Woods, "International Financial Institutions and the Mexican Crisis," in *The Post-NAFTA Political Economy,* edited by Wise, p. 153.

20. For a technical discussion of the J-curve, see Paul Krugman and Maurice Obstfeld, *International Economics: Theory and Policy* (New York: Addison Wesley, 2000), p. 466.

21. Kessler, "The Mexican Peso Crash," p. 53.

22. Ibid.

23. See Kessler's "The Mexican Peso Crash" for a discussion of the Fobaproa case. Also see "Latin Lessons for Asian Banks," *The Economist,* July 23, 1998, p. 22.

24. Kessler, "The Mexican Peso Crash," p. 55.

25. "Putting 'Missed' Chances Behind," *Financial Times,* December 14, 2000, p. 5.

26. For more on Mexico's response to the 1997–1998 Asian economic crisis, see Riordan Roett and Russell Crandall, "The Global Economic Crisis, Contagion, and Institutions: New Realities in Asia and Latin America," *International Political Science Review* 20, no. 3 (July 1999): 271–283.

27. For more on Mexico's early IMF payment, see Henry Tricks, "Mexico Likely to Make Early IMF Payment," *Financial Times,* August 31, 2000, p. 11.

28. "Fiscal Reform," *Merrill Lynch,* July 17, 2001.

29. "The Lady Vanishes," *Economist,* December 6, 2003, p. 33.

30. Elisabeth Malkin, "U.S. Economy Recovery Begins to Trickle into Mexico," *New York Times,* February 18, 2004, section W, p. 1.

31. John Lyons, "Mexico Seeing Few Advances; In First World Race, Nation Falling Behind," *Houston Chronicle*, November 26, 2003, Business, p. 1.

32. John Authers, "Bank of Mexico Acts on Inflation Before Wage Round," *Financial Times*, February 21, 2004, p. 4.

33. "Mexico's NAFTA Boom Cools Off," *Tulsa World*, November 30, 2003, p. E7; M. Delal Baer, "Mexico at an Impasse," *Foreign Affairs* 84, no. 1 (January–February 2004): 101–113.

34. This section on the maquiladora industry was first published in Russell Crandall, "Mexico's Changing Domestic and International Dynamics," in *Latin America in a Changing Global Environment,* edited by Riordan Roett and Guadalupe Paz (Boulder, CO: Lynne Rienner Publishers, 2003), pp. 171–187.

35. As explained in Chapter 6 by Gary Gereffi and Martha Martínez, the maquiladora program officially ended on January 1, 2001. Nonetheless, many firms in Mexico still provide in-bond services, even if they are no longer required to hold maquiladora permits to import inputs or export finished goods to and from the United States. As in Chapter 6, the term maquiladora will be used to describe these firms.

36. "Central States Dominate the Action," *Financial Times*, December 14, 2000, p. 4.

37. Susan Ferriss, "Broken Promises: Mexicans Rely on Dwindling Export Assembly Work," *Cox News Service*, October 30, 2003.

38. Kevin G. Hall, "NAFTA at 10: Predicted 'Sucking Sound' of Job Losses More Like a Whimper," *Knight Ridder/Tribune News Service*, December 17, 2003, p. K2399; Susan Ferriss, "Broken Promises: Mexico's Cash Economy a Symptom of Failed Reforms," *Cox News Service*, December 16, 2003.

39. "Central States Dominate the Action."

40. Ferriss, "Broken Promises: Mexicans Rely on Dwindling Export Assembly Work."

41. "Strictly Macro," investment memorandum, Santander Central Hispano Investment, May 3, 2002.

42. Ibid.

43. Alan M. Field, "Headed South; The Economy and China's Emergence as a Low-Cost Manufacturing Center Are Taking a Toll on U.S–Mexico Trade," *Journal of Commerce*, April 14, 2003, p. 19.

44. "The Sucking Sound from the East," *Economist*, July 26, 2003, p. 35.

45. "The Effect of SARS on Mexico," *Mexico & NAFTA Report*, May 16, 2003.

46. Lyons, "Mexico Seeing Few Advances"; Authers, "Bank of Mexico Acts on Inflation."

47. Ferriss, "Broken Promises: Mexicans Rely on Dwindling Export Assembly Work."

48. Earl H. Fry, "North American Economic Integration: Policy Options," *Policy Papers on the Americas* 14, study 8, p. 14; "The Sucking Sound from the East."

49. "Fiscal Reform," *Merrill Lynch*, July 18, 2001.

50. "Food for Argument," *Economist*, November 22, 2003, p. 37.

51. "A System That Needs Some Simplifying," *Financial Times*, December 14, 2000, p. 3.

52. "Fiscal Reform," *Merrill Lynch*, July 18, 2001.

53. A common expression in Spanish, "borrón" refers to the act of having erased something clean and "cuenta nueva" literally means new account.

54. Paul Day, "Gridlocked," *Business Mexico*, November 2001, pp. 26–27.

55. "Food for Argument"; "The Lady Vanishes."

56. John Authers, "Mexico Boosts Tax Collection Despite Sluggish Growth," *Financial Times*, February 23, 2004, p. 3.

57. Baer, "Mexico at an Impasse."

58. Javier Aguilar García, "El perfil de la política laboral y sindical de Vicente Fox," *Estudios Políticos* (January–April 2001): 153–170.

59. Heath, "The Impact of Mexico's Trade Liberalization," pp. 185–187.

60. Ibid.

61. "Fox's Moment of Truth," *The Economist*, September 1, 2001, pp. 31–32.

62. Day, "Gridlocked," pp. 26–34.

63. José de Córdoba and Russell Gold, "Pemex to Increase Spending on Energy Exploration," *Wall Street Journal*, September 16, 2003, pp. A3, A8.

64. Ibid.

65. Ibid.

66. "World Gas: Mexico; Reform or Bust," *Petroleum Economist*, May 19, 2003, p. 23; Lyons, "Mexico Seeing Few Advances."

67. "Peculiar Practices," *Economist*, May 31, 2003, p. 36.

68. JP Morgan, "Emerging Markets Outlook," May 2, 2002.

5

The Fox Administration and the Politics of Economic Transition

Manuel Pastor and Carol Wise

After beating back the regional trend toward the simultaneous liberalization of markets and politics during the 1980s and 1990s, Mexico finally joined step with its Latin American neighbors with the July 2000 election of National Action Party (Partido Acción Nacional, PAN) presidential candidate Vicente Fox. In the short period since the end of the Institutional Revolutionary Party's (Partido Revolucionario Institucional, PRI) 71-year reign over the presidency, the once "perfect dictatorship" has succumbed to the rough-and-tumble politics typical of many transitional democracies. This has made Fox's transition efforts more challenging: With the advent of competitive politics in Mexico, the president no longer has autocratic control over his own party, much less over the diverse political forces now catapulting the country toward modernization.

At the same time, as confirmed by the data and analysis presented by Gary Gereffi and Martha Martínez in Chapter 6 in this volume, the Mexican economy has been completely transformed over the past 20 years. Mexico, once a typical model of debt-dependent import-substitution industrialization (ISI), has become a leading light for export promotion and trade integration. Primary sector exports have been largely outpaced by higher-value-added manufacturing goods, and—in contrast to the fragile reliance on portfolio inflows that helped trigger the 1994–1995 peso crisis—since 1996, flows of fixed direct investment into the Mexican economy have consistently exceeded more volatile financial instruments (see Figure 5.1).[1]

Figure 5.1   Foreign Investment Flows to Mexico, 1990–2002

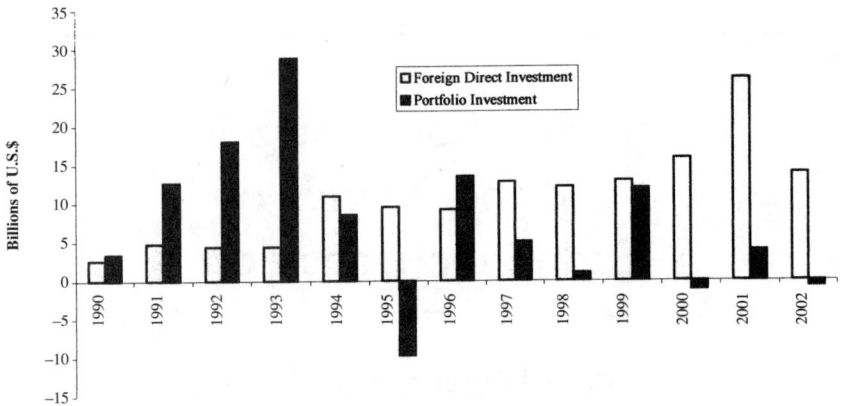

Source: Banco de México. See www.banxico.org.mx.

However, the pressures of the U.S. and Mexican recessions and mounting competition from China served to dampen foreign direct investment in 2002. Some have argued that this recent vulnerability underscores problems in Mexico's model of trade and financial liberalization. Moreover, the gaps in Mexico's economic reform are still formidable, especially with regard to the regressive pattern of income distribution and the new liberal model's ability to sustain a dynamic growth momentum. Although distributional pressures have generated a storm of popular criticism, there seems to be limited domestic interest for the pursuit of a fundamentally different economic strategy—especially with the avowed benefits from the country's ready access to the U.S. market since the implementation in 1994 of the North American Free Trade Agreement (NAFTA)—but rather an appetite for softening the blows from change.

Already, a rich literature has emerged with regard to Mexico's political liberalization and economic transformation.[2] On the political side, the most convincing explanations for the PRI's long decline at the ballot box (the once-ruling party's share of the presidential vote eroded from 77.4 percent in 1982 to just 36.1 percent in 2000) have centered on the interplay of rapid socioeconomic change, electoral reforms, and the internationalization of Mexican politics in the NAFTA era.[3] Economic variables, such as external shocks, financial disruptions, and the market reforms implemented since the 1982 debt crisis, have also been factored into these explanations but generally not in a systematic way. Our own view is that these cumulative political and economic challenges were further exacerbated by the PRI's overselling of its reform agenda, which in turn raised the electorate's expectations for positive returns that were not realized in time for the PRI to benefit at the voting booth.

But rather than revisiting the standing explanations and debates, this chapter uses these various insights as a departure point for analyzing the political economic dynamics that have underpinned efforts at democratic governance during the first half of the Fox administration (2000–2003). Though little dispute encompasses the issues that remain on the country's economic reform agenda (e.g., fiscal restructuring, greater labor market flexibility, deeper social targeting, industrial upgrading, and a renewed round of smaller-scale privatizations),[4] the nature of Mexico's political opening has thus far obstructed the process of reform.

Because the advent of democracy was not accompanied by the kinds of enduring coalition politics and deal making that marked other democratic transitions in the region (such as those in Argentina and Chile), the Fox administration has been impaired in its efforts to accomplish its stated goals. In short, because political liberalization in Mexico resulted more from the internal unraveling of long-standing alliances within the former ruling PRI party and the weakening of the PRI's corporatist ties to civil society, the country has seen the weakening of an old-style political coalition without the construction of other viable or lasting alternatives to replace it. Additionally, Mexico has no prior experience with democratization to help curb continuing excesses in the political arena.

In other Latin American cases of democratization, the former perpetrators of authoritarian rule have been disarmed (e.g., Argentina, Brazil, Chile) or sent into exile (e.g., Bolivia, Paraguay, Peru). Not so in Mexico, where the PRI still holds the largest number of elected seats in both the Senate and the Chamber of Deputies, and even managed to win an additional 14 seats in the latter as a result of the July 2003 midterm elections (raising its Chamber total to 222). The remainder of the midterm spoils went to the leftist Party of the Democratic Revolution (Partido de la Revolución Democrática, PRD), which nearly doubled its total seats in the Chamber of Deputies to 95. The odd one out was the PAN, which lost 54 seats in the Chamber of Deputies and is now reduced to holding just 151 seats.[5] This marked the first time since the Mexican Revolution that the president's party failed to win the highest number of votes in a midterm race; however, the percentage breakdown in the Chamber will still require interparty cooperation to advance reforms. Yet, the political winds continue to blow in the opposite direction. Although it would be premature to speak of a full-blown PRI comeback, even the remote possibility of recapturing the presidency in 2006 has been a strong disincentive for once-omnipotent PRI politicians to engage in the kinds of coalition politics that Mexico's current economic and social situation clearly calls for.

Against this backdrop of a highly fluid political situation and a faltering economic reform agenda, our analysis of the political economy of governance in Mexico is divided into four parts. We begin with a brief summary of the political economic antecedents to the Fox administration, which is meant to complement the analyses put forth by the other authors in this volume. We then turn to the Fox reform agenda proper, and in doing so, we analyze the most pressing challenges, and the political dynamics that have unfolded around them, from three separate but overlapping standpoints: (1) the need to spur higher economic growth and employment expansion, (2) the imperative to reduce income inequality, and (3) those national and subnational trends that cry out for another round of serious political reform in Mexico.

The Political Economic Antecedents to the Fox Administration: Four Main Themes

In this section we offer a brief overview of the post-1982 transformation of the Mexican political economy in terms of four themes of "bounce back" that have spanned the past two decades: (1) the shift from microeconomic challenges to macroeconomic tasks and now back to microlevel restructuring; (2) the transition from a heavily state-sponsored development strategy to a market-based one, and now to a need to bring innovative public policy and the state back in; (3) the change from socially motivated policymaking to more economically driven concerns, and the current need to tackle the country's burgeoning social deficit; and (4) the shifting fortunes of Mexican politicians and technocrats, with the former having been largely shoved aside during the heyday of market reforms in the early 1990s, yet now essential for rendering these same reforms compatible with Mexico's increasingly democratic polity.

The Shift from Micro to Macro to Micro

Many of the imbalances that characterized the ISI model and that propelled Mexico into the debt crisis in the 1980s were essentially microeconomic in nature: inappropriate tariff protection, a long-standing urban policy bias, blanket subsidies to inefficient firms, and a social safety net based on price controls for key products and other market distortions. Petroleum revenues and the ability to borrow abroad helped paper over those problems, but when a severe macroeconomic crisis erupted in 1982, it was not just because of an overvalued peso and the large trade and fiscal deficits that accompanied it. Rather, the underlying microeconomic parameters were simply not sustainable.

Although the Miguel de la Madrid administration (1982–1988) realized the microeconomic imperative and tried to promote trade liberalization, sell off state companies, and undertake a sweeping set of market measures, its efforts were virtually swamped by the need to tame inflation and stabilize the macroeconomic imbalances of the early 1980s. Unfortunately, the typical orthodox remedies adopted by the government—depreciating the currency, lifting price controls, initiating steep spending cuts, and allowing a sharp decline in real wages—failed to stabilize the aggregate economy, let alone revive it. Rightfully worried about their own political survival at the polls, PRI policymakers eventually adopted a more pragmatic macroeconomic strategy, including pegging the exchange rate to the U.S. dollar and negotiating incremental wage and price hikes through the 1990s. Even policies that seemed microeconomic in their logic, such as trade liberalization and the pursuit of NAFTA, were driven by these macroeconomic concerns, with enhanced trade competition initially designed to tame the political risk of inflation.[6]

In turn, macroeconomic outcomes, lower inflation, and the rising appreciation of the peso helped to cover up the lack of dynamic microeconomic change. For example, while real gross national product (GNP) per capita increased an average of 2.2 percent per year from 1988 to 1994 during the entire Salinas *sexenio* (a Mexican six-year presidential term), much of that increase was lost in the wake of the 1994 peso crash: real per capita GNP at the end of 1995 sank back down to the level achieved in the first year of President Carlos Salinas de Gortari's administration. Throughout the crisis, concerns for macroeconomic balance continued to dominate, as policymakers sought to control the economic damage with a haphazard rescue of the banking system, a more explicit reliance on export-driven growth, and a huge multilateral bailout led by the United States. This tenacious attention to the macroeconomic fundamentals finally began to pay off after 1997; as the peso stabilized and adjusted under a new flexible exchange rate regime, exports boomed and wages finally rose.

Now, as reflected in the Fox administration's economic program, policymakers have recognized the need to attend more assertively to the microeconomic realm. The Fox team has undertaken this task in the context of a sharp economic recession caused by the slowing of the U.S. economy in early 2001 as well as the aftershocks of the September 11, 2001, terrorist attacks in New York and Washington, D.C. Still, there are few who would argue that Mexico runs the risk of another significant financial crisis, such as economic depression or raging inflation. The risk, rather, is that of succumbing to mediocrity, and this fate can only be avoided by taking on the difficult microeconomic tasks: repairing the segmentation of credit markets to allow small enterprises a fuller opportunity to participate in the market; encouraging stronger backward linkages from exporters to domestic suppliers; expanding banking services to include more Mexicans;[7] and aggressively investing in human capital. Microeconomic reform is admittedly tedious, or as one local Mexican official told us, "It's boring . . . it's one firm at a time, a lengthy modernization of every economic unit, and you cannot simply do it by decree."[8] But this observation makes a telling point: the era of spectacular crises must now give way to one of plodding improvements.

The Shift from State to Market to State

While the initial goal of Mexican reform was the reduction of heavy-handed state intervention, the market has not shown itself to be the elixir for Mexico's economic woes. Left to their own devices, privately held banks ran themselves into the ground. In addition, haphazard privatization in other sectors confirmed that the state is not the only bad manager (e.g., efforts at privately run toll roads collapsed), and for the most part, small enterprises have yet to board the express train toward trade competitiveness. A concerted Chilean-style public policy to promote efficiency, productivity, and an export orientation in smaller domestic firms has become at least a voiced cornerstone of the Fox administration's domestic economic strategy. Left on its own, Mexico's microeconomic restructuring has enabled some of the smaller companies to move further up the value-added production chain. Yet, because the NAFTA negotiations took off under the leadership of an economic team whose ideology regarded more explicit public policy interventions as taboo, discussions about microeconomic restructuring were swept under the carpet for fear that investors would interpret the restructuring as tantamount to the return of ISI.

But Mexico today faces a reality far different from that of 1982. There is now a long list of emerging-market countries where selective interventions, such as technical support, tax incentives, subsidized credit, and even limited controls on capital movements, have helped to bridge the gap between macroeconomic success and microeconomic stress. More generally, research has shown that constructive state sponsorship matters greatly—the fastest growing Latin American economies in the 1990s, Chile and Peru, were also those that had revived public spending and renovated state institutions in ways that complemented and bolstered market reforms.[9]

The Fox administration has made positive inroads in revitalizing government institutions in ways that enhance transparency and accountability. The completion of key fiscal reforms is now of the essence, partly because state spending needs to be revived and redirected in ways that strengthen the ability of individuals and firms to succeed within the market economy.[10] The Fox administration will need to remain resolutely nonideological in its choices of state and market approaches to particular problems, drawing upon research that demonstrates which interventions work best and when. Fortunately, the president has shown himself to be both pragmatic and quite heterodox on this front. The drawback, as reflected in the drubbing the PAN took in the 2003 midterm elections, has been Fox's inability to work constructively within his own party or with the PRI and the PRD in actualizing a more active and effective state policy.[11]

The Shift from Social to Economic to Social Considerations

The Mexican revolution and the national mythology it promoted were rooted in a promise of development and social justice. Even the ISI model, adopted in many countries for its capacity to further capitalist industrial development, had, in Mexico, more social roots. It originated in the 1930s when revolutionary notions were kept alive by the nationalization of the petroleum industry, massive land reform, and the passage of comprehensive labor legislation. While the "revolutionary" promises most often remained unfulfilled, social justice was the benchmark by which government performance was judged; even the PRI's corporatist efforts to organize all sectors and tie them tightly to the ruling party were done under the guise of privileging those of lesser means.

Over time, but particularly in the 20-year period since the launching of market reforms in 1982, the interplay between social and economic concerns eventually became lodged in a conflict between the PRI traditionalists, who pursued social policy through patronage, and the ascendant technocrats, who saw patronage as both a waste of resources and inimical to the market model. But the traditionalists and the technocrats enjoyed an uneasy alliance based on mutual need: once the debt crisis was underway, only the technocrats held the keys to the necessary International Monetary Fund (IMF) financial assistance and debt rescheduling. Yet, as demonstrated during the 1988 elections, only the traditionalists could round up the vote and produce the electoral alchemy necessary to keep the technocrats' economic program in place.

The alliance between traditionalists and technocrats was strained by the 1994 peso crash. After suffering through fiscal austerity and market restructuring in the 1980s, it was expected that Salinas's successor, Ernesto Zedillo (1994–2000), would have the resources to again spread the wealth in ways that would shore up the PRI's rural and urban constituencies. The peso debacle of 1994–1995 meant that such largesse was unaffordable, and, as Andreas Schedler points out in Chapter 2, President Zedillo began trading away political reforms in order to pursue his economic agenda, weakening PRI hegemony along the way.

Despite the urgency of the economic problems, the Zedillo team did find time to address social problems, changing the slush-fund approach of Salinas's National Solidarity Program (Programa Nacional de Solidaridad, PRONASOL) safety net scheme to the more targeted interventions of the National Education, Health, and Nutrition Program (Programa Nacional de Educación, Salud y Alimentación, PROGRESA). Although PROGRESA's spending has been put to a more specific and professional use in terms of human capital investments, it has also been limited. Neither PROGRESA nor waiting for macroeconomic soundness to spur higher growth will be sufficient to significantly improve the lives of the country's many poor people. While on the 2000 campaign trail, Fox's strongest selling point was his insistence that more targeted and weighty social investments— enhanced education, improved health systems, adequate housing—were still urgently needed. In the following section we detail the progress that has been made on that front since the advent of the Fox administration.

The Shift from Político to Técnico to Político

In Mexico, as in the rest of the region, the ISI period was not marked by tremendous economic expertise in the government. The post-1982 scarcity of foreign exchange quickly raised the value of economists, and technocrats soon ruled the day. It had been expected that de la Madrid's technocratic team would be followed by a cohort from the more political wing of the PRI, in line with the past practice of alternating selected presidential candidates from the different factions of the party. The *dedazo,* or handpicking, of Carlos Salinas as the PRI presidential candidate in 1988 enraged traditionalists, who saw him as an accountant and opportunist rather than a seasoned politician. But the traditionalists fell in line—only to be disappointed once again by Ernesto Zedillo, a man for whom the word technocrat seems to have been invented.

Zedillo's was an accidental candidacy. When presidential hopeful Luis Donaldo Colosio was assassinated while campaigning for the office in 1994, Zedillo was one of the few high-level PRI leaders who had spent enough time out of the federal government (because he was managing Colosio's campaign) to be eligible to run under Mexico's convoluted electoral rules. As a former secretary of budget and planning, and then as secretary of education under Salinas, Zedillo's credentials were sound. Nevertheless, he did demonstrate the tin ear to politics typical of the PRI's technocratic wing: For example, the Zedillo team rescued the private banks at a cost of more than 20 percent of gross domestic product (GDP) and then asked taxpayers to foot this bill. His chosen policy course, one that would have earned a high grade in a U.S. graduate seminar in public economics, fell flat when pitched to an electorate suffering from intense reform fatigue and now courted by up-and-coming political operatives from competing parties.

President Fox represents a return to a político style, albeit one with more sophistication and democratic propensities than the PRI políticos of an earlier era. He has shown an uncanny ability to read the public's mood, capitalize on symbols that celebrate the country's democratic transition, and respond to real and perceived needs. But he has also fumbled, as reflected in self-inflicted spats within his own PAN party and the numerous delays in implementing his ambitious reform agenda. To his credit, Fox orchestrated a National Political Accord in late 2001 as an attempt to lend some order to the political chaos that has marred the halls of the Mexican Congress since the PRI's departure from the executive office. On paper, the accord committed the three main parties to work toward a common set of social and economic policy goals.[12] In practice, no specific policies or procedures were actually agreed upon. The PRI, in particular, remains a loose political cannon and, if anything, its 2003 midterm gains will further exacerbate this stance. The former ruling party is not at all willing to assume the role of loyal opposition long played by the PAN and is split between rival factions that are still vying to take back the presidency.

As we see it, the country's ability to progress along these four thematic lines will govern whether Mexico can forge a political economic transformation on a par with Chile's, or will be condemned to the same mediocre growth and development indicators that characterized Mexico in the 1990s, regardless of having implemented deep structural reforms, joining the Organization for Economic Cooperation and Development (OECD), and gaining entry into NAFTA. There is, of course, solid ground for optimism: with a reformed economy, a revamped political system, and an increasingly active civil society, Mexico faces a very different panorama from the economic turmoil and authoritarian obstacles that confronted the nation as recently as in the 1980s. Still, the current challenges

are both significant and complicated. On the one hand, fiscal modernization, penetrating state reform, and the aggressive tackling of inequality
will require strong doses of executive leadership. On the other hand, these
goals must be achieved in the context of an open and increasingly transparent political system, a situation that may cause some observers—and
some voters—to long nostalgically for the old days of PRI hegemony.

Reconciling Democratic Politics with Economic Change: Squaring the Circle?

Though spared the usual economic blowup that had long marked Mexico's
passing of the presidential torch every six years,[13] Fox still inherited a
bundle of unresolved issues that quickly became part of his own pro-
grammatic agenda. Those issues included the problems of a peace settlement with the Zapatista guerrillas; the long overdue need for a tax reform
bill, as non-oil public revenues continued to stagnate at just 11 percent of
GDP (compared with 25 percent for Chile and 25 to 30 for the United
States and most European countries); the need to forge ahead with privatization and/or the introduction of competitive measures in the electricity,
transportation, and energy sectors; and the imperative to advance more
quickly in rectifying the worsening income inequalities portrayed in Figure 5.2 (including the significant redistribution away from the middle
income brackets as well as from the poor). Less pressing, although equally
problematic, was the need to launch a deeper round of reforms in the
banking and labor sectors and to move forward with electoral reforms that
would tighten campaign finance rules and create an orderly alternative to
the highly conflicted process still surrounding elections at the state and
municipal levels.[14]

Just as Zedillo had done in his 1994 presidential campaign, Fox, too,
had phrased those challenges in terms of second-phase market reforms
meant to strengthen institutions, assure competition and oversight, and
more aggressively target a wide range of the country's human capital
needs.[15] Despite the lack of strong differences between the PRI and the
PAN 2000 presidential campaign platforms and the healthy macroeconomic backdrop that prevailed prior to that election, the PRI had finally
lost all credibility as the champions of political and economic reform. The
tendency for voters to take a chance on other parties and candidates once
the economic house has basically been put in order has been an integral
part of the political economy of democratic transition in post–debt crisis

Figure 5.2   Shifts in Overall Income Distribution, 1984–2000

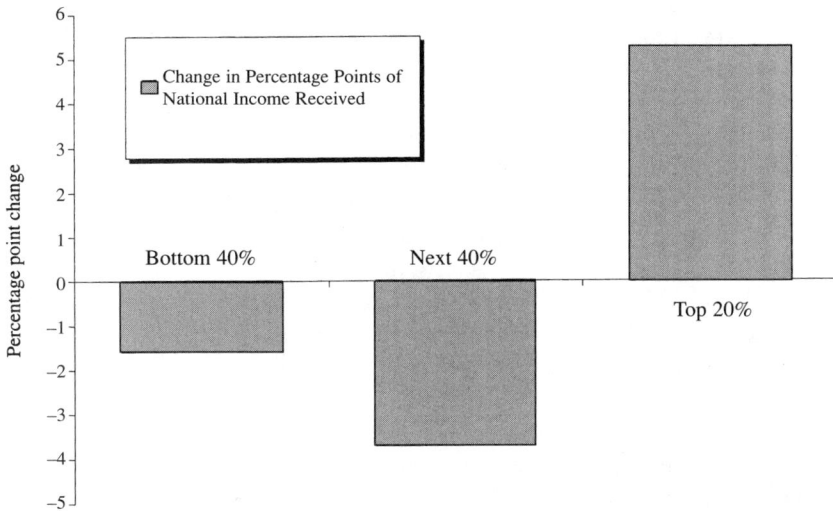

Sources: Instituto Nacional de Estadística, Geografía e Informática (INEGI), *Ingreso-Gasto de los Hogares,* CD-ROM database, covers 1984, 1989, and 1992; and *Encuesta Nacional de Ingresos y Gastos de los Hogares-98,* CD-ROM database, covers the 1992, 1994, 1996, and 1998 surveys; the 2000 distribution figures were downloaded from preliminary results available on the INEGI website, www.inegi.gob.mx. We concentrate on monetary rather than total income; total income includes nonmonetary flows, such as imputed rent, and we have argued earlier that the characterizations are potentially too arbitrary. See Manuel Pastor and Carol Wise, "State Policy, Distribution, and Neoliberal Economic Reform in Mexico," *Journal of Latin American Studies,* 29 (May 1997): 419–456.

Latin America. The PRI was, of course, hoping to avoid participation in that regional trend.

However, as the 2003 midterm results confirmed, it would be premature at this point to speak of a "post-PRI" era for Mexican politics. For different reasons, all three of the major parties have been wrought with internal strife since the 2000 transition, and the lack of a working majority bloc in Congress is one manifestation of this problem. Like it or not, the former ruling party continues to be a force majeure in the domestic political arena. The PRI's loss of executive power has emboldened the party's traditional wing; unfortunately for the party, the authoritarian and populist tendencies represented by that group, led by party bosses like Roberto Madrazo, are painfully out of touch with a more democratically minded and forward-looking electorate.

The PRD, having resurged just once since its near win of the presidency in 1988—in the 1997 midterm elections—staged a mini-comeback in the 2003 midterm race. However, disputes concerning political strategy—whether to focus on winning elections versus promoting democracy—and squabbles over leadership continue to take a toll on the PRD. For the PAN, which has had few qualms about pursuing a fairly straight electoral route toward political liberalization, the 2000 victory has been bittersweet. Prior to the midterm elections of 2003, Fox's insistence on appointing an ideologically diverse cabinet (only three cabinet posts went to the PAN at the outset of Fox's term in 2000) and his independent stance on numerous policy issues have been a source of tension within the PAN since the campaign.[16] After suffering considerable midterm losses, even some within the president's own party are anxious to declare him a lame duck.

Now that the political playing field has been leveled, the Mexican political system is in the process of shifting from two parallel two-party systems (the PRI versus the PAN, or the PRI versus the PRD) to a competitive system proper.[17] The difficulty that all three of the main parties have had in acting as competitive players has meant that most of the Fox policy agenda (e.g., fiscal reform, an indigenous rights bill, and privatization of the electricity and transport sectors) has either been stalled or watered down as it winds its way through a Mexican Congress that has ceased to be a mere rubber stamp. Still, the Congress, as a whole, is not much greater than the sum of its parts. Already, the Fox administration has come to represent more the departure point for Mexico's democratic transition rather than any ultimate destination.

Despite the electorate's clear disappointment with the PAN, can Fox overcome the current political hurdles and fulfill the hefty expectations that have unavoidably accompanied his accession to power? We now analyze Fox's progress within the three main issues facing his administration identified at the outset of this chapter: the need to spur higher levels of economic growth and employment expansion; the imperative to reduce the severe income differentials, by class and by region, that have plagued Mexico for decades; and the need for additional political reforms that ensure a greater degree of transparency, accountability, and sustainability. It is not out of the question for the highly capable Fox team to make the necessary progress in all three areas. But the problem is that inroads on one front may require concessions on at least one of the others, and the tenacious slowdown of the economy may hamper progress on any front. If recession and stalemate become the main descriptors of Fox's sexenio, there will be little in this new era of competitive politics to buffer today's incumbents from the voters' wrath. Clearly, those symbols and myths surrounding short-term prosperity and democratic accountability must be turned into everyday realities.

Spurring Higher Economic Growth and Employment Expansion

The Fox administration began with a commitment to achieve 7 percent annual growth rates and to create 1.4 million jobs each year; in the past two decades, policymakers have not hit anywhere near these targets. The Fox team's initial level of optimism was partly warranted by the economic indicators inherited from the outgoing Zedillo team (including an average annual growth rate of 6 percent since 1997, a moderate fiscal deficit, the highest levels of foreign direct investment [FDI] in the country's history, and a long-waited recovery of real wages), all of which suggested that Mexico was finally about to realize its tremendous postreform potential for high growth. However, as reflected in Figure 5.3, the economy experienced an abrupt slowdown in 2001, partly because of the downturn in the United States. With the recession lingering into its third year, even as the United States has had a tepid, albeit jobless, recovery, it has become increasingly apparent that the failure of Mexican legislators to forge ahead with second-generation reforms has become a growth trap in and of itself.[18]

This performance is particularly disappointing since the country has never been better positioned to break out of its post-1982 status as an underachiever. First, the economy is no longer driven by debt-backed state intervention but rather by trade and private investment set against a back-drop of sustained macroeconomic stabilization (see, for example, Figure 5.4 for the growing importance of private investment). Critics, however, have rightfully questioned whether there are sufficient domestic linkages to the more dynamic export and maquiladora sectors where much of private investment has been concentrated; the slippage of maquiladora employment through 2001 and 2002 gave even maquiladora proponents cause for concern (see Figure 5.5). These concerns aside, there are sound reasons to be optimistic about the export sector as a whole. Second, as Gereffi and Martínez point out in Chapter 6, the transformation of Mexican exports has been substantial: the type of tradable goods produced contain increasingly more value-added, and supply links between Mexican and foreign (mostly U.S.) firms are growing.

How will the Fox team harness these new competitive advantages such that the gains are more sustainable and widespread? What will be the impulse for forging those backward domestic linkages that were so highly touted by Salinas and his NAFTA coalition? Thus far, the basically lais-

Figure 5.3   Real GDP Growth, 1981–2002

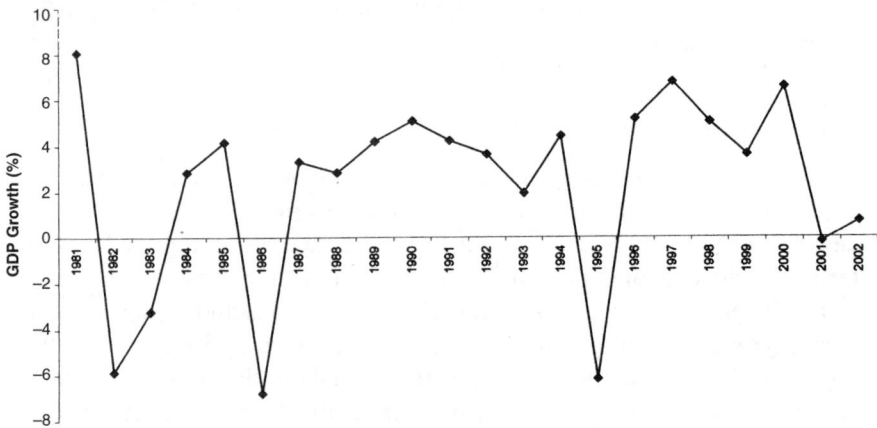

Sources: World Bank, *World Development Indicators, 2001* (WDI 2001 on CD-ROM); the 2000–2002 figures taken from the real GDP series available from the Banco de México.

Figure 5.4   Private and Public Investment in Mexico, 1980–2000

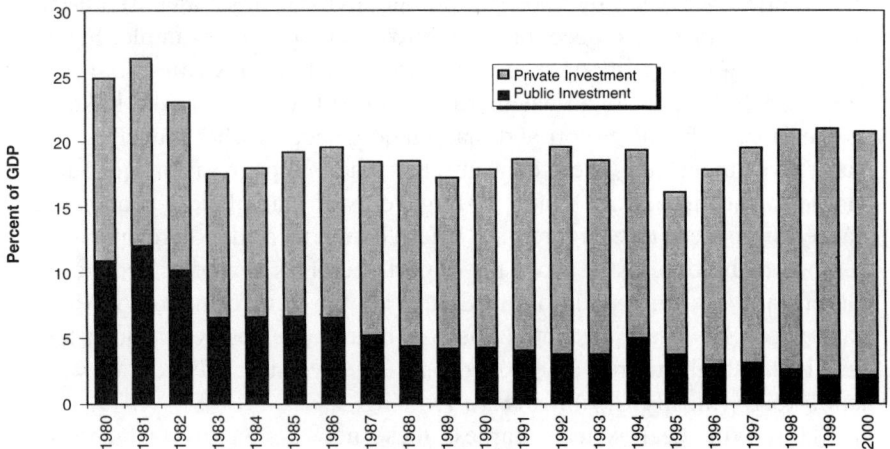

Sources: Stephen Everhart and Mariusz A. Sumlinski, *Trends in Private Investment in Developing Countries: Statistics for 1970–2000* (Washington, DC: International Finance Corporation [IFC], forthcoming); the database is available at www.ifc.org/economics/data/dataset.htm.

Figure 5.5 Maquiladora Employment, 1994–2002

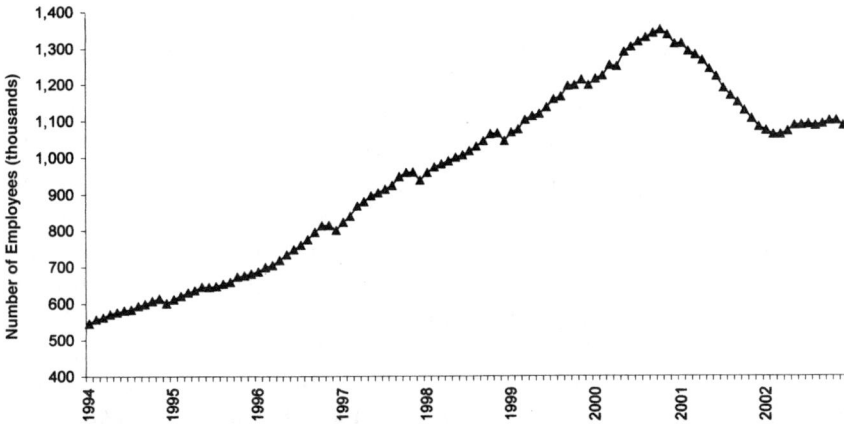

Source: Instituto Nacional de Estadística, Geografía e Informática (INEGI), www.inegi. gob.mx.

sez-faire industrial policy inherited from the Zedillo administration has remained in place, but there has been much greater budgetary leeway at the state level for directly channeling support for the development of small and medium-sized firms (SMEs).[19] As one high-ranking official put it, the thinking now is not so much about what Mexico will do for small businesses but more that a prosperous small business sector is essential for the country to achieve higher growth rates.[20] The federal government has thus taken a more active role by targeting resources for firms with strong potential to participate in higher-value-added export activities.

Various SME promotion efforts (e.g., programs such as the Industrial Policy and Foreign Trade Program [Programa de Política Industrial y Comercio Exterior, PROPICE], the National Committee for Productivity and Technological Innovation [Comité Nacional de Productividad e Innovación Tecnológica, COMPITE], and the Regional Centers for Business Competitiveness [Centros Regionales para la Competitividad Empresarial, CRECE]) are now consolidated under one main office, the Intersecretarial Commission for Industrial Policy (Comisión Intersecretarial de Política Industrial, CIPI) in the Secretariat of Economy (formerly the Secretaría de Comercio y Fomento Industrial, SECOFI),[21] which itself has been assigned an unprecedented mandate to focus on microeconomic restructuring—including ambitious plans to double its share of the federal budget.[22]

The goal is to reach at least 10 percent of those firms in need of support and to do so by the end of the Fox term. In addition to offering assistance in such areas as technology upgrading, skills training, and diagnoses for improving efficiency, the Fox microeconomic strategy also commits to greater accountability in the allocation of credit to SMEs. In particular, the current reform package demands much higher levels of transparency from those development banks that are the main conduits through which smaller firms access credit; it will be more difficult for those banks to return to the old practices of bending the rules or playing favorites, as the banks will now be subject to external audits and public disclosure of all aspects of their ongoing loan portfolios.[23] Still, with respect to the overall support of SMEs, resources have been scarce. So the president has also relied on symbolic politics, referring to micro enterprises in colloquial terms, as *changarros*,[24] and generally suggesting that they are an engine of growth, albeit an overlooked and long-neglected one.

The need to invest more vigorously in education, skills, and human capital, partly to position Mexico higher up on the value-added hierarchy, was also a prominent theme in the 2000 Fox campaign. Once an afterthought during the era of ISI and heavy state patronage, the sweeping liberalization of the Mexican economy over the past two decades has made it impossible to ignore the country's serious education deficit. Most troublesome is the disconnect between a low-skilled workforce and the rising wage premium for skills and education, especially in those sectors that have been liberalized.[25] Thus far, the most concrete plans to boost human capital include a pledge to raise the average level of schooling from seven to ten years by deepening the inroads made by the Zedillo administration in shifting a greater share of the education budget toward basic education. That crucial category of schooling captured about 58 percent of the education budget in 1990, a proportion that rose to 66 percent[26] by the end of the Zedillo presidency and is slated to go higher under the Fox administration.[27]

With regard to reforming domestic labor markets to encourage employment opportunity and mobility, Fox is stepping gingerly, proposing to loosen the labor code in such areas as severance payments and the ability of employers to offer temporary contracts.[28] The Fox administration is also in the process of breaking the hold of those unions with long-term ties to the traditional wing of the PRI, some of which still control entire sectors through a web of corruption and coercion. One strategy to weaken union power involves moving toward plant-level—rather than sector-level—negotiations, mostly to avoid the sector-wide rules that basically block labor market mobility. Unions were further weakened by a Supreme Court ruling in 2001 that reversed an age-old dictate directing companies to fire workers who leave their unions.[29] But the upshot of the reduction in union power is a potential lowering of wages, albeit for the purpose of creating employment. Given the administration's income distribution goals and the lingering power of the country's labor bosses, this presents both a contradiction and a political challenge that will require much greater intermediation than any of the main stakeholders have yet displayed.

The Fox administration has sought to circumvent gridlock on this crucial labor market issue by placing the question of migration firmly on the agenda—a key issue because escape to U.S. labor markets has been a safety valve for Mexican workers, one that will be needed if current employment growth at home remains slow. Although the NAFTA negotiations would have been a propitious time to address the upward secular flow of migrant labor from Mexico to the United States, the United States was adamantly opposed to bringing such a controversial issue to the NAFTA negotiating table.[30] Fox has once again raised the issue, and although he quickly backed down on his bold campaign calls for the free movement of labor within the NAFTA bloc, President Fox has attempted to launch at least sporadic discussions with U.S. President George W. Bush about a more orderly framework for migration between Mexico and the United States.[31]

With a lingering recession in the United States, and conservative opposition to immigration on the rise in the U.S. Congress, it was doubtful from the start that discussions between Bush and Fox concerning immigration issues would amount to a comprehensive migration accord.[32] The September 11, 2001, terrorist attack and the security concerns it has posed further undermined Fox's prospects for negotiating a meaningful migration reform. However, by raising the issues of increased border violence associated with the illicit movement of people northward and the often-poor treatment of Mexican workers in the United States—topics regarded as taboo under Salinas and Zedillo—Fox has raised expectations for reform that still must be met.[33] The gap between expectations and progress on migration questions continues to haunt Fox politically, even after President Bush unveiled in early 2004 a proposal to grant three-year visas to temporary immigrant workers in the United States, a plan that has met with considerable opposition from both Republicans and Democrats in Congress.

Reducing Income Inequality

While Mexico's regressive distributional trends were most pronounced in the 1980s, policymakers did not really focus on lifting the bottom until the launching of the PROGRESA program midway through the Zedillo administration. Policymakers' earlier reluctance to move more assertively on that front seemed to be a matter of fiscal shortfalls coupled with a sense that "adjustment without a safety net" would enhance the government's image of liberal toughness and hence improve credibility with international lenders. When Salinas came to power with a narrow and hotly disputed victory in 1988, the government shifted to compensatory measures basically meant to contain social strife and secure the necessary votes around election time—for example, using PRONASOL to disburse funds to politically targeted communities. It was only when such compensatory measures failed to accomplish even those modest goals that key technocrats were able to wrest some control of social policy and shift attention toward enhancing the productivity of the poor and a more careful targeting of resources to those most in need.

Though there is little debate about the importance of macroeconomic stabilization as a necessary condition for growth and income gains, the evidence overwhelmingly confirms that poverty declines more quickly if income inequality is tackled through the direct targeting of resources to those most in need.[34] In Mexico, even in the short time that a more targeted distributional approach has been in effect, there is evidence that selective antipoverty programs like PROGRESA are having a positive impact on the bottom 40 percent of the income pyramid.[35] The PROGRESA program, which by 2001 covered some 2.6 million families in poverty-stricken rural areas, has increased government spending on basic needs by an annual increase of 20 percent, on average, and the government's spending on poverty alleviation has now surpassed 1 percent of Mexico's GDP.

Of course, those improvements occurred against the synergistic backdrop of strong growth since 1997 and the heightened export demand for unskilled labor under NAFTA. Since there is no guarantee that those favorable macroeconomic trends will continue in the medium term and long term—indeed, as noted, they have already cooled considerably—the Fox administration must promote improvements to income redistribution all the more, including devising new strategies to meet his campaign vow to reduce poverty by 30 percent. PROGRESA, for example, has now been expanded to urban areas in Mexico,[36] the so-called *cinturones de miseria* (misery belts)—with some of the rationale for this not just economic but also the political need to deliver benefits to PRD-dominated metropolitan areas around Mexico City and thereby quell organized social protest in those areas.

In terms of broader investments in human capital, even though total programmable public spending has been reduced by about 5 percent since

1994, social spending per capita was 19 percent higher in 2001 than it was in 1994.[37] Within this category, health spending has increased by 17 percent per capita from 1994 to 2001, while health spending for the uninsured in the lowest income deciles has increased by 67 percent. In addition to the aforementioned shift toward basic education, overall spending on education has increased by 24 percent since 1994. Despite such inroads on inequality, it continues to have a tenacious hold on the country, with current trends confirming that policies for targeted redistribution must be accelerated. But that will require an even greater allocation of scarce public resources, which means that the Fox government simply must increase tax revenues (see Figure 5.6).

While petroleum revenues have often been used to balance the books, the country needs to address the relatively low level of tax collection that stems from a combination of granting too many exemptions to big business and the fact that at least 40 to 50 percent of the workforce is now operating in the informal economy. By definition, fiscal reform implies drawing yet another set of lines between winners and losers and this has rendered the domestic debate especially contentious. At the same time,

Figure 5.6   Public Sector Income in Mexico, 1980–2002

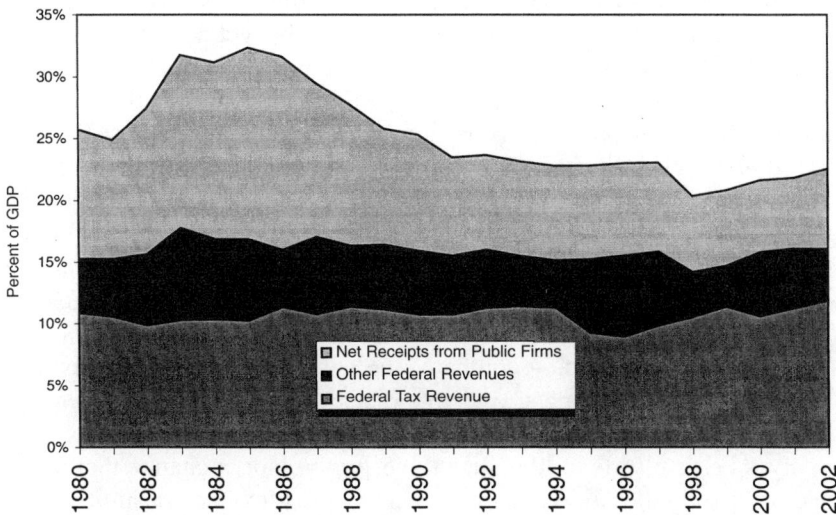

Source: Banco de México, http://www.banxico.org.mx/eInfoFinanciera/FSinfoFinanciera. html, with values determined from the yearly summary reported in December of each year. Net receipts from public firms refers to the profits of those firms minus the public subsidies afforded them. These net receipts have declined over the years as the state sector has privatized more firms.

given the right mix of tax measures, Mexico's future fiscal policies could infuse greater dynamism into its income redistribution strategy and move the country further in the Chilean direction: raising public revenues in order to aggressively target distributional needs and broadening the social safety net in ways that encourage productivity rather than the old-style compensation (e.g., subsidies, food baskets, public vouchers).[38]

The difficulty of getting down to serious business with a fiscal reform bill in the Mexican Congress was reflected in the mid-2001 decision to postpone the vote on the tax package until the end of that year. In principle, all of the major political parties in Congress were in agreement as to the urgency of passing a sound package of fiscal reforms that would bolster and complement the designated distributional goals. However, the PRI and the PRD were determined to stack the debate such that they could take credit for breaking the country's long-standing tax logjam, while shifting the blame onto the PAN for the less appealing trade-offs that fiscal reform inevitably entails. The challenge of reconciling Mexico's new competitive politics with this particular set of economic reforms was compounded by the efforts of some PAN deputies to distance themselves from their own party's proposals.

The stated fiscal reform goals were to increase the government's revenue intake by 2.5 percent of GDP in 2002 and at least 4 percent per year thereafter.[39] When combined with public spending cuts, it was expected that the fiscal reform package would reduce the budget deficit to less than 1 percent of GDP, with the tax increases dampened by the fact that the government's bank bailout scheme, the Institute for the Protection of Bank Savings (Instituto para la Protección al Ahorro Bancario, IPAB), had placed undue stress on the fiscal balance.[40] In principle, further revenues could be raised from privatization, although the Zedillo team muddied the political waters for that strategy with that administration's rescue of a disastrously privatized banking system, resulting in the resource-draining acquisition of bad bank debt. The Fox administration has thus targeted a rather low-profile group of assets for sale, including the state's remaining shares in an airline holding company, the public insurance company, privatized railway companies, and the Banco Bilbao Vizcaya Argentaria (BBVA)–Bancomer financial group. A longer-term revenue-raising goal involves Fox's efforts to liberalize the energy sector, a change that in the medium term will require an amendment to the Mexican constitution[41]— something not likely until Congress settles down into a legislative rhythm more akin to the give-and-take of democratic governance.

Thus, the politically realistic options for raising revenue in the short run were identified as, first, a widening of the tax base and, second, the elimination of various tax loopholes including exemptions on the payment of a 15 percent value-added tax (VAT) for food, medicine, books, and educational fees. Not surprisingly, the administration's proposals concerning the extension of the VAT, a prima facie regressive tax, provoked the most furors in Congress. As the tax bill started to stall in the legislature in mid-2001, the Fox team quickly circulated a study that suggested that those in the top income decile were paying nearly 90 percent of the country's taxes and receiving only 7 percent of government spending while those in the bottom 60 percent were paying no taxes and receiving nearly 75 percent of government spending.

That assessment did not square with the public's sense of the relative tax burden and benefits, particularly in light of the bank bailout for billionaires, and the release of those figures understandably deflated the public's confidence in the government's political priorities, not to mention its methodology for income redistribution.[42] This occurred in the context of minimal trust already: Many Mexicans, for example, do not necessarily connect increased taxes with improved services, because their past experiences with the government had been so spotty on that count. Moreover, although the Fox team had gone to great lengths to convince the public that those in the lower income deciles would be compensated for the VAT increases through direct relief, historical experience offered little reason to believe that a regressively collected tax would be spent in a progressive way.

In the end, the Mexican Congress passed in December 2001 a tax reform bill that fell far short of the revenue targets identified by the administration when the testy debate over tax reform began the year before.[43] The congress did succeed in passing a uniform tax rate of 35 percent for individuals and businesses in the top tax brackets, a rate due to fall by 1 percentage point per year until 2005. But other proposed measures collapsed, such as Fox's efforts to close special tax loopholes and the passage of a uniform 15 percent VAT tax with extended coverage to food, medicine, education, and health care.

The result was a projected revenue increase of just 1 percent of GDP, versus earlier goals to collect 2.5 percent of GDP in 2002 and at least 4 percent per year thereafter. As the budget deficit had already surpassed its targets, a panicky round of new taxes were levied in early 2002, including those on cell phones, high-speed Internet services, tobacco, and alcoholic beverages. With any further talk of tax reform patently shelved until after the July 2003 elections, the government also raised effective electricity rates for commercial users by 300 percent as another quick deficit-cutting play. The cumulative result of the long tax battle and its generally unsatisfactory outcome is that the political opposition succeeded in driving down Fox's approval ratings and overall standing in the public opinion polls,[44] a hint of the losses that the PAN would eventually suffer in the 2003 midterm elections.

Pursuing Political Reform

The Fox government wasted no time in advancing political reforms that upheld earlier campaign promises to combat crime and corruption and instill much greater levels of transparency and accountability into everyday political and economic life. Most prominent among these initiatives was the creation of a new Secretariat of Public Security (Secretaría de Seguridad Pública, SSP) that replaced its corruption-infested correlate in the attorney general's office and took over the policing duties of the PRI-permeated Secretariat of the Interior. The Secretariat of the Comptroller and Administrative Development (Secretaría de la Contraloría y Desarrollo Administrativo, SECODAM) was also scrapped and replaced with a new Government Audit Office (Secretaría de la Función Pública, SFP).[45] Other measures, such as the Law of People's Savings and Credit (Ley de Ahorro y Crédito Popular), will regulate financial intermediaries that focus on low-income groups, and a new stock market law will similarly protect small investors and seek to limit insider trading. One of Fox's earliest legislative moves was to veto a rural development bill on the stated grounds that it did not offer sufficient relief to small farmers; however, it is clear that he also vetoed it because the bill stipulated that government funds be channeled indirectly to these groups through the National Peasants Confederation (Confederación Nacional Campesina, CNC), one of the PRI's last remaining corporatist footholds in the countryside.[46] Even though some of these gestures represent as much symbol as they do substance, it is noteworthy that political symbolism is being employed to deepen, rather than derail and distract from, the democratization process.

As with the fiscal reform package, those political reforms that dig into much deeper tissue with regard to Mexico's democratic transition—including the highly contested indigenous rights bill and the need for yet another generation of electoral reforms—are taking longer to hammer out in Congress. On the indigenous rights bill, Fox has been plagued by an audacious campaign comment where he claimed that, in contrast to the PRI's bungling of this issue, he could resolve it in "fifteen minutes." While it appears that Zedillo's negotiators could have done more to avoid the shaky stalemate that developed between the Zapatista National Liberation Army (Ejército Zapatista de Liberación Nacional, EZLN) and the government in 1997, it cannot be said that Fox has done all that much better to date. At stake is the resumption of good-faith peace negotiations between the government and the EZLN, although the latter has demanded that the following conditions must first be met: the Fox administration must close most of the military bases in Chiapas and release those guerrillas still being held as political prisoners, and the Congress must pass the indigenous rights bill generated in 1996 by the multiparty congressional Commission for Peace and Reconciliation (Comisión de Concordia y Pacificación, COCOPA).

The COCOPA indigenous rights bill was indeed the first piece of legislation that the Fox administration sent to Congress, and the president's strategy was to basically concede to the EZLN's demands. The problem, obviously, is that Fox alone cannot seal this deal, and his attitude of collegiality toward the Zapatistas is not shared by the more conservative elements within his own party. For once, the PRD backed the president on this particular issue, but the PRI's position on indigenous rights has wavered erratically because that party's control over the poor southern states with large indigenous representation requires treading carefully for fear of further alienating a main constituent base. An indigenous rights bill was passed by Congress in April 2001, but the content did not meet the desire of indigenous groups to establish autonomy in local political matters, including land and natural resource rights and judicial matters. In addition, any autonomy granted in the bill was made precarious by congressional insistence that it could be usurped when it conflicts with federal law. As a result, there is a lack of "buy-in" by affected groups and continuing discord among all concerned parties about how to make peace and achieve reform. In short, the time frame is longer than 15 minutes, and, for Fox, this remains a sticky problem.

Given that fiscal reform and the unexpected standoff on indigenous rights have consumed the bulk of the new administration's time and energy, it is worth noting that discussions launched prior to the 2000 presidential race among the major parties about the need for another wave of electoral reforms have yet to be resumed in any serious way. Especially since the PRI's widespread losses in 1997, virtually every state-level gubernatorial contest involving a possible PRI defeat has erupted into the equivalent of a mini–civil war. It is indisputable that there is a definite need for further electoral reform to help prevent these lapses into old authoritarian practices. As prominent Mexican political analyst José Antonio Crespo has noted, there is a particular need "not only to eliminate lingering inequalities . . . but also to adjust the electoral system to propagate greater electoral competition, power distribution, party checks and balances, and citizen mobilization."[47]

A next crucial, yet ill-defined, step for Mexican politics will be rally-ing a new proreform coalition from the vestiges of the 2000 debate over electoral modernization. Although no state-level elections were slated until 2003, when all 500 seats in the lower house of Congress went up for grabs, on the reform front all three of the major political parties squan-dered this respite from the immediate pressures of electoral politics.[48] Apart from the still-vague political accord mentioned earlier, only minor political reforms were implemented within the three parties. Nevertheless, glaring gaps in political reform, such as those in the areas of candidate selection and campaign finance, continue to cry out for action. Nowhere is this more apparent than with the "Pemexgate" scandal, involving some $120 million in illicit presidential campaign funds channeled in 2000 from the state petroleum company, Pemex, to the PRI via the coffers of the oil workers' union.[49]

Mexico's increasingly sophisticated public opinion pollsters have declared the current juncture—economic recession, political stalemate, and Congress's deliberate slowdown of the entire reform agenda—as too fluid and uncertain to point solidly toward any single victorious party or bloc of parties now gearing up for the 2006 presidential contest. To be sure, past the midpoint of the Fox administration it does not look good for the PAN. Moreover, the uncanny ability of the PRI's mainly traditional wing to reverse its local-level losses in 2000 and 2001 and win numerous subsequent municipal races, not to mention its 2003 gains in the Chamber of Deputies, suggests that it is indeed far too soon to speak of the "post-PRI" era in Mexican politics. As academic analysts continue to debate the Mexican electorate's past and future voting allegiances in terms of party identification, political socialization, or pocketbook concerns, we caution that Mexico's protracted democratic transition continues to defy easy cat-egorization—especially with the standard-bearers of authoritarianism still happily running for office and winning.[50]

As in the rest of Latin America, Mexico's current incumbents have been punished for failing to deliver in any visible manner.[51] Perhaps the strongest message from the 2003 midterm elections is that Mexican vot-ers will continue to opt for alternative candidates and parties as an expres-sion of their key concerns, just as they did in the 1997 and 2000 elections. Thus, the race is on for deliverable results, be it jobs, education, infra-structure, or access to affordable working capital for small firms. This is a message that some state-level leaders have readily responded to, and they have done so regardless of party affiliation. For example, in Jalisco (the PAN), Hidalgo (the PRI), and Zacatecas (the PRD), state governors and their staffs have pragmatically tackled adverse development indicators and worked effectively to increase the ranking of their respective states in all areas.[52] Rather than waste another three years of the electorate's time with political arbitrage, this war of attrition at the federal level could be readily won by intense reform efforts of the kind now witnessed in some states and municipalities across Mexico.

Conclusion: Reconciling the Political and the Economic

The challenges inherited by the Fox team are significant, as reflected in the political difficulties already encountered as his administration seeks to push through its economic measures and legislative reforms. With no legitimate democratic past to draw on and the unraveling of old political pacts still superseding the establishment of new viable ones, the learning curve for Mexico's democratic transition has perhaps been unexpectedly steep. The bigger question, of course, is whether the broad tasks of political economic restructuring and second-generation reform—creating employment, ameliorating income inequities, strengthening representative structures—can be accomplished in Mexico's new institutional terrain of nascent competitive politics and enhanced accountability. Certainly, the scramble for party advantage has resulted in stalled initiatives and overly tempered policies.

In general, this emerging interplay between politics and economics in Mexico is the opposite of what ascendant PRI technocrats had originally envisioned in the 1980s. Rather than achieving the vision of PRI reformers—a dominant ruling party maintaining control through its accommodation to a more competitive economic system—Mexican politics have been swept up in change as well. In some sense, the Mexican experience squares with typical reform models in which political liberalization inevitably follows on the heels of economic liberalization—in this case, with members of the dominant party dragged kicking and screaming into an authentic democratic transition, somewhat bewildered that the party's technocratic leadership sold out to the vagaries of fair elections in order to ensure the sustainability of their own economic reforms. In other ways, the Mexican case differs from classic accounts, particularly in the lengthy lag between economic restructuring and political reform, but also in the interplay of technocrats and traditionalists within the same ruling party, with the former group adopting political reforms mostly to buy time for further economic adjustments.

In any case, the political transition, while tentative, is authentic. It is hard to imagine Mexico making the sort of democratization retreats evidenced by Fujimori's *autogolpe* in Peru, Menem's embrace of constitutional change to ensure himself a second term in Argentina, Hugo Chávez's disbanding of Venezuela's Congress to draw up a new constitution, or the Ecuadorian parliament's removal of Adbalá Bucaram, a duly elected president, by declaring him psychologically incompetent. Rather, in Mexico, economic and political reform will continue their uneasy march forward. Both will continue to be subjected to the microscopic scrutiny of public opinion and the increased competition from truly participatory decisionmaking structures, as the decree-heavy reform approaches of de la Madrid and Salinas have been firmly relegated to the past. The cacophony of civic demands and interparty squabbling will continue to frustrate President Fox, who is unused to blending his own headstrong opinions with those of others. But listen he must, as the economic and political changes in Mexico now form a reciprocal loop—a dynamic set of interactions that the PRI can no longer control on its own and which Fox must finesse in order to steer Mexico onto the path of economic and political reform.

Notes

1. Manuel Pastor and Carol Wise, "A Long View on the Mexican Political Economy," in *Mexico's Politics and Society in Transition,* edited by Joseph S. Tulchin and Andrew Selee (Boulder, CO: Lynne Rienner Publishers, 2003), pp. 179–213.

2. On Mexico's political liberalization, see Maxwell Cameron and Carol Wise, "The Political Impact of NAFTA on Mexico," *Canadian Journal of Political Science,* forthcoming; Vikram Chand, *Mexico's Political Awakening* (Notre Dame, IN: University of Notre Dame, 2001); Joseph Klesner, "Electoral Politics and Mexico's New Party System," paper presented at the American Political Science Association Meetings, San Francisco, September 4–6, 2001; and Daniel Levy and Kathleen Bruhn, *Mexico: The Struggle for Democratic Development* (Berkeley: University of California Press, 2001). On Mexico's economic transformation, see Nora Lustig, *Mexico: The Remaking of an Economy* (Washington, DC: Brookings Institution Press, 1998 [second edition]); Enrique Dussel Peters, "Industrial Policy, Regional Trends, and Structural Change in Mexico's Manufacturing Sector," in *Confronting Development: Assessing Mexico's Economic and Social Policy Challenges,* edited by Kevin Middlebrook and Eduardo Zepeda (Palo Alto, CA: Stanford University Press, 2002), pp. 241–274; and Jorge Máttar, Juan Carlos Moreno-Brid, and Wilson Peres, "Foreign Investment in Mexico after Economic Reform," in *Confronting Development,* edited by Middlebrook and Zepeda, pp. 123–160.

3. See Denise Dresser, "Falling from the Tightrope: The Political Economy of the Mexican Crisis," in *Mexico 1994: Anatomy of an Emerging-Market Crash,* edited by Sebastian Edwards and Moisés Naím (Washington, DC: Carnegie Endowment for International Peace, 1997), pp. 55–79; and Carol Wise, "Mexico's Democratic Transition: The Search for New Reform Coalitions," in *Post-Stabilization Politics in Latin America: Competition, Transition, Collapse,* edited by Carol Wise and Riordan Roett, with Guadalupe Paz (Washington, DC: Brookings Institution Press, 2003), pp. 159–198.

4. See, for example, Marcelo M. Giugale, Olivier Lafourcade, and Vinh H. Nguyen, *Mexico: A Comprehensive Development Agenda for the New Era* (Washington, DC: World Bank, 2001).

5. Cámara de Diputados, H. Congreso de la Unión, "Composición de la Cámara por Partido," and "Integración LVIII Legislatura," available in the official Chamber of Deputies website: www.cddhcu.gob.mx (last accesed September 26, 2003).

6. This has been a recurring theme in numerous interviews that we conducted with high-level Mexican policymakers between 1992 and 2003. See Manuel Pastor and Carol Wise, "The Origins and Sustainability of Mexico's Free Trade Policy," *International Organization* 48, no. 3 (1994): 459–489.

7. For example, according to one public official, as recently as 2001 only 27 percent of Mexicans were considered to be active participants in the formal banking system. Authors' interview with Vicente Arredondo, former national coordinator of PROGRESA, Mexico City, March 22, 2001.

8. The quote stems from the authors' interview in Mexico City in March 2001 with an official in the Secretariat of Economy who wishes to remain anonymous.

9. See Rachel Schurman, "Chile's New Entrepreneurs and the 'Economic Miracle': Invisible Hand or a Hand from the State?" *Studies in Comparative International Development* 31, no. 2 (1996): 83–109; and Carol Wise, *Reinventing the State: Economic Strategy and Institutional Change in Peru* (Ann Arbor: University of Michigan Press, 2003).

10. Moreover, the administration will need to cultivate an esprit de corps within a public sector that has often been demoralized by PRI scandals and is still overly controlled by select pockets of favored technocrats tied to the former ruling party.

11. See Jonathan Heath, "El voto y la economía," *Reforma,* July 8, 2003, Negocios section.

12. Economist Intelligence Unit, "Country Report: Mexico," *EIU Country Report,* January 2002, p. 13.

13. See Jonathan Heath, *Mexico and the Sexenio Curse: Presidential Successions and Economic Crises in Modern Mexico* (Washington, DC: Center for Strategic and International Studies, 1999).

14. José Antonio Crespo, "Raising the Bar: The Next Generation of Electoral Reforms in Mexico," Policy Papers on the Americas, Center for Strategic and International Studies, Washington, DC, 2000.

15. Manuel Pastor and Carol Wise, "The Politics of Second-Generation Reform," *Journal of Democracy* 10, no. 3 (1999): 34–48.

16. Soledad Loaeza, "An Unhealthy Distance Between Fox and the National Action Party," *Enfoque* (Fall 2000–Winter 2001), p. 3.

17. Klesner, "Electoral Politics."

18. We thank Jonathan Heath for this insight.

19. "Fox's Trade Plan to Focus on Smaller Firms," *Mexico & NAFTA Report*, December 12, 2000, p. 1. Governors in such states as Hidalgo, Jalisco, and Zacatecas have taken this increased budgetary leeway and run with it by aggressively targeting support for micro and small business ventures. Authors' interviews: Governor Manuel Núñez Soto (Hidalgo, July 10, 2003); Governor Francisco Ramírez (Jalisco, July 15, 2003); Governor Ricardo Monreal (Zacatecas, July 17, 2003).

20. Authors' interview with Luis de la Calle, former Undersecretary for International Trade Negotiations, Secretariat of Economy, Mexico City, March 22, 2001.

21. For more detail on these programs see Dussel Peters, "Industrial Policy."

22. Authors' interview with CIPI Director, Luis Melgar, Secretariat of Economy, Mexico City, March 22, 2001.

23. "Country Report: Mexico," *EIU Country Report*, April 2001, p. 17. The government also intends to offer tax incentives to encourage SME export activities outside of the maquiladora sector and more vigorously enforce anti-trust policies already on the books, but it remains to be seen whether these goals will be pursued in the event that the congress remains difficult to traverse.

24. The term *changarro* is a Mexican colloquialism for a modest business or street stand.

25. See Gordon Hanson and Ann Harrison, "Trade Liberalization and Wage Inequality in Mexico," *Industrial and Labor Relations Review* 52, no. 2 (1999): 271–288.

26. Santiago Levy, "Reorienting Mexico's Social Policy," in *Mexico in Transition,* edited by Andrew D. Selee (Washington, DC: Woodrow Wilson Center Reports on the Americas, No. 1, 2001), pp. 28–29.

27. Authors' interview with Ignacio Chávez, Office of Health, Education, and Labor, Ministry of Finance ("Hacienda"), Mexico City, March 23, 2001.

28. "Country Report: Mexico," *EIU Country Report*, April 2002, p. 8.

29. "Country Report: Mexico," *EIU Country Report*, July 2001, p. 15.

30. See Maxwell A. Cameron and Brian W. Tomlin, *The Making of NAFTA: How the Deal Was Done* (Ithaca, NY: Cornell University Press, 2000).

31. Wayne A. Cornelius, "Death at the Border," *Population and Development Review* 27, no. 4 (2001): 661–685.

32. Among the proposals for a more orderly migration framework between the United States and Mexico are a new guest worker program for Mexicans in the United States, an increase in legal immigration from Mexico, and/or an amnesty bill for undocumented Mexicans now residing in the United States.

33. See Peter Andreas, *Border Games: Policing the U.S.-Mexico Divide* (Ithaca, NY: Cornell University Press, 2000).

34. See Inter-American Development Bank, *Facing Up to Inequality in Latin America* (Baltimore: Johns Hopkins University Press, 1998); and Jere Behrman,

Nancy Birdsall, and Miguel Székely, "Economic Reform and Wage Differentials in Latin America," Working Paper 435, Inter-American Development Bank, Washington, DC, 2000.

35. Secretaría de Desarrollo Social (SEDESOL), *¿Está dando buenos resultados Progresa? Informe de los resultados obtenidos de una evaluación realizada por el IFPRI* (International Food Policy Research Institute) (Mexico City: SEDESOL, 2000).

36. Authors' interviews with Gonzalo Hernández (Director of Program Evaluation) and Gustavo Merino (Director of Planning), Secretariat of Social Development (SEDESOL), July 11, 2003, Mexico City.

37. Santiago Levy, "Reorienting Mexico's Social Policy," pp. 27–34.

38. To ensure that increases in education and other social spending actually translate into improved outcomes, there is also a need to improve administrative capacity. In the words of one public official, under Zedillo, "You pitched and there was no catcher"—that is, at a local level, the capacity to absorb spending and use it productively was limited. Partly as a result, the development secretariat (SEDESOL) has been putting more funds and energy into capacity building. Authors' interviews with Gonzalo Hernández (Director of Program Evaluation) and Gustavo Merino (Director of Planning), Secretariat of Social Development (SEDESOL), July 11, 2003, Mexico City.

39. "Budget Sent to Congress," *Latin American Mexico & NAFTA Report*, December 12, 2000, pp. 6–7.

40. See Timothy Kessler, "The Mexican Peso Crash: Causes, Consequences, Comeback," in *Exchange Rate Politics in Latin America,* edited by Carol Wise and Riordan Roett (Washington, DC: Brookings Institution Press, 2000), pp. 43–69.

41. "Country Report: Mexico," *EIU Country Report*, April 2002, p. 8.

42. Part of the method combined income taxes with social security contributions and payments, a strategy that resulted in a calculation that those in the top income decile were paying 140 percent of direct taxes on income. While the rest of the incidence estimates were more reasonable, the analysis wound up suggesting that those in the bottom 60 percent of wage earners were actually paying negative taxes (this is even without calculating what are normally construed as benefits to arrive at a net fiscal revenue figure).

43. "Country Report: Mexico," *EIU Country Report*, April 2002, p. 8.

44. Ibid., pp. 13–16.

45. This section draws on various issues of "Country Report: Mexico," *EIU Country Report*, from July 2000 to July 2001.

46. "President Wields the Veto," *Mexico & NAFTA Report*, March 20, 2001, p. 9.

47. José Antonio Crespo, "Raising the Bar," p. 27.

48. Gubernatorial races in six states took place in July 2003: Campeche, Colima, Nuevo León, San Luis Potosí, Sonora, and Querétaro.

49. All dollar amounts are in U.S. dollars. Ibid., pp. 15–16.

50. See Jorge Buendía, "Economic Reform, Public Opinion, and Presidential Approval in Mexico, 1988–1993," *Comparative Political Studies* 29, no. 5

(1996): 575–576; and Robert Kaufman and Leo Zuckerman, "Attitudes Toward Economic Reform in Mexico: The Role of Political Orientations," *American Political Science Review* 92, no. 2 (1998): 359–374.

51. See Karen Remmer, "Elections and Economics in Contemporary Latin America," in *Post-Stabilization Politics in Latin America: Competition, Transition, Collapse,* edited by Carol Wise and Riordan Roett, with Guadalupe Paz (Washington, DC: Brookings Institution Press, 2003), pp. 31–55.

52. Authors' interview with Luis de la Calle, former Undersecretary for International Trade Negotiations, Secretariat of Economy, Mexico City, March 22, 2001.

6

Mexico's Economic Transformation Under NAFTA

Gary Gereffi and Martha A. Martínez

Profound structural changes have beset the world economy in the past two decades. These transformations have been particularly radical in Latin America, where in the mid-1980s, after almost a decade of economic crisis that included devaluations and zero or negative growth, countries were forced to reconsider the benefits of their import-substitution industrialization (ISI) strategy of self-sufficiency and internally driven growth. Motivated by the ultimate failure of ISI (which prompted many to refer to the 1980s as Latin America's "lost development decade")[1] and by the contrasting and almost miraculous success of the so-called East Asian Tigers (South Korea, Hong Kong, Taiwan, and Singapore), Latin American countries have shifted the focus of their industrial policies from the ISI strategy to an export-oriented development model.[2]

Mexico is perhaps the most extreme example of that development model shift. Despite its initial success between 1940 and 1970, ISI turned out to be an unsustainable development strategy for Mexico, which relied excessively on petroleum as the main export. Although signs of economic decline can be found in the 1960s, the shortcomings of the ISI model became most apparent in the 1970s period plagued by trade deficits and devaluations, culminating in the debt crisis during the early 1980s. Mexico's high external debt burden required the allocation of 25 to 30 percent of the country's foreign exchange proceeds merely to cover interest payments. It was in this context that Mexico decided to reverse its long-standing allegiance to ISI and, during the Miguel de la Madrid and Carlos Salinas presidential administrations (1982–1988 and 1988–1994, respectively), adopted a development model based on economic liberalization and export expansion.

This chapter examines how Mexico's radical experiment in economic liberalization is a story of undeniable success, but also one of missed opportunities and real losses. The export-oriented development strategy is a doubled-edged sword. It has allowed Mexico to correct many of the economic problems present in the 1980s, but the strategy has not been sufficient to ensure sustainable growth and stability. Although many companies are thriving, the strategy has brutally and negatively affected many other individuals and firms. Furthermore, an export economy, at least as practiced by Mexico, has unique vulnerabilities. For Mexico, export-oriented industrialization seems to be one necessary component of what should be a more well-rounded development strategy. Rather than analyzing Mexico's transformation under the North American Free Trade Agreement (NAFTA) among Mexico, the United States, and Canada merely as an economic system or as a management agenda, this chapter also examines NAFTA as a development strategy with distinct advantages and disadvantages. In particular, we review NAFTA's impact on industrial upgrading and the criticisms of NAFTA's impacts on Mexico's development, including discussions of sectoral grievances, dependency, the maquiladora debate, inequality, and employment.

The Emergence of Mexico's Export-Oriented Development Model

The export-oriented model applied by Mexico has two main components: first, it emphasizes growth through exports; and second, foreign investment is used to finance this growth, instead of foreign loans. According to this model, successful exportation requires higher levels of quality and productivity that promote healthy industrialization and growth. Mexico spent the 1980s immersed in profound crises, partly as a consequence of prior mistakes, but also because of the severe adjustments required to create a safe environment for attracting foreign investment and increasing productivity. In the 1990s, Mexico's economic performance under the export model was relatively robust, with annual growth rates of 4 to 5 percent in the early part of the decade. Following a major downturn in 1995, in which the gross domestic product (GDP) dropped 6.2 percent as a result of the 1994–1995 peso devaluation, real GDP growth averaged more than 5.5 percent from 1996 to 2000 (see Table 6.1).

Mexico's turn toward an externally oriented development strategy formally began with the country's entrance to the General Agreement on

Table 6.1   Mexico's Economic Performance, 1990–2001

Year	Population (millions)	Gross Domestic Product (GDP) (billions 1995 $)	GDP % Annual Growth	GDP Per Capita (1995 $)	GDP Per Capita % Change
1990	83.2	265.3	5.1	3,187	NA
1991	84.8	276.5	4.2	3,260	2.3
1992	86.4	286.5	3.6	3,317	1.7
1993	88.0	292.1	2.0	3,321	0.1
1994	89.5	305.0	4.4	3,406	2.6
1995	91.1	286.2	−6.2	3,140	−7.8
1996	92.6	300.9	5.2	3,251	3.5
1997	93.9	321.3	6.8	3,421	5.2
1998	95.3	337.2	5.0	3,540	3.5
1999	96.6	349.9	3.8	3,623	2.3
2000	98.0	374.1	6.9	3,819	5.4
2001	99.4	371.4	−0.8	3,739	−2.0

Source: World Development Indicators, World Bank. Available online (with subscription) at http://publications.worldbank.org/subscriptions/WDI.
Note: NA = not available.

Tariffs and Trade (GATT) in 1985, and since then Mexico has become one of the world's most open economies. In the 1990s, Mexico signed free trade agreements with 32 countries, including the United States, Canada, and all the members of the European Union (EU).[3] The interesting fact is not so much that these agreements have been negotiated and implemented in less than a decade with countries presenting quite different economic characteristics and political systems, but that, in a very short time, Mexico has used these partnerships to boost its bilateral trade flows.

NAFTA has dominated discussion of the Mexican economy in recent years and formed part of the broader debate about whether globalization is good or bad for Mexico's national development. NAFTA certainly changes the incentives regarding what will be made in Mexico, because the agreement removes tariff barriers for Mexican exports to the United States. It also changes the rules of origin for foreign investors who want to gain access to the U.S. market from a North American production base.

Despite Mexico's many free trade agreements, the process of regionalization promoted by NAFTA has been by far the greatest force for economic structural transformation in Mexico. Mexico's most important trading partners remain the United States and Canada, in part because of their geographic proximity, but also because of the sheer size of the U.S. and Canadian economies as well as Mexico's comparative advantage owing to disparities in labor and other costs. Nonetheless, one should not exaggerate

NAFTA's impact. Many of the trends toward regional economic integration involving Mexico and the United States began long before the trade agreement went into effect on January 1, 1994. By itself, NAFTA does not guarantee that Mexican firms will become successful exporters.[4]

As Table 6.2 shows, between 1993 and 2001 Mexico at least doubled the value of its trade with all the countries with which it has negotiated free trade agreements, with the exception of Bolivia. This increase in trade started prior to the implementation of the agreements themselves and continues afterward. Mexico's trade with Chile, Costa Rica, and Honduras in 2002 was more than triple its 1993 value. NAFTA, however, has played a key role in the transformation of the Mexican economy. Trade with the United States, Mexico's most important trade partner, has almost tripled, going from $88 billion in 1993 to $250 billion in 2002 (see Table 6.2).[5]

Free trade agreements have been the primary instrument used by Mexico to fulfill the first goal of its new strategy: make exports the main motor of the economy. A closer look at trade data shows that Mexico has been incredibly successful in this area. Table 6.3 provides a longitudinal analysis of foreign trade during the past decade. From these numbers, it is easy to see that exports have greatly increased their importance in Mexico's economic life. Exports are by far the fastest growing sector of the Mexican economy,

Table 6.2   Mexico's Free Trade Agreements

Country	Implementation Year	Total Trade 1993 (millions $)	Total Trade 2002 (millions $)	% Change
Chile	1992	330	1,269	285
United States	1994	88,146	249,719	183
Canada	1994	2,744	7,293	165
Bolivia	1995	33	44	33
Costa Rica	1995	121	760	528
Colombia	1995	323	908	181
Venezuela	1995	455	1,119	146
Nicaragua	1998	32	118	269
European Union	2000	10,587	21,659	105
Israel	2000	149	301	102
El Salvador	2001	127	302	138
Guatemala	2001	266	631	137
Honduras	2001	45	233	420
EFTA[a]	2001	682	1,337	96

Source: Estadísticas Comerciales, Aranceles y Normatividad, Comercio Exterior, Anual, Mexican Secretariat of Economy (Secretaría de Economía), available online at www.economia-snci.gob.mx/sic_php/1s23al.php?s=54&p=1&1=1.

Note: a. European Free Trade Association, which includes Iceland, Norway, Switzerland, and Liechtenstein.

Table 6.3   Mexico's International Trade: Main Indicators, 1991–2003

Year	Exports (millions $)	% Change Previous Year	Imports (millions $)	% Change Previous Year	Exports as % GDP
1991	42,688	NA	49,967	NA	16
1992	46,196	8.2	62,129	24.3	15
1993	51,886	12.3	65,367	5.2	15
1994	60,882	17.3	79,346	21.4	17
1995	79,542	30.6	72,453	-8.7	30
1996	96,000	20.7	89,469	23.5	32
1997	110,431	15.0	109,808	22.7	30
1998	117,459	6.4	125,373	14.2	31
1999	136,391	16.1	141,975	13.2	31
2000	166,455	22.0	174,458	22.9	31
2001	158,443	-4.8	168,397	-3.5	28
2002	160,682[a]	1.4	168,678[a]	0.2	NA
2003	164,922[a]	2.6	170,546[a]	1.1	NA

Source: Instituto Nacional de Estadística, Geografía e Informática (INEGI), Banco de Información Económica (BIE), Sector Externo, Resumen de Comercio Exterior, Presentación Actual, Importaciones y Exportaciones.   Available online at http://dgcnesyp.inegi.gob.mx/BDINE/bancos.htm. The source for Exports as percentage of GDP is: World Development Indicators. Query: Mexico, Exports of Goods and Services (% GDP), 1991–2001, available online at http://publications.worldbank.org/subscriptions/WDI.
Notes: NA = not available.
a. Preliminary data.

and their share of the country's GDP increased from an already high 16 percent in 1991 to 28 percent in 2001. However, during the 1990s, imports (notwithstanding their uneven pattern on an annual basis) expanded even faster than exports. Overall, the proportion of exports to imports has stayed relatively stable, with a trend toward a small trade deficit.

Mexico has also proven remarkably successful at fulfilling its other objective for the export-oriented strategy, attracting foreign direct investment (FDI). Under the new economic model, FDI has been the preferred strategy to finance both export growth and trade deficits. An important part of NAFTA is the liberalization not only of trade but also of investment flows between the countries. Mexico has lifted barriers to foreign investment in almost all sectors of the economy, with the notable exception of energy. Even that once untouchable stronghold will probably be liberalized soon because the regional energy crisis[6] has triggered discussions about and initiatives for privatization in Mexico's Congress, and foreign companies are preparing financial plans to invest in Mexico's energy sector in the near future.[7] However, changes in this sector have been delayed by partisan politics. Although annual FDI inflows vary depending on the implementation of free trade agreements, privatization schedules, and firms' strategic choices, FDI has averaged more than $10 billion per year in Mexico since the implementation of NAFTA in 1994, reaching a peak of nearly $27 billion in 2001 (see Table 6.4).[8]

These numbers indicate that Mexico's export-oriented strategy indeed has ushered in an extraordinary economic transformation in the past decade. Government deficits have been kept to a minimum, interest rates are at a 20-year low, and inflation, once the scourge of the Mexican economy, has been held to single digits during the past few years (a remarkable feat, considering the hyperinflation suffered by Mexico in the 1980s).

However, Mexican society still seems restless and dissatisfied with this turn of events. Overall, the Mexican economy is not necessarily more competitive than before the reforms. Exports and investments are high, but the domestic economy continues to be depressed. Open unemployment still exists, the informal economy accounts for a significant share of the workforce,[9] and wages, although higher than in the 1980s, have not triggered a consistent improvement in the quality of life. Despite a solid macroeconomic record, Mexico was hit by a deep recession in 2001 that included the loss of more than 270,000 jobs in the exceptionally dynamic maquiladora sector.[10] Skeptics do not question the country's efficiency in implementing the export-oriented model, but rather the adequacy of the model itself as a development strategy for a country as big and diversified as Mexico. Clearly, because of its aggressive and sustained application of the free trade model, Mexico is the best-case scenario for defining both the benefits and the limits of the global trend toward open market economies.

The Industrial Upgrading of Mexico's Export Industries

The evaluation of industrial upgrading requires the analysis of several dimensions of the capabilities and configurations of firms and industries within a country. To examine Mexico's industrial development one must address the question: What is made where, by whom, and for whom? *What* refers to types of products, including both industry classification and whether they are finished goods or intermediate inputs; *where* refers to the location of production, including countries as well as regions within a country; *by whom* refers to the kinds of companies that lead Mexico's industrialization efforts, including transnational firms, local private companies, and state enterprises; and *for whom* refers to whether production is for the domestic or the export markets.

Table 6.4 Foreign Direct Investment in Mexico (FDI), 1994–2003

Year	Total FDI (billions $)	% of Total FDI by Activity[a]						
		Agriculture	Manufacturing	Trade	Transport and Communications	Banking Services	Community Services	Other
1994	10.6	0.1	58	12	7	9	11	3
1995	8.3	0.1	58	12	11	13	5	1
1996	7.7	0.4	61	9	6	16	6	2
1997	12.1	0.1	60	16	6	9	7	2
1998[b]	8.2	0.4	62	12	5	9	10	2
1999[b]	13.2	0.6	68	9	2	6	11	3
2000[b]	16.4	0.6	57	14	-14	28	11	3
2001[b]	26.6	0.02	22	6	11	54	5	2
2002[b]	13.3	0.04	40	10	6	32	7	5
2003[b]	9.4	0.1	48	8	16	19	6	3

Source: INEGI, Banco de Información Económica, Inversión Extranjera Directa, Nueva Metodología, Actividad Económica, available online at www.inegi.gob.mx/est/contenidos/espanol/tematicos/mediano/med.asp?t=sext04&c=5006.

Notes: a. Total may not be 100% due to rounding.

b. Data is considered preliminary.

The concept of industrial upgrading encompasses several related levels: intersectoral shifts, intrasectoral shifts, economic roles, and product characteristics.[11] At the most general level, industrial upgrading may be viewed as intersectoral shifts from primary products to manufactured goods, and within manufacturing, from low-value, labor-intensive industries to capital- and technology-intensive ones (e.g., going from clothes to cars to computers). A second type of industrial upgrading involves an intrasectoral progression, typically from the manufacture of finished items to the production of higher-value goods and services involving forward and backward linkages along the supply chain. If intersectoral and intrasectoral upgrading takes place, both economic roles and product characteristics change. A country's economic role is transformed when it performs activities that involve increasingly sophisticated production, marketing, and design tasks, and at the product level production moves from simple to more complex goods of the same type (e.g., going from cotton shirts to men's suits).[12] Given that they are the source of any other transformations, we will concentrate on intersectoral and intrasectoral upgrading.

Although firms typically are the agents of industrial upgrading activities, the spatial context in which such activity occurs includes local, national, and regional economies. Government policies that affect each of these levels can facilitate (or impede) the upgrading process. Mexico's new strategy has produced transformations in each of these levels.

Industrial Upgrading as Intersectoral Shifts: From Primary Products to Manufactured Goods

This chapter focuses on Mexico's exports, rather than on production for the domestic market. Export production is a stringent indicator of industrial development, because it deals only with those products in which Mexico has demonstrated an international competitive edge. Focusing on exports is appropriate when one considers that Mexico's emphasis on export promotion is a cornerstone of its current development strategy. Not surprisingly, the most radical structural transformations in the Mexican economy have taken place within the export sector. In purely quantitative terms, exports have entered an unprecedented phase of expansion and have increased their relative importance in the Mexican economy. From representing only 7.6 percent of Mexico's GDP in 1980, exports jumped to 31 percent of the GDP in 2000.[13]

However, the transformations are more impressive when considering industrial upgrading in terms of the shift from primary products to manufactured goods. In 1980, primary products dominated Mexico's top 10 exports to the world: fuels (petroleum and natural gas), raw materials (metalliferous ores and textile fibers), and food (vegetables and fruit, coffee, and fish). Mexico's main export item in 1980 was petroleum, which accounted for an exceptionally high 61.6 percent of all exports. In 1990, petroleum's share of total exports fell to 35.2 percent, and vegetables and fruit and three intermediate goods (nonferrous metals, iron and steel, and organic chemicals) remained among Mexico's top 10 exports. By 2000, Mexico's export profile was dramatically different: petroleum had been reduced to a mere 7.3 percent of overseas sales, while manufactured products accounted for 89.9 percent of export earnings.[14]

Comparing Mexico with its North American neighbor Canada shows that Mexico has undergone a more significant degree of industrial upgrading between 1985 and 2000, as measured by both countries' exports to the United States. Canada's exports to the United States were far larger than Mexico's in 2000 ($256 billion and $153 billion, respectively), although the gap has shrunk very rapidly since 1990, when Canada had five times more exports to the United States than Mexico ($100 billion and $20 billion, respectively).[15] Canada's top exports have remained very stable for the past decade, while Mexico shows considerable diversity and upgrading in its export profile. Motor vehicles, petroleum, natural gas, and paper were among Canada's top 5 export items in 1985, 1990, 1995, and 2000, and three other products (cork and wood, nonferrous metals, and power-generating machinery) are in the Canadian top 10 in each of these 4 years.

In contrast, Mexico has made significant strides in diversifying its exports from primary products and intermediates to manufactured goods, increasingly making more sophisticated export items. Although in 1985 primary products like oil and its derivatives, coffee, vegetables, and crustaceans were in the top 10 export items for Mexico, by 2000 no primary products can be found in Mexico's top 10 exports list. In 15 years, primary products were displaced by such goods as motor vehicles, telecommunications equipment, data processing equipment, television receivers, and electronic apparatus.

A fuller understanding and evaluation of the causes and consequences of the intersectoral upgrading shifts would require a more detailed look at Mexican, U.S., and Canadian government policies toward each of the sectors, international market conditions, and the kinds of firms engaged in exporting. At a minimum, however, one needs to recognize that Mexico's export sector has become much more dynamic and diversified than Canada's, especially since 1990.

Although most of Latin America has switched away from ISI and toward an export-oriented strategy, following the script of the so-called

Washington Consensus,[16] Mexico's results in terms of exports have been the most impressive in the region, even when compared with Argentina, Brazil, and Chile, the largest economies in a similar regional market: Mercosur.[17] From 1990 to 2000, exports rose in Latin America as a whole. However, Mexico's exports increased sixfold (from $29 billion to $179 billion), whereas Argentina's and Chile's exports more than doubled (to $28 billion and $20 billion, respectively, in 2000) and Brazil's exports increased approximately 80 percent (to $60 billion).[18] The combined exports of Argentina, Brazil, and Chile in 2000 ($107.7 billion) represented only 60 percent of Mexico's export total in that year.[19]

Mexico's competitive advantages in the manufacturing sector are revealed by a closer look at each country's export mix. In the 1980s, Mexico, Argentina, Brazil, and Chile all had similar export profiles, ones based on raw materials (e.g., minerals, agricultural products, and petroleum products). Argentina, Brazil, and Chile have maintained that export pattern for the past two decades, with the exception of the growth in the automotive sector in Argentina and Brazil. In contrast, Mexico has decreased the importance of raw materials in its total export mix, evidenced by increased shipments in capital-intensive or high-technology sectors, such as the automobile, electrical, telecommunications, and computer industries.[20]

If most Latin American countries, in particular Argentina, Brazil, and Chile, have adopted an export-oriented industrialization strategy, then why have they not achieved results similar to those of Mexico? There are many reasons. One is that Mexico applied its economic liberalization reforms in a more radical fashion than did any of its Latin American counterparts. For example, although Mercosur is almost exclusively oriented toward the free export and import of products, Mexico's trade agreements, following the scheme established by NAFTA, include provisions for the free flow of capital, the protection of intellectual property, and the regulation of government contracting.

Another factor contributing to the difference in export profiles between Mexico and other Latin American countries is the specific destination within and sources of FDI in the various countries. In 2001, Mexico received 35 percent of all net FDI inflows for Latin America, Brazil was second with 32 percent, and Chile was a distant third with 6 percent.[21] Even though foreign corporations that invest in Mexico have concentrated on creating efficient manufacturing bases for export products (with the exception of the recent acquisition of Mexico's biggest banks), FDI in Mercosur countries has been used by transnational firms to enter local markets in areas that were formerly closed to foreign investment. During the first six months of 2000, Mexico's manufacturing sector received 46 percent of the country's FDI, whereas manufacturing in Brazil received only 24 percent of national FDI.[22]

The process of intersectoral upgrading is but one dimension in the industrial development of any country. A second type of industrial upgrading involves an intrasectoral progression, typically from the manufacture of finished items to the production of higher-value goods and services involving forward and backward linkages along the supply chain of a particular good.

Industrial Upgrading as Intrasectoral Shifts: Forward and Backward Linkages

Analyzing the industrial upgrading process within national development in terms of forward and backward linkages is common among economists.[23] The idea is best illustrated in Mexico by looking at the apparel and automotive sectors. The Mexican apparel industry demonstrates how assembly firms can evolve toward activities with a higher degree of complexity, including developing national supply chains with local linkages and increasing the participation of Mexican entrepreneurs.[24] In becoming the number one exporter of apparel to the United States, Mexico relied heavily on a handful of items (including blue jeans, cotton underwear, and cotton shirts) to gain a strong foothold in the U.S. market during the 1990s. In contrast, the auto industry is a story of increased product sophistication and variety.

The passage of NAFTA in 1994 began to remove the trade restrictions that had virtually locked Mexico into an assembly role. In the past, the maquiladora system effectively conditioned Mexico's access to the U.S. market on the use of U.S. inputs. The phase-in period for NAFTA allows one to see, step by step, how different segments of the apparel supply chain (such as textile production, cutting, washing, and sewing) are relocating to Mexico as specific tariff restrictions on each segment are eliminated. As these activities relocate, both Mexican and American manufacturers invest in more modern equipment, software, and facilities, particularly when big customers with famous brand names are involved. New customers (particularly brand marketers and retailers) have been attracted to Mexico by the possibility created by NAFTA of full-package production (i.e., the coordination of all production-related activities, including sourcing, needed to deliver finished products).

Despite the relocation of most apparel production activities to Mexico, two important aspects in the process are still beyond the reach of

Mexican manufacturers: design and marketing. These aspects also happen to have the highest profit margins in the industry. However, lack of direct experience in the U.S. consumer market, not restrictions created or maintained by NAFTA, keeps Mexican entrepreneurs from entering those sides of the business. Concentrating on full-package, business-to-business transactions is safer, if less profitable, for Mexican entrepreneurs than trying to develop their own brands for fickle American consumer tastes.[25]

In the automobile industry, many of the most significant intrasectoral shifts have resulted from government policies. In Mexico, the automobile industry has been regulated by a series of decrees issued from 1962 to 1989.[26] The two main goals of the decrees were to make Mexico an automobile producer, rather than a mere assembler, and to lower the automobile industry's perennial trade deficit.[27] A variety of specific industrial policy objectives were incorporated in Mexico's automotive decrees to push the transnational automakers to contribute more to the domestic development of the industry. These include (1) increasing the domestic content of finished vehicles, (2) ensuring that engines and drive trains would be made in Mexico, (3) regulating the proliferation of models, and (4) reducing the industry's trade deficit by imposing export requirements to balance an automotive firm's imports with an equal or greater amount of exports. Although some of these policies could not be implemented and others have since been rescinded, the state's role in the automobile industry was critical in establishing a relatively sophisticated automotive parts sector in Mexico.[28]

The automobile industry represents a case of advanced manufacturing in which Mexico has gone beyond mere assembly: the industry produces technologically complex components and even engages in some research and development activities. By the late 1990s, the automobile industry was Mexico's single most important manufacturing business. More than 500,000 Mexicans were employed making parts and assembling vehicles for eight of the world's biggest automakers, including the U.S. Big Three (General Motors, Ford, and DaimlerChrysler), Nissan, Honda, Volkswagen, BMW, and Mercedes-Benz. In 1995, about 80 percent of the vehicles produced in Mexico by the Big Three were for export, compared with just 48 percent in 1994.[29] NAFTA's rules of origin, which require high North American–made content in cars, have forced European and Asian parts suppliers to follow their automakers to Mexico. In Puebla, 70 parts suppliers cluster around Volkswagen's sprawling factory, which churns out 600 new Beetles and 900 other Volkswagen cars per day.[30] Induced by NAFTA's rules, many other U.S., Asian, and European automobile parts firms have also set up manufacturing operations in Mexico.

NAFTA has played a major role in promoting the industrial upgrading of the Mexican motor vehicle industry. From 1994 to 2000, Mexico's motor vehicle exports (SITC 78) to the United States more than tripled (from $7.3 to $26.2 billion), while Canada's U.S. exports rose by only 48 percent (from $40.6 to $60.3 billion). During that time, the most dynamic sector for Mexico was light trucks (SITC 782), exports of which grew nearly sixfold (from $945 million to $5.3 billion), while automobile parts (SITC 784) exports also increased sharply (from $2 billion to $5.4 billion).[31]

With regard to exports, Mexico has clearly improved its position in the North American automobile commodity chain. The country has attracted all the major global assemblers and, despite the economic recession in the mid-1990s, auto assembly levels seem to be returning to pre-devaluation levels of exports. (The year 2001 was an exception: the slowdown of the American economy curtailed export growth.) In addition, the prospects of further expansion are good because three new assemblers (Honda, Mercedes-Benz, and BMW) entered Mexico in 1996.[32] Using the industrial upgrading logic, two routes for continued development seem particularly promising.[33] One option is to use the most dynamic assemblers (Volkswagen and Ford) as a basis for developing more integrated supplier networks in Mexico, because they can tap export demand in the U.S. market. A second option would be for Mexico to encourage major first-tier suppliers to set up advanced manufacturing and research and development facilities in the country,[34] because these systems integrators are becoming the new drivers of global change in the automobile industry.[35]

Criticisms of NAFTA's Impact on Mexican Development

The sheer growth in the value of Mexico's exports and the upgrading of goods and services exported are impressive accomplishments by any standard. Many Latin American countries envy Mexico's situation, with its geographic proximity and open access to the biggest market in the world, the United States. Mexicans have faced NAFTA with a high degree of pragmatism. In less than a decade, NAFTA has become an integral and almost taken-for-granted part of the Mexican economy, and institutions, firms, and individuals have strategically adapted to the new conditions.

But NAFTA and Mexico's export-oriented model are not without their critics. Some oppose free trade in principle; others specifically oppose free trade with the United States based on the argument that NAFTA represents a loss of autonomy and cultural independence. In terms of Mexican development issues, NAFTA has increasingly become the favorite scapegoat. For many, free trade is the all-encompassing explanation for most of the problems and difficulties faced by Mexico today, and everything wrong with the country is somehow related to NAFTA. This attitude is understandable when the strong and ambiguous love-hate relationship between the United States and Mexico is taken into account. For those Mexicans who believe in conspiracies, or who simply are wary of the United States' overwhelming power, NAFTA is seen as the first step in the economic, cultural, and political assimilation of Mexico to the United States.[36] Those critics represent only one set of the voices against NAFTA or at least against particular effects of free trade.

Many scholars ask not for the eradication of free trade but for the revision and modification of free trade agreements in light of recent experiences.[37] Others ask for a complementary public policy to correct the intrinsic vulnerabilities of an export economy. The following section organizes these more specific criticisms of the export-oriented strategy into five distinct but somewhat related topics: sectoral grievances, the dependency dilemma, the maquiladora debate, polarization and inequality, and jobs and labor market dynamics.

Sectoral Grievances

Specific sectoral grievances have become quite important in the trade liberalization debate. Critics in this camp point out that, although NAFTA has indeed increased overall exports and fueled economic growth, NAFTA also has contributed to the utter crumbling of certain sectors and industries in Mexico. Some sectors have been hurt directly by the implementation of free trade; others have suffered from the lack of institutional arrangements that would ensure the proper application of the explicit and implicit terms of the free trade agreement. Though many sectoral issues are tied to the labor and environmental "side agreements" that actually have been central to NAFTA since its inception, only agriculture and transportation are discussed in this chapter.[38]

Agriculture. Most of the losers in the free trade game have been in the primary sector (agriculture, fishing, forestry, and livestock).[39] Although in 1999 the primary sector produced a little more than 4 percent of the GDP, it provides the means of subsistence for 25 percent of the Mexican population.[40] Considering that one in every four Mexicans depends on the primary sector for his or her livelihood, agriculture, fishing, forestry, and livestock are not, by any means, unimportant economic activities in the Mexican context.

During the past 20 years, agriculture and related activities have experienced a dramatic decline. Since the early 1980s, the production of the following key commodities has decreased substantially: grains by 27.6 percent, red meat by 34.6 percent, milk by 15.5 percent, and wood by 37.4 percent.[41] Although some internal factors may account for falling production, free trade has played an active role in the demise of agriculture. Agricultural output in Mexico is highly concentrated: 1,490 firms produce 80 percent of the total volume, whereas the other 400,000 small firms and entrepreneurs account for the rest.[42] In the past three administrations, public funding to the primary sector decreased from 2.5 percent of total federal expenditure in 1982 to 0.8 percent in 1997.[43]

Given the depressed situation of Mexican agriculture in 1994, imagine the effect of the sudden opening of the border to agricultural imports from the United States and around the world. Farmers that manage to produce high enough volumes to obtain a profit now must deal with low international prices and transnational marketing channels that tend to shrink farming's profit margins even more. Mexican farmers who grow corn, for example, find it almost impossible to compete with American farms that are highly automated and have the world's highest level of productivity per worker. Although there is a quota on the amount of corn that can be imported totally free of duties, the Mexican government has allowed corn to be imported with just symbolic taxes of 1 to 3 percent. Given the excess of supply, the big corporate buyers in the United States and elsewhere are able to set prices that in some cases are below the production costs for Mexican farmers.[44]

Transportation. The U.S. refusal to comply with some of the terms set by NAFTA is another source of criticism. While not unique, the most infamous example is transportation. Although NAFTA allows Mexican, U.S., and Canadian drivers to cross the border freely to deliver products, the U.S. border is effectively closed to Mexicans. The U.S. Congress, citing security and safety reasons, has created legislation seeking strict requirements for Mexican drivers who want to cross the border (requirements that are not applied to Canadians), but it has not approved funding for the necessary inspections, de facto blocking the border. Although the panel for the resolution of controversies in charge of solving disputes related to NAFTA has already reached a verdict in favor of Mexico, the controversy is far from resolved. Mentioning disparities in the size of the Mexican and American transportation industries (Mexican companies have 370,000 vehicles, whereas the United States has almost eight million), Manuel

Gómez García, leader of the carrier's union, has asked Mexican President Vicente Fox not to pursue the opening of the border, but rather to close the Mexican market to Canadian and U.S. drivers. According to García, Mexicans do not need to enter the United States but they do have a vested interest in protecting the domestic market.[45] Transportation is only one example of trade disputes that have not been resolved by the mechanisms embedded in NAFTA.

The Dependency Dilemma

Dependency theory has a long history in Mexico, and Latin America more generally.[46] The dependency argument highlights Mexico's inability to become the driving force of its own economic development and well-being. Excessive dependence on foreign investments, markets, inputs, technology, and products weakens a country's bargaining position in the international arena and restricts the range of options for internal policies in order to accommodate the needs and requests of external actors. Furthermore, heavy reliance on foreign investment also means that big transnational players are the main actors capable of seizing the opportunities created by the Mexican economy, particularly those related to the privatization of big state-owned enterprises.[47] The government and leading domestic economic actors are perceived as serving the interests of transnational capital, thereby hindering local justice and preserving asymmetries in power.[48]

Technological dependence is a special case in this argument. Export-oriented strategies are criticized for their inability to solve disparities in the use and creation of technologies. In the global economy, although technology transfer occurs, developing countries such as Mexico become simply users and copiers of technology, whereas stronger economies are traditionally the only ones capable of the research and development that drives the world's technological revolutions.[49]

A significant amount of empirical evidence seems to support the dependency perspective. Opening the doors to foreign investment can create instability, since speculative capital may leave a country as fast as it entered, as the 1994–1995 peso crisis proved.[50] But even the more stable and apparently advantageous form of foreign capital, FDI, has negative consequences. FDI is the main source of investment capital in Mexico, but the distribution of this investment is related more to foreign profitability than to internal needs.[51] In the search for macroeconomic health and balanced budgets, the role for government investment in the Mexican economy has been greatly reduced, and business loans for Mexicans are still difficult to obtain and extremely expensive when compared with international standards.[52] In short, FDI provides access to substantial amounts of capital but does a pretty poor job of distributing the capital in a sustainable and development-friendly way.[53]

Table 6.4 shows the distribution of FDI from 1994 to 2003. The distribution of FDI and the dollar amounts depend a lot on the sociopolitical and business environment. For example, following a change in Mexican legislation in 1998 that basically allowed foreigners to take over domestic banking institutions, FDI to the banking sector was 28, 54, and 32 percent of the total FDI in the years 2000, 2001, and 2002, respectively. However, there are a few consistent trends. In every year, with the exception of 2001, the largest share of FDI was channeled toward manufacturing, the most active export sector in the Mexican economy. By the same token, foreign investment in agriculture has been practically nonexistent (between 1994 and 2003, the percentage of FDI in agriculture never reached 1 percent). Although FDI has been one of the main forces behind Mexico's export boom, FDI has not advanced the domestic economy and has clearly disadvantaged rural communities, in turn increasing migration and related social problems.

Dependence on the United States is a by-product of the export-oriented economy in Mexico. Despite Mexico's clear efforts to diversify the sources of international commerce through free trade agreements with countries worldwide, the United States remains Mexico's main trade partner and has become even more dominant in the past few years. During the 1990s, the United States increased its share of Mexico's exports from 70 percent in 1990 to more than 85 percent in 2001. Mexican exports to Canada have remained small and stable, fluctuating around 4 percent, whereas the percentage of Mexico's total exports sent to other countries has steadily decreased from 27 percent in 1990 to a mere 10 percent in 2001 (Table 6.5). Thus, Mexico's trade dependence on the United States has increased markedly during the NAFTA era.

Dependence on the U.S. market may seem like a reasonable trade-off for economic growth, but it has its drawbacks. Under free trade, sudden devaluations and financial crisis in one country affect the status of all the other parties involved. With a very stable economy, low inflation, relatively attractive interest rates, and abundant investment capital, the United States has provided a solid foundation for Mexico's transformation. A close relationship with the United States—the most important capitalist economy in the world—however, has unique vulnerabilities. One vulnerability is the presence of economic cycles. Although they exist in all countries, U.S. business cycles tend to be very strong and have worldwide repercussions. Mexico is particularly sensitive to any change in the U.S.

Table 6.5   Mexico's Exports by Destination, Total (all commodities), 1990–2001

	Export Value (millions $)			% of Total Exports		
Year	United States	Canada	Rest of the World	United States	Canada	Rest of the World
1990	20,423	799	7,958	70.0	2.7	27.3
1991	20,150	1,354	7,854	68.6	4.6	26.8
1992	38,937	1,903	8,425	79.0	3.9	17.1
1993	44,440	2,479	7,427	81.8	4.6	13.7
1994	54,364	3,102	8,162	82.8	4.7	12.4
1995	69,043	3,728	11,872	81.6	4.4	14.0
1996	83,214	4,346	14,931	81.2	4.2	14.6
1997	95,888	4,842	16,177	82.0	4.1	13.8
1998	104,605	4,883	14,914	84.1	3.9	12.0
1999	122,639	6,092	14,931	85.4	4.2	10.4
2000	150,140	7,866	17,623	85.5	4.5	10.0
2001	144,167	7,416	16,667	85.7	4.4	9.9

Source: World Trade Analyzer, CD-ROM describing trade flows from 1985 to 2000, based on United Nations trade data and compiled by the International Trade Division of Statistics Canada. Query for Mexico's total exports by destination.

economy. As the popular Mexican adage says, "When the United States gets a cold, Mexico gets pneumonia."

A few years before the signing and implementation of NAFTA, the United States had entered an unprecedented phase of economic expansion due to the resources liberated by the collapse of communism, the rise of the digital economy, and increases in productivity. At the start of the twenty-first century, it seems as if this phase has come to an end. The collapse of the dot-coms, the excessive accumulation of inventories, and the September 11, 2001, terrorist attacks contributed to the downturn in the U.S. economy.[54] Unfortunately for Mexico, the crisis has hit hardest those industries on which the country has relied for its export boom, namely, the computer, electronics, and auto industries.

This crisis has blocked a Mexican economic expansion that in the early 2000s seemed unstoppable. The psychological effects of such a calamity are as important as the real and potential jobs that are lost. Since 1982 every Mexican crisis has been related to government deficits, bad public administration, or corruption. However, none of these conditions seems to have caused the slump that Mexico encountered in 2001 and 2002. From a net growth of 7 percent in 2000, Mexico plummeted to less than 0.5 percent growth in GDP in 2001,[55] and only 0.65 in 2002. For a developing country such as Mexico, a year of close-to-zero growth is a national catastrophe. Mexicans are discovering for the first time in almost two decades of reforms that macroeconomic health does not ensure economic progress. At present, Mexico's growth seems to be completely dependent on the reactivation of the American economy, and the dependency dilemma continues.

The Maquiladora Debate

One of the main criticisms of Mexico's export-oriented development model relates to the so-called maquilization of Mexico, a thesis that states the entire Mexican economy is becoming a giant export-processing zone to make low-value-added products for the U.S. market. The prominent role of maquiladora firms in Mexico's export-led growth model has been associated with an increasingly unequal income distribution and falling real wages for the majority of the country's workers.[56] NAFTA's rules and provisions have rendered the maquiladora program, officially terminated on January 1, 2001,[57] obsolete but have not eliminated the criticisms attached to such exports: low-value-added activities, emphasis on assembly, concentration on simple or standardized products, and lack of connection with the domestic economy.

Broad structural changes during the past 10 to 15 years, many as a result of NAFTA, however, have challenged the popular stereotypes concerning the maquiladora sector. In the 1980s, a new wave of maquiladora plants began to push beyond the enclave model of maquiladoras to a more advanced type of production, making components for complex products such as automobiles and computers. Although the amount of domestic materials and inputs used in the maquiladora industry as a whole remains low, some signs indicate that certain maquiladoras are becoming more integrated with the domestic economy, particularly in the cases of apparel, automobile, and electronics production.[58]

Most criticisms of the maquiladora model are becoming outdated. A study of Mexico's export manufacturing industry in the late 1990s challenges five outmoded generalizations:[59]

1. Maquiladoras are said to be found almost exclusively along Mexico's northern border. This is no longer true. Since the mid-1980s, the maquiladoras in the interior have been growing rapidly. In 2002 they accounted for one-fifth of national maquiladora employment.
2. The maquiladora labor force is thought to be dominated by young women. However, the proportion of female workers in maquila-

doras has plunged, and the gender structure of maquiladora employment is approaching parity.

3. Labor compensation in maquiladoras is purported to be extremely low and exploitative. However, maquiladora wages, although low by U.S. standards, compare quite favorably to other industrial wages in Mexico. Furthermore, there appears to be little difference between working conditions in maquiladoras and those in domestic manufacturing plants.

4. Maquiladoras are said to be primarily foreign owned. However, the origin of the capital invested in maquiladoras now is divided almost evenly between the United States and Mexico.

5. Finally, maquiladoras are characterized as export enclaves totally dependent on imported components. The situation is changing. Even though maquiladoras still import an average of 98 percent of their material inputs, maquiladoras in the interior show a greater propensity to use domestic inputs than those along the border. In addition, there has been a sharp growth of inter-maquiladora trade in certain sectors (such as electronics and automobiles).

Maquiladora-type exports are very important for the Mexican economy. In 1991, Mexico's maquiladora industry generated $15.8 billion in exports and employed 466,000 Mexicans; by 2003, the industry had grown to $77 billion in exports with over 1 million employees (Table 6.6). In 2001, approximately 15 percent of Mexico's GDP corresponded to maquiladora exports. The main destination for these products is the United States.

Until the mid-1980s, maquiladora export firms were located in the northern part of Mexico, nearest to the U.S. market. Since then, several factors have favored the establishment of maquiladoras in southern and central Mexico. First, the legal requirement of having a border location to take advantage of the maquiladora model has disappeared. Second, the possibility of using domestic components free of U.S. import taxes reduced the main advantage of a border location, since transportation between countries can be reduced. Finally, the success of the maquiladora program along the border has radically increased labor demand, causing rising wages and high turnover rates.[60]

Because of these factors, maquiladoras have consistently, although slowly, moved to nonborder municipalities across the country. In 2002, less than one-third of the maquiladora establishments and around one-fifth of maquiladora employees were located in nonborder states. Table 6.6 shows the expansion of maquiladora industries into the interior of Mexico. Between 1990 and 2003, nonborder states almost doubled their proportion

Table 6.6   The Maquiladora Industry in Mexico, 1990–2003

| | Total | Establishments[a] | | Jobs[a] | | Remunerations |
Year	Exports (millions $)	Total Number	% Located in Interior States	Total Number	% Located in Interior States	% in Interior States
1990	NA	1,695	14.1	451,375	9.9	6.9
1991	15,833	1,921	15.4	465,944	11.6	9.2
1992	18,680	2,069	15.7	510,162	12.7	10.1
1993	21,853	2,112	16.6	537,929	14.2	11.5
1994	26,269	2,056	17.5	582,111	13.9	11.0
1995	31,103	2,093	20.9	645,376	15.9	11.7
1996	36,920	2,398	22.3	747,137	18.6	13.3
1997	45,166	2,699	22.7	903,330	19.5	13.8
1998	53,083	2,952	24.2	1,005,778	20.7	15.2
1999	63,853	3,294	26.4	1,134,616	22.0	16.4
2000	79,468	3,582	27.4	1,301,947	22.5	17.3
2001	76,881	3,735	27.9	1,210,825	23.1	18.9
2002	78,040	2,976	28.2	1,074,476	22.5	17.8
2003	77,467	2,868	27.7	1,057,765	23.3	19.3

Source: INEGI, Banco de Información Económica, Industria Maquiladora de Exportación, Indicadores Mensuales y Anuales. Percent jobs and establishments located in interior states calculated using Total Nacional y Subtotal Estados Fronterizos. Remunerations calculated using nominal value. Total exports are located in the following section: Indicadores Económicos de Coyuntura, Balanza Comercial, Resumen de Comercio Exterior, Maquiladoras y No Maquiladoras. Available online at: www.inegi.gob.mx/difusion/espanol/fbie.html.
Notes: NA = not available.
a. Data are for the month of June of every year.

of maquiladora establishments, and maquiladora jobs and worker remunerations in those states have grown even faster. In addition, there appears to be a growing realization by government and business interests alike that even in southern states such as Yucatán, new high-tech factories employing more skilled workers will give Mexico the best chance to create new jobs, replacing those in low-wage maquiladora plants in sectors such as apparel.[61]

Polarization and Inequality

As in all countries in Latin America, inequality is pervasive in Mexico. Educational inequality, income inequality, and regional inequalities were prevalent under the ISI strategy. But what happens when free trade is introduced in an already unequal society? The answer is simple: more inequality. Free trade benefits only those capable of seizing the opportunities of free trade and, in the Mexican case, few have the necessary ability.[62]

The structure of economic activities has a direct effect on the distribution of wealth within a country. Critics of an export-oriented strategy state that market mechanisms in an open economy benefit certain industries, industry segments, firms, regions, and workers while disadvantaging others. From this viewpoint, dominant economic groups shape liberalization, and domestic interests are secondary to the hegemonic needs of other countries, in particular the United States.[63] Aside from the rhetoric against international capital, polarization may also be a natural by-product of an export-oriented, highly market-driven economy,[64] because investment flows only to the most profitable activities, those for which the country can have a clear and decisive competitive advantage. In an export-oriented economy, firms within industries become highly specialized and disconnected, and the economies of scope in integrated sectors are never achieved.

The main advantage of free trade is that producers have the opportunity to increase their economies of scale because of bigger markets. Only 20 percent of Mexican firms supply 70 percent of all jobs, and just 15,000 of a total of 150,000 Mexican firms export at all.[65] Therefore, only a handful of firms can actually achieve high enough volumes to really benefit from an integrated regional market.

The distribution of FDI is also a form of polarization. One of the few ways in which companies can become more competitive, efficient, and generate higher production volumes is through capital-intensive investments. FDI is closely related to exports, so nonexporters become stagnant.[66] In such an environment, productivity gains therefore are unevenly distributed within and across industries.[67]

In summary, economic liberalization by itself is an incomplete and inadequate strategy for development. Free trade accompanied by a restrictive role for the government is an under-institutionalized approach that cannot consistently and broadly improve the quality of life, eradicate poverty, boost environmental protection, or improve labor conditions.[68] For all its influence in the Mexican economy, NAFTA cannot and should not be expected to solve all of Mexico's development problems.

Jobs and Labor Market Dynamics

Export-oriented development and industrial upgrading are ultimately supposed to lead to an improvement in the quality of life for Mexicans. Looking at the overall picture of the 1990s, there is reason for cautious optimism, although many critics would insist that the opportunities missed in this area are as important as the advances made.

Between 1990 and 2001, Mexico's population went from 83.2 million inhabitants to 99.4 million, an overall increase of 20 percent. During the same time, absolute GDP figures (corrected for inflation) show a 40 percent increase. In other words, the Mexican economy grew considerably faster than the population and generated a 20 percent increase in GDP per capita (see Table 6.1). At least in terms of wealth creation, the 1990s was not a lost decade. However, Mexico's income per capita is still quite low when compared with other economies in Latin America. According to World Bank figures for 2001, Brazil's GDP per capita (in constant 1995 U.S. dollars) was $4,633, Chile's was $5,385, and Argentina's was $7,468, compared with only $3,739 for Mexico. Comparisons with the GDP per capita of the United States ($31,592) and Canada ($23,081) are even less favorable.[69]

However, GDP per capita is not a good measure of how much ordinary people have benefited from growth. From a development point of view, the creation of wealth is more relevant when evenly distributed among the population. It is possible for a country's economy to grow considerably without having an improvement in the quality of life for the majority of the population. Therefore, new jobs and the evolution of wages are better measures of the overall benefits reaching Mexicans as a result of the export-oriented strategy.

Since the early 1990s, the loss of about 600,000 farm jobs in Mexico has been attributed to lower import barriers on agricultural products, mainly as a result of NAFTA. Mechanization by Mexican growers and constitutional changes that allow private ownership of agricultural land in Mexico have contributed to the job destruction in rural areas. The job losses in agriculture have fueled rural migration into urban areas, as well as the surge of undocumented workers into the United States. Currently, it is estimated that 40 percent of the labor force in Mexico, approximately 12 million workers, does not have stable employment.[70] Increasing migration flows from rural areas make it evident that there is a clear link between free trade and the heightened volatility in Mexico's labor markets.

On the other hand, the export economy must also be credited with playing a major role in employment creation during the 1990s. Though jobs in agriculture have declined, manufacturing has been, by far, the most active sector in adding jobs. Between 1990 and 2001, 1.2 million permanent jobs were created in manufacturing, an increase of 42 percent. During the same period, employment in commerce grew by 53 percent and in other service areas by 50 percent. However, noncommercial services continued to be the most important source of jobs in the 1990s. Although not the industry with the most employment, construction boasts the biggest growth rates during the decade, with an increase of 327 percent in the number of employees between 1990 and 2001.[71]

In addition, between 1990 and 2001 formal employment showed consistent growth, except during a period when the economy suffered a sharp contraction immediately following the 1995 peso devaluation. The maquiladora industry is responsible for creating 768,000 of the five million permanent jobs established between 1990 and 2001, a respectable 15 percent of total jobs created. Yet overall export activities (including maquiladora and nonmaquiladora activities) are responsible for creating a percentage of jobs considerably higher than 15 percent, since non-maquiladora, nonpetroleum products corresponded to 43 percent of all Mexican exports in 2001.[72]

Although numbers of jobs have risen, wage levels fluctuated during the 1990s. The minimum salary for 2002 was about $120 per month, an amount whose real value has remained unchanged since 1980. But the minimum wage is frequently insufficient to attract workers in the most dynamic areas of the country, such as Mexico's northern cities where about 300,000 jobs have been created since NAFTA. The Mexican Secretary of Economy calculates that wages in the export sector are 33 percent higher than those offered in the rest of the economy.[73] Nonetheless, as a whole, maquiladora workers today receive compensation roughly equivalent to that received in 1993—approximately one-sixth of what workers in similar jobs receive in the United States.[74] Furthermore, the productivity of Mexican workers in the export sector, which has increased substantially during the 1990s, is not reflected in real wages; they have remained stagnant.

Mexico is in a difficult position. Its efforts to attract higher-value industries and industrial segments have elevated wages, at least compared with other developing countries. As Mexico fights to become a more sophisticated economy, it loses competitiveness to low-wage economies, most notably the People's Republic of China.[75] The situation reflects the harsh economics of globalization: as cheap as Mexico's labor is, it is not as cheap as that found in Asia, Eastern Europe, or even Central America. Countries in these regions now attract the kinds of jobs that initially flocked to Mexico. The only way to stay ahead (or more realistically, to avoid losing ground) in the global race is to move toward higher-value industries, economic activities, and export roles that allow a country to take advantage of both its comparative and competitive advantages and to diversify production for both the domestic and the export markets to avoid the boom and bust patterns typical of global competition.

Conclusion

Mexico's industrial development since the late 1970s has been marked by a shift from ISI to a more export-oriented strategy of economic growth. Examining Mexico's performance in the 1980s and 1990s shows that the country has clearly progressed from primary products to manufactured exports, as well as to a more diversified set of export items. Three broad factors have affected Mexican development: globalization, liberalization, and regionalization. Globalization dates from the 1970s, and refers, among other things, to the increased significance of decentralized international trade and production networks.[76] Liberalization refers to Mexico's mid-1980s creation of an open economy with fewer trade and investment restrictions, a policy that favored the entry of record amounts of FDI. Regionalization refers to the process in the 1990s by which Mexico became officially linked to the U.S. economy through NAFTA. All of these factors, especially the latter, have greatly accelerated the pace of Mexico's industrial development.

Mexico has had considerable success with its export-oriented development strategy. Mexican exports have grown and diversified dramatically. Some Mexican industries and firms have become highly competitive as they improved their standing in the global division of labor. Such improvements have been reflected in a GDP growth rate that outstrips population growth and generates considerable wealth and employment. Mexico now has more jobs that offer better pay than at the beginning of the 1990s. Thus, Mexico has definitely improved its position in terms of economic development.

Are these improvements sufficient to call Mexico's export-oriented development strategy an unmitigated success? Probably not. Trade liberalization is a necessary and very powerful development tool, but it is not sufficient as a means to achieve continuous and sustainable economic growth in the era of globalization. FDI is a very powerful motor that drives Mexico's economic growth, and international competition has triggered productivity gains and technology transfer. In addition, the U.S. market has provided a myriad of opportunities that the battered Mexican economy at the beginning of the 1990s could never have offered. Goals such as economic stability, the eradication of poverty, and the reduction of inequality seem to require something else, however. An export-oriented strategy may have helped improve Mexico's macroeconomic health, but it has not shielded the country from cyclical crisis. Without the protection of a strong domestic market, the effects of international crises are magnified. Mexico is more vulnerable than ever to U.S. policies and circumstances.

Even in the best of conditions with flourishing international markets, free trade is not a mechanism that naturally corrects disparities among industries, firms, and individuals. Quite the contrary: competition favors those who are already in a position of strength. Many Mexican companies have been unable to change fast enough to face heightened competition— the agricultural sector is an example. Change requires appropriate conditions, but Mexico's development model lacks the institutional and policy elements to ensure that a majority of firms and individuals evolve into entities that can take advantage of free trade and face the competition of international firms. Learning can only take place in an institutionally favorable environment, and many Mexicans do not have access to appropriate knowledge. Even with knowledge, the capital required to change production systems into more competitive ones is not available. Without more aggressive government measures, Mexican entrepreneurs face almost impossible odds.

Unless the institutional and policy elements of Mexico's development model are corrected, the average worker will not be able to benefit from Mexico's export strategy. Jobs seem to grow at a much slower pace than general exports, and many disappear overnight. Between 1991 and 2001, exports increased more than 300 percent, while formal employment grew by only a little less than 50 percent in the same period. It might be argued that the amount of time since the implementation of the new Mexican strategy is too short for passing judgment and that many of these problems will be solved eventually. Although possible, it is not likely. The export-oriented model offers great opportunities that have to be accompanied by the proper policies aimed at integrating the gains from export growth with the needs of the national population. This is a lesson that not only Mexico, but also many other countries in the world, still has to learn.

Notes

1. Víctor L. Urquidi, "The Prospects for Economic Transformation in Latin America: Opportunities and Resistances," *LASA Forum* 22, no. 3 (1991): 1–9.

2. For a detailed comparison of the ISI and export-oriented development strategies in Latin America and East Asia, see Gary Gereffi and Donald L. Wyman, eds., *Manufacturing Miracles: Paths of Industrialization in Latin America and East Asia* (Princeton, NJ: Princeton University Press, 1990). The World Bank offers an overview of the East Asian development experience that attributes their sustained international competitiveness largely to the application of fundamentally sound, market-friendly policies, including stable macroeconomic management, high investments in human capital (especially education), and openness to foreign trade and technology; see World Bank, *The East Asian Miracle* (New York: Oxford University Press, 1993).

3. René Villarreal and Rocío Villarreal, *México Competitivo 2020: Un Modelo de Competitividad Sistémica para el Desarrollo* (Mexico City: Océano, 2002), p. 18.

4. East Asia's export success was gained in large part without special access to the U.S. market. Indeed, U.S. and European quotas and other trade barriers

have actually made it more difficult for East Asian exporters to sustain their process of trade-led industrialization.

5. All dollar figures are in U.S. dollars unless otherwise noted.

6. Predicted levels of energy demand for Canada, Mexico, and the United States in the next decade are higher than the projected production capacity of the three countries. If no strong corrective measures are taken, in the particular case of Mexico radically increasing the amount of investment in energy production facilities, sustained economic growth will be jeopardized. The blackouts in California during 2001 are but the first manifestation of this potential crisis.

7. Víctor Rodríguez Padilla, "La política de precios desangra a la planta productiva," *Petróleo y Electricidad* (February 6, 2001).

8. Between 1970 and 1985, Mexico's inflows of foreign direct investment averaged less than $1 billion per year, with the highest levels coming during the debt crisis of 1980 to 1982. After Mexico's entry into the GATT in 1985 until the NAFTA treaty of 1994, FDI inflows grew steadily, averaging $5.4 billion from 1990 to 1994. From 1995 to 2000, Mexico's FDI inflows averaged more than $10 billion. Economic Commission for Latin America and the Caribbean (ECLAC), *Foreign Investment in Latin America and the Caribbean, 2000 Report,* LC/G.2125-P (New York: United Nations, 2001), p. 39.

9. Francisco Zapata, "NAFTA: Few Gains for Mexico's Workers," *Perspectives on Work* 6, no. 1 (2002): 22–24.

10. Mexico's maquilas were foreign- or domestically owned factories traditionally geared to assemble products for export from imported components. These inputs were imported to Mexico duty free, and when they were exported after assembly, only a minimal duty was assessed on the value added in Mexico, chiefly labor. Maquilas existed in a number of manufacturing sectors, although the main products assembled in maquilas are autos and auto parts, consumer electronics, and apparel. As legal entities, maquiladoras disappeared with NAFTA because for all firms the value of both inputs and labor is duty free. However, firms primarily performing assembly using imported inputs still exist. In-bond export industry employment in Mexico fell from a peak of 1,347,803 jobs in October 2000 to 1,076,224 in January 2003. Instituto Nacional de Estadística, Geografía e Informática (INEGI), Banco de Información Económica (BIE), Industria Maquiladora de Exportación, "Indicadores Mensuales por Entidad Federativa, Total Nacional," available online at www.inegi.gob.mx/difusion/espanol/fbie.html (last accessed April 2003).

11. Gary Gereffi, "International Trade and Industrial Upgrading in the Apparel Commodity Chain," *Journal of International Economics* 48, no. 1 (June 1999): 37–70.

12. One typology includes assembly, original equipment manufacturing (OEM), original brand-name manufacturing (OBM), and original design manufacturing (ODM). See Gary Gereffi, "Global Production Systems and Third World Development," in *Global Change, Regional Response: The New International Context of Development,* edited by Barbara Stallings (New York: Cambridge University Press, 1995), pp. 100–142.

13. Juan Ramiro de la Rosa Mendoza, "Relaciones entre apertura y crecimiento económico en México," *Comercio Exterior* 51, no. 5 (May 2001): 438–445.

14. Figures are from the World Trade Analyzer, CD-ROM describing trade flows from 1985 to 2001, based on United Nations trade data and compiled by the International Trade Division of Statistics Canada. (Query for Mexico's main exports to the world using the two-digit SITC code.)

15. Ibid. (Query for Mexican and Canadian exports to the United States, total value.)

16. Charles Gore, "The Rise and Fall of the Washington Consensus as a Paradigm for Developing Countries," *World Development* 28, no. 5 (May 2000): 789–804.

17. The Common Market of South America, known as Mercosur, is a customs union composed of four full members—Argentina, Brazil, Paraguay, and Uruguay—plus two associate members—Bolivia and Chile.

18. World Trade Analyzer. (Query for Mexican, Chilean, Brazilian, and Argentinean exports to the World, total value.)

19. This is a striking reversal of the picture a decade earlier. In 1990, Brazil by itself exported more than Mexico, and together with Argentina and Chile, the three economies exported nearly twice as much as Mexico.

20. In 2000, more than half of Mexico's total world exports were accounted for by four categories of advanced manufactured products: road vehicles (16.8 percent), electrical machinery and appliances (15.6 percent), telecommunications (11.5 percent), and office machines and automatic data processing equipment (7 percent). In 1990, these same items represented only 16 percent of Mexico's exports.

21. ECLAC, *Foreign Direct Investment in Latin America and the Caribbean, 2001 Report,* p. 28.

22. ECLAC, *Foreign Investment in Latin America, 2000 Report,* pp. 40 and 44.

23. Albert O. Hirschman, "A Generalized Linkage Approach to Development, with Special Reference to Staples," *Economic Development and Cultural Change* 25, Supplement (1977): 67–98.

24. See Gary Gereffi, David Spener, and Jennifer Bair, eds., *Free Trade and Uneven Development: The North American Apparel Industry After NAFTA* (Philadelphia: Temple University Press, 2002); Jennifer Bair and Gary Gereffi, "Local Clusters in Global Chains: The Causes and Consequences of Export Dynamism in Torreon's Blue Jeans Industry," *World Development* 29, no. 11 (November 2001): 1885–1903; and Gary Gereffi, "The Transformation of the North American Apparel Industry: Is NAFTA a Curse or a Blessing?" *Integration and Trade* 4, no. 11 (May–August 2000): 47–95.

25. Gary Gereffi, Martha Martínez, and Jennifer Bair, "Torreon: The New Blue Jeans Capital of the World," in *Free Trade and Uneven Development* (Philadelphia: Temple University Press), pp. 203–223.

26. The auto decrees were issued in 1962, 1972, 1977, 1983, and 1989. See Dale B. Truett and Lila J. Truett, "Government Policy and the Export Performance of the Mexican Automobile Industry," *Growth and Change* 25 (Summer 1994): 301–324.

27. Ibid.

28. Douglas C. Bennett and Kenneth E. Sharpe, *Transnational Corporations Versus the State: The Political Economy of the Mexican Auto Industry* (Princeton, NJ: Princeton University Press, 1985).

29. United States International Trade Commission (USITC), *Production Sharing: Use of U.S. Components and Materials in Foreign Assembly Operations, 1992–1995* (Washington, DC: USITC, 1997), p. 3-8.

30. "Mexico's Makeover," *Business Week,* December 21, 1998 (International Edition), pp. 50–51.

31. Standard International Trade Classification (SITC) is a statistical classification of the commodities entering external trade designed to provide the commodity aggregates needed for purposes of economic analysis and to facilitate the international comparison of trade-by-commodity data. World Trade Analyzer. (Query for Canadian and Mexican Motor Vehicles Exports to the United States, SITC 78 and 781–784.)

32. See Gary Gereffi, "Mexico's Industrial Development: Climbing Ahead or Falling Behind in the World Economy?" in *Confronting Development: Assessing Mexico's Economic and Social Policy Challenges*, edited by Kevin J. Middlebrook and Eduardo Zapata (Stanford: Stanford University Press and Center for U.S.–Mexican Studies, University of California–San Diego, 2003), pp. 216–217 (195–240).

33. See Gary Gereffi, "Shifting Governance Structures in Global Commodity Chains, with Special Reference to the Internet," *American Behavioral Scientis* 44, no. 10 (June 2001): 1623–1625 (1616–1637).

34. Jorge Carrillo and Alfredo Hualde, "Third Generation Maquiladoras? The Delphi-General Motors Case," *Journal of Borderlands Studies* 13, no. 1 (Spring 1998): 79–97.

35. While there are no Mexican systems integrators as yet, a growing number of second-tier suppliers are Mexican.

36. For examples of this position, see Luis González Souza, "¿Alianzas con EU?" *La Jornada,* September 25, 1999, opinion, online at www.jornada.unam.mx/1999/sep99/990925/gonzalez.html (last accessed April 2003); Luis González Souza, "Entre el TLC y el EZLN," *La Jornada,* January 9, 1999, opinion, online at www.jornada.unam.mx/1999/ene99/990109/souza.html (last accessed April 2003); Horacio Labastida, "Globalización y soberanía nacional," *La Jornada,* March 3, 2002, opinion, online at www.jornada.unam.mx/2000/mar00/000303/labastida.html (last accessed April 2003); Jorge Camil, "Sexenios monotemáticos," *La Jornada,* January 7, 2000, opinion, online at www.jornada.unam.mx/2000/ene00/000107/camil.html (last accessed April 2003); and Claudia Sheinbaum Pardo, "¿Petróleo para México o para EU?" *La Jornada,* February 22, 2000, opinion, online at www.jornada.unam.mx/2000/feb00/000222/pardo.html (last accessed April 2003).

37. For example, provisions in the labor side agreement to NAFTA have been brought into the main statutes of U.S. trade agreements with Jordan and Cambodia, which entered into effect in December 2001. The pending U.S.–Central American Free Trade Agreement (CAFTA) is also being targeted to go beyond NAFTA in adopting more specific objectives and transparent enforcement mechanisms with regard to labor issues. See Sandra Polaski, "Central America and the U.S. Face Challenge—and Chance for Historic Breakthrough—on Workers' Rights," Carnegie Endowment for International Peace, *Issue Brief*, February 2003, pp. 1–8; and Sandra Polaski, "Trade and Labor Standards: A Strategy for Developing Countries," Carnegie Endowment for International Peace, Washington, DC, 2003, pp. 1–23. (These reports can be downloaded from www.ceip.org/pubs.)

38. The main NAFTA agreement deals with the trade of goods and services, capital flows, intellectual property, and government contracts. NAFTA also describes the mechanisms to resolve trade controversies. In response to criticisms from environmental groups and labor unions, two parallel agreements were signed defining cooperation strategies in these two areas. For more on NAFTA, see Frederick W. Mayer, *Interpreting NAFTA: The Science and Art of Political Analysis* (New York: Columbia University Press, 1998).

39. Luis Rubio, "El TLC en el desarrollo de México," in *Tres Ensayos: Fobaproa, privatización y TLC* (Mexico City: Cal y Arena, 1999), pp. 117–163.

40. INEGI/BIE, Indicadores Económicos de Coyuntura, "Producto Interno Bruto Trimestal a Precios Corrientes por Gran División de Actividad Económica," available online at www.inegi.gob.mx/difusion/espanol/fbie.html (last accessed April 2003); and Jesús Ramírez Cuevas, "El Campo: En el Ojo del Huracán," *La Jornada,* March 13, 2003, available online at www.jornada.unam.mx/2003/ene03/030112/mas-campo.html (last accessed April 2003).

41. Fernando Paz Sánchez, "Grave crisis en el sector agropecuario y comercial," *MacroEconomía* (Mexico City), no. 94 (May 15, 2001).

42. Ibid.

43. Alberto Ruiz de la Peña, "La quiebra del sector agropecuario, tempestad sobre el campo," *MacroEconomía* (Mexico City), no. 97 (August 15, 2001).

44. Paz Sánchez, "Grave crisis."

45. Cristina Meave Avila, "La Canacar le exige a Fox cerrar la frontera a transportistas de E.U." *Siempre* (Mexico City), no. 2505.

46. For a review of dependency theory as it applies to Latin America and Mexico, see James L. Dietz, *Latin America's Economic Development: Confronting Crisis*, 2nd ed. (Boulder, CO: Lynne Rienner Publishers, 1995); and Gary Gereffi, "Dependency Theory and Third World Development," in *The Pharmaceutical Industry and Dependency in the Third World,* edited by Gary Gereffi (Princeton, NJ: Princeton University Press, 1983), pp. 3–49.

47. Arturo Ortiz, Héctor Núñez, and Arturo Bonilla, *Cambios Urgentes de la Política Económica a Partir del Año 2000* (Mexico City: Editorial Paz, 2000).

48. Raúl García Barrios, "Free Trade and Local Institutions: The Case of Mexican Peasants," in *Economic Integration in NAFTA and the EU,* edited by Kirsten Appendini and Sven Bislev (New York: Palgrave MacMillan, 1999), pp. 34–50.

49. Enrique Dussel Peters, *Polarizing Mexico: The Impact of Liberalization Strategy* (Boulder, CO: Lynne Rienner Publishers, 2000).

50. For a more complete review of this effect, see Chapter 4, by Russell Crandall, in this volume.

51. Claudia Villegas Cárdenas, "La economía, rehén de la inversión externa," *Proceso,* no. 1327, April 6, 2002.

52. "Mexico Finance: Recovery in Corporate Lending Still Distant," *Country Briefing,* Country ViewsWire Mexico, Economist Intelligence Unit, July 19, 2002.

53. Oscar Contreras, *Empresas Globales, Actores Locales: Producción Flexible y Aprendizaje Industrial en las Maquiladoras* (Mexico City: El Colegio de México-Centro de Estudios Sociológicos, 2000).

54. Robert D. Hof, Peter Elstrom, Steve Hamm, Marcia Stepanek, William Echikson, and Peter Burrows, "The Tech Slump," *Business Week*, no. 3712, December 18, 2000, pp. 54–59; John Shinal, "Dead Dot-Coms Can Still Cause Havoc," *Business Week,* no. 3723, March 12, 2001, p. 50; and Michael Mandel, "Big Spending on IT Has Made Labor More Vulnerable Than Ever," *Business Week,* no. 3718, February 5, 2001, pp. 42–43.

55. "México prevé crecimiento PIB 1.74 por ciento en 2002," *América Economía*, October 17, 2001; and "Merrill Lynch espera mayor crecimiento PIB México 2002: de 1.2 a 1.4 por ciento," *México Analytica*, March 11, 2002.

56. Enrique de la Garza, "The Restructuring of State-Labor Relations in Mexico," in *The Politics of Economic Restructuring: State-Society Relations and Regime Change in Mexico,* edited by Maria Lorena Cook, Kevin J. Middlebrook, and Juan Molinar Horcasitas (La Jolla: University of California–San Diego, 1994), pp. 195–219; William I. Robinson, "Latin American and Global Capitalism," *Race & Class* 40, no. 2/3 (1998–1999): 111–131; Enrique Dussel Peters, *Polarizing Mexico*; and Abelardo Mariña Flores, "Factores Determinantes del Empleo en México," *Comercio Exterior* 51, no. 5 (2001): 410–424.

57. Firms no longer require maquiladora permits in order to import inputs from the United States or export finished products. Although maquiladoras as legal entities do not exist anymore, we will continue to use the term to describe manufacturing exporting firms that provide "incomplete" or fragmented production services for foreign companies. USITC, *Production Sharing*, p. 4-3 (Note: in this publication page numbers include the chapter number; thus, 4-3 refers to Chapter 4, page 3).

58. Gary Gereffi, "Mexico's 'Old' and 'New' Maquiladora Industries: Contrasting Approaches to North American Integration," in *Neoliberalism Revisited: Economic Restructuring and Mexico's Political Future,* edited by Gerardo Otero (Boulder, CO: Westview Press, 1996), pp. 85–105; Jorge Carrillo and Alfredo Hualde, "Third Generation Maquiladoras?"; Luis A. Berlanga-Albrecht, "Maquiladoras japonesas en Tijuana: Estructura productiva y cadenas mundiales de insumos," *Comercio Exterior* 49, no. 9 (1999): 821–829; and Bair and Gereffi, "Local Clusters in Global Chains."

59. Ian MacLachlan and Adrián Guillermo Aguilar, "Maquiladora Myths: Locational and Structural Change in Mexico's Export Manufacturing Industry," *Professional Geographer* 50, no. 3 (1998): 315–331.

60. For a review of some of the mechanisms related to labor demand, see Gereffi, Martínez, and Bair, "Torreon."

61. Two new factories that make airplane parts for General Electric have recently opened up in Yucatán. This form of technological upgrading is an essential part of the development process, according to economist Sidney Weintraub: "Mexico's going to have to graduate the way all other countries do. It's inevitable that countries that earn their money through relatively cheap labor, as their situation improves and the labor costs go up, they just have to move up the technology scale." Quoted in Ginger Thompson, "Mexico Is Attracting a Better Class of Factory in the South," *New York Times,* June 29, 2002, p. A3.

62. For an analysis of how regional disparities within the U.S. South and the Mexican South reinforce inequalities, see Richard Tardanico and Mark B. Rosenberg, eds., *Poverty or Development: Global Restructuring and Regional Transformations in the U.S. South and the Mexican South* (New York: Routledge, 2000).

63. Sven Bislev, "Introduction," in *Economic Integration in NAFTA and the EU,* edited by Kirsten Appendini and Sven Bislev (New York: Palgrave MacMillan, 1999), pp. 1–16.

64. Dussel Peters, *Polarizing Mexico.*

65. Rubio, "El TLC en el desarrollo de México."

66. Bodil Damgaard, "Labour and Economic Integration: The Case of the Electronic Sector in Mexico," in *Economic Integration in NAFTA and the EU,* edited by Appendini and Bislev, pp. 89–105.

67. María Flor Chávez, María Beatriz García, Heliana Monserrat, Josefina Robles, Eunice Taboada, and Leticia Velásquez, *Estudios Sectoriales de las Manufacturas Mexicanas* (Mexico City: Universidad Autónoma Metropolitana, 2000).

68. Blanca Torres, "Environmental Cooperation Before and After NAFTA," in *Economic Integration in NAFTA and the EU,* edited by Appendini and Bislev, pp. 106–123; and Ricardo Grinspun and Roberto Kreklewich, "Institutions, Power Relations and Unequal Integration in the Americas: NAFTA as Deficient Institutionality," in *Economic Integration in NAFTA and the EU,* edited by Appendini and Bislev, pp. 17–33.

69. World Bank, World Development Indicators, available online at http://devdata.worldbank.org/dataonline/. Data in 1995 dollars.

70. Francisco Zapata, "NAFTA: Few Gains for Mexico's Workers," *Perspectives on Work* 6, no. 1 (2002): 22 (22–24).

71. INEGI/BIE, Empleo y Desempleo, "Asegurados Permanentes en el IMSS por Sectores de Actividad Económica," available online at www.inegi.gob.mx/difusion/espanol/fietab.html (last accessed April 2003).

72. INEGI/BIE, Industria Maquiladora de Exportación, "Personal Ocupado Renumerado," "Valor Agregado de Exportación," and Sector Externo, "Exportaciones Petroleras y No Petroleras," available online at www.inegi.gob.mx/difusion/espanol/fbie.html (last accessed April 2003).

73. "Las negociaciones comerciales internacionales en la nueva estrategia de desarrollo de Mexico." Available online www.economia-snci.gob.mx/sic_php/1s23al.php?s=54&p=1&1=1 (last accessed July 2004).

74. Zapata, "NAFTA," p. 23.

75. Julián Reséndiz, "Sin apoyo de la Federación saldrían 50 por ciento de maquiladoras," *El Diario,* July 17, 2002.

76. There is a large literature on global commodity chains that looks at the impact of diverse types of international production and trade networks on development outcomes. See Gary Gereffi, "The Global Economy: Organization, Governance, and Development," in *Handbook of Economic Sociology,* 2nd ed., edited by Neil Smelser and Richard Swedberg (Princeton, NJ: Princeton University Press, 2004).

PART 3

Foreign Policy Dynamics

7

Mexico and the
Western Hemisphere

Riordan Roett

In Mexico today, there is a sense of nostalgia about the well-intentioned foreign policy ambitions of the Mexican government that followed the July 2000 election of Vicente Fox as president. At the start of the Fox administration (2000–2006), three major foreign policy issues topped the agenda: (1) there would be a burgeoning partnership between the United States and Mexico;[1] (2) the possibility of expanding the North American Free Trade Agreement (NAFTA) to the Southern Cone countries of South America;[2] and (3) Mexico, under Fox, would have a newly active international role.[3] The period of the transition from election to inauguration appeared to confirm those ambitions: U.S. President George W. Bush and President Fox held an amicable meeting at the Mexican leader's ranch in February 2001—the first trip abroad of the newly inaugurated American president. Almost immediately, negotiations opened on a wide range of issues, including immigration, the border, and drugs, and it was announced that the first White House state dinner in early September 2001 would honor President Fox. At the glittering dinner, President Bush stated that the United States had no more important relationship in the world than its relationship with Mexico.[4]

Dramatically and tragically, the agenda shifted on September 11, 2001, with the terrorist attacks on the World Trade Center and the Pentagon. The concerns of the White House turned abruptly toward fighting terrorism, while bilateral and regional issues previously on the agenda were quickly relegated to a back burner. In addition, 2001–2002 saw a number of other changes that made the promises and hopes of Mexico prior to

September 11 less relevant. A new wave of economic and financial uncertainties appeared in Latin America, and opposition to open markets and to further liberal economic reforms surged across the hemisphere. Difficulties continued in the negotiations for a Free Trade Area of the Americas (FTAA), even though the White House finally obtained congressional approval for presidential trade promotion authority (TPA)—an updated version of fast-track—in August 2002. As Fox entered the second half of his *sexenio*, it was far from clear that he would achieve his goals of casting himself as a political equal of the U.S. president and as the leader of Latin America.[5]

Furthermore, as the July 2003 midterm elections demonstrated, the Mexican president's leadership skills at home came increasingly under question, making it difficult to imagine that he would be able to play a broader hemispheric or global role when he faced mounting challenges on the domestic front. The talk of a permanent seat for Mexico on the United Nations Security Council receded, as did the concept of a new and innovative Mexican regional diplomacy. As it became clear that President Fox was not master of his own political house—given the stalemate between the Mexican legislature and the presidential palace on almost all important policy issues—the early initiatives by Mexico toward the conflict in Colombia, a hope of reviving the G-3 (the group of three comprising Colombia, Venezuela, and Mexico), and a role in the internal politics of Venezuela faded.

It is possible—but not probable—that the high hopes most observers held for Fox upon his election to the presidency will ultimately be met in the latter half of his administration. The U.S. administration's continued focus on homeland security and preoccupation with the war on terrorism has occupied center stage in U.S. foreign policy, and although there remain good relations between Mexico and the United States, it is difficult to imagine the goals of the first nine months of 2001 returning full force to the table in the foreseeable future. This chapter reviews the basic foreign policy initiatives of the Fox administration in the Western Hemisphere, indicates where they stand as Fox begins the final years of his *sexenio*, and examines the likelihood that they will prosper.

The Bilateral Agenda with the United States

Although Mexico has adopted a highly visible diplomatic role in the Western Hemisphere, as explained later in this chapter, it is in its bilateral relations with the United States that the real issues of policy will be played out. On the economic and financial side, the integration process begun with NAFTA in 1994 is inexorably broadening and deepening the economic integration process, with very positive results for all three NAFTA members—Mexico, the United States, and Canada. But it is in the noneconomic, nonfinancial realm that the Fox administration had, in 2001, placed high hopes on the evolving special relationship with the United States.

Vicente Fox and George W. Bush met for the fifth time in Washington, D.C., for President Fox's first state visit to the United States. From the perspective of a longtime U.S.–Mexico observer, the state visit offered President Bush "a unique opportunity not only to redefine relations with Mexico but also to lay the foundation for a North American community."[6] It was suggested that the two leaders should invite Canadian Prime Minister Jean Chrétien to a North American summit and establish a North American commission to develop an agenda for that and future summits. To deal with immigration and customs at the border, it was suggested that the leaders propose "North American passports" for frequent travelers, and the three leaders were urged to establish a "North American Development Bank" to connect the border to central and southern Mexico.

At the center of Fox's concerns were the two-thousand-mile U.S.–Mexico border and the challenge of a new set of policies for Mexican workers in the United States. The hope in Mexico prior to Fox's visit was that the two chief executives would be able to sign new agreements in Washington, D.C., but as Fox prepared to travel north he acknowledged that it would likely take four to six years to complete comprehensive U.S.–Mexico immigration reform. The issue was an important one for both leaders. Fox needed a victory on the immigration front to quiet increasingly vocal critics at home who said he had promised much but delivered little since taking office. Bush counts on Fox to help him woo the fast-growing Hispanic vote in the United States, which is seen as critical to his reelection in 2004.

In the past, the usual bilateral agendas of the two countries differed. Mexico's first concern has been immigration; the United States has focused on drugs and trade. The dialogue began to shift in February 2001 when Bush visited Fox at Fox's ranch. During that visit, discussions began over the possibility of expanded guest worker programs, as well as a policy change that Mexico considers critical: legalizing the status of at least some of the 3 to 4.5 million undocumented Mexicans living in the United States and already paying U.S. taxes.

The facts are clear. Undocumented workers contribute significantly to the U.S. economy through work in construction, farming, gardening, housecleaning, child care, and other areas. Without Mexican workers, it is argued by supporters of reform, the U.S. economy would suffer. But there is a strong bloc of members of the U.S. Congress who remain adamantly opposed to any arrangement that seems to reward undocumented immigrants who are viewed as simply breaking the law.

Arriving to fanfare in Washington, D.C., on September 5, 2001, Fox stated: "We must, and we can, reach an agreement on migration before the end of this very year, which will allow us, before the end of our respective terms, to make sure that there are no Mexicans who have not entered this country legally, and that those Mexicans who have come into the country do so with the proper documents."[7] Responding later in the day, White House National Security Advisor Condoleezza Rice was cautious, commenting that Bush had to negotiate immigration agreements with the U.S. Congress and various political and business sectors, stating that the discussions involved "a lot of moving parts."[8]

The following day, President Fox took his campaign to the U.S. Congress. In a joint session of Congress, Fox urged U.S. lawmakers to grant legal rights to millions of undocumented Mexican immigrants, saying they generate significant economic and cultural ties to the United States. Fox also urged the legislators to show confidence in his new, democratic government by supporting legislation that would address two other important concerns for Mexico in the bilateral agenda: exempting Mexico from the U.S. drug certification program and easing the restrictions on the use of U.S. highways for Mexican commercial trucks.

The American press greeted the visit with great enthusiasm, characterizing Fox as an equal of Bush.[9] But the tide turned dramatically with the events of September 11, 2001. The effects in Mexico were immediate. The attacks curtailed U.S. consumer spending and travel, which depressed the Mexican manufacturing and tourism industries (85 percent of foreign visitors to Mexico arrive from the United States), the leading sources of jobs for many Mexicans. The U.S. economy went into a slide that continued into 2002, while tighter security at the border slowed the shipment of goods.

In response to the attacks, Mexico's foreign secretary, Jorge Castañeda, was quick to offer unqualified support for the United States. Castañeda defended the right of the United States to avenge the attacks and said that Mexico "should not hold back its support" for the United States, urging for solidarity and cooperation with the U.S. government, the definition of a common international position, and in particular to follow the stance of the United Nations Security Council.[10] Castañeda was immediately criticized by members of the Mexican Congress, fearful that such support could open the door to direct involvement of Mexico in the war against terrorism. Soon after, resolutions were drafted to remove the foreign secretary. The three political parties in the Mexican Senate issued a joint statement rejecting any effort by Mexico to offer military support to the United States. Though the criticism died down within the Mexican political and intellectual classes, it did not disappear.

It was noted in the U.S. press that the reactions to September 11 in the Mexican government and Mexican society were lukewarm. After September 11, Mexican flags were raised as usual, while capitals from Madrid to Moscow lowered theirs to half-staff. Mexico failed to observe a moment of silence in memory of the victims, an unknown number of whom were Mexicans. While tens of thousands across Europe and Asia held vigils and lit candles to show their solidarity with the United States, only a few dozen people, most of them Americans, attended a hastily organized vigil in Mexico City. While President Fox attempted to convey solidarity with the United States in press meetings and public statements, it was clear that the weight of history was more important for many Mexicans. It was noted that textbooks in the schools still emphasize that the United States went to war against Mexico, resulting in the loss of half of Mexico's territory.

Even though the Mexican executive branch attempted to show solidarity with the United States regarding border and security issues in 2002, there was little reciprocity from the Bush administration. In a speech in New York City in May 2002, Fox stated that he and Bush had set a new, positive tone in bilateral relations. But he argued that by then, 18 months after he took office, Washington should have adopted some fundamental changes in immigration policy, including an increased number of permanent visas for Mexicans and legal status for approximately four million undocumented Mexicans living in the United States. And, addressing his own political future, President Fox indicated the lack of progress was making it increasingly difficult for him to maintain political and public support for the shift in Mexican foreign policy.[11]

As if to demonstrate Fox's weakened position at home because of his inability to deliver on immigration policy, in April 2002 the Mexican Senate embarrassed him by using—for the first time ever—its constitutional power to deny presidential travel in order to prevent Fox from visiting the United States. Fox argued, as well, that the lack of response by the United States was an indication to other countries in the hemisphere that there was no U.S. policy for the region other than security.

In 2003 little was accomplished in the area of immigration reform, but in early 2004, when President Bush welcomed President Fox to his ranch in Texas, some signs of progress were evident. The White House announced that it was seriously considering a plan that would exempt many Mexicans from strict new requirements that all visitors to the United States be finger-printed and photographed. In addition, the White House issued a proposal to grant temporary visas to undocumented workers in the United States. If implemented, the initiative would help Fox at home, where he is under intense pressure to win concessions from the United States. In addition, the plan could help President Bush with Hispanic Americans, who are emerg-ing as one of the most contested groups of voters in the 2004 presidential elections, but the proposal has run into strong opposition from both Repub-licans and Democrats in Congress.

President Fox's situation at home was further complicated by the growing perception that Mexico is developing the politics of stalemate. As stated in the *New York Times*, "though Mr. Fox won incremental victories against entrenched corruption and red tape, the sweeping reforms he prom-ised in everything from energy to economic policy have not come to pass, partly because he has not built a political coalition capable of persuading the old party's [Institutional Revolutionary Party (Partido Revolucionario Institucional, PRI)] diehards to support the changes he seeks."[12] And that perception has grown in Washington, D.C., as well. Because bilateral pol-icy innovations with the United States will require action by the Mexican Congress as well as the U.S. Congress, Fox's weak leadership and the fail-ure of his policy agenda are not encouraging to the White House.

Although Fox's victory in an oil workers' strike over a new wage set-tlement in late 2002 helped restore some of his authority, it did not appear to herald rapid progress on fiscal and other reform initiatives, such as opening the electricity sector. To make matters worse, the general eco-nomic malaise in the world economy from 2001 to 2003 reduced expecta-tions for Mexico's growth. Mexico's growth in 2003 was a disappointing 1.5 percent, and growth in 2004 is projected to be 3.5 percent with a belief that U.S. economic recovery will stimulate the Mexican economy in 2005.[13] The linkage to the U.S. economy, of course, plays a large role in the ultimate economic situation for Mexico in 2004 and 2005.

Mexico and the Rest of Latin America

Although its degrees of freedom for strengthening ties with South Amer-ica are limited and its links with Cuba are undergoing reassessment, Mex-ico's inter-American role remains an active one. In an effort to expand its diplomatic role in the Caribbean region, in January 2002 Mexico con-vened a Caribbean Conference on Maritime Borders. In addition, President Fox has sought to reinvigorate the G-3, a diplomatic grouping of Mexico, Colombia, and Venezuela, with the goal of playing a constructive role in the Colombian peace process. But Mexico is having little apparent success. The U.S.-sponsored Plan Colombia, which aims to strengthen the Colombian government's hand in its struggle against guerrillas and paramilitaries, is the dominant policy initiative in the Andes at the present time.

In a broader diplomatic and political context, in October 2001 the United Nations General Assembly elected Mexico as a nonpermanent member of the United Nations Security Council. Traditionally, Mexico's authoritarian governments eschewed international publicity at the UN and similar international organizations. The Fox administration has taken an active role in promoting a higher Mexican profile in inter-American and international organizations.

All of these initiatives have been generally welcomed in the Western Hemisphere. Mexico is recognized as an important player in the region and, with its expanding economic and financial influence, a future player of growing importance. In an effort to consolidate Mexico's leadership role in the hemisphere, President Fox has pursued innovative policy initiatives to engage Mexico's Latin American partners. But, as explained in this section's overview of some of Fox's main foreign policy initiatives in the region, the issue will always return to the deepening integration of the country into North America, raising important questions about culture, history, and economic growth and development for Mexico.

Central America: The Puebla-Panama Plan

In 2004, it is difficult to remember that one of the most innovative and visionary foreign policy initiatives of the Fox government was the Puebla-Panama Plan (PPP). For decades, there had been discussions within the Mexican government about the need to better integrate poor and marginal southern Mexico into the nation-state. Fox, as a presidential candidate, raised the idea of a progressive regional integration effort that would go beyond the southern states of Mexico. As president-elect, in 2000 he toured Central America with the governors of nine Mexican states and indicated a new policy emphasis. In Mexico City on inauguration day, December 1, 2000, Fox held a working breakfast with the Central American presidents who attended the ceremony. In June 2001, a summit of regional heads of state was held in San Salvador to kick off the PPP, and President Fox hosted a second summit in Yucatán in June 2002 at which the regional leaders again reiterated their commitment to the initiative.

Regional integration has been a stated goal in Mexico for decades, if not centuries. Border disputes, financing, historical antagonisms, and a wide range of other obstacles have often prevented any concrete planning. The PPP was conceived as encompassing seven Central American countries and nine states in the south-southwest of Mexico. The portion of Mexico included in the program represents 24 percent of the nation's territory and holds 23 percent of the nation's population. It has long been the redoubt of some of the most conservative dinosaurs of the long-ruling PRI, the party that Fox, the candidate of the National Action Party (Partido Acción Nacional, PAN), defeated in national elections in 2000. The region also includes the headquarters of the Zapatista National Liberation Army (Ejército Zapatista de Liberación Nacional, EZLN) that launched military action against the Mexican government in January 1994 on behalf of the local population. The region also holds about one-half of the petroleum reserves of Mexico.

The PPP encountered immediate opposition. The Zapatista rebels argued that the regional integration plan was nothing more than a pro–free market plot that would harm indigenous cultures, resulting primarily in the selling of their land to foreign companies. Subcomandante Marcos, the EZLN spokesman, stated that "instead of using riches to support poor peasants and small business owners, Fox has a plan to use the money to support those who want to fill the land with gas stations, malls and plastic play lands," turning indigenous villages into "amusement parks."[14] Armando Bartra, the director of the Mayan Institute, which studies rural and agricultural issues, said the plan represented a new version of the old colonial ways, arguing that "there is no sign that the plan will improve the lives of those living in indigenous communities."[15]

In addition to local opposition, the regional integration objectives face important challenges in the security realm. Even before September 11, 2001, security issues in the region had escalated. It was reported in June 2001 that the Mexican government planned to considerably increase the presence of soldiers, police officers, naval patrols, and immigration checkpoints near its porous southern border.[16] The purpose of such increased security at Mexico's borders is to choke off flows of illegal immigrants, drugs, and guns entering Mexico from Central America. Most of the illicit human and drug traffic coming into Mexico is heading to the United States, and Washington has long urged Mexico to control its 750-mile border with Guatemala and Belize more tightly. Following September 11, there has been an escalation in pressure from the United States for the Mexicans to act on this front. Given the emphasis in Washington, D.C., on homeland security it is difficult to imagine the United States looking favorably on any

plan that would imply the movement of large numbers of people or potential social unrest in the region.

Mexico and South America

When one considers the close, if wary, ties between Mexico and the
United States, traditionally the issue of Mexican relations with the Southern Hemisphere was largely ignored. "Latin" America includes Mexico,
Central America, the Caribbean, and South America, but the realities of
history and geography increasingly indicate that, informally, hemispheric
dynamics are divided into "North America" and "South America." That
divide did not need to be stressed until the creation of NAFTA and of Mercosur, a free trade agreement between Southern Cone countries of South
America, two important foreign policy and economic integration developments in the early 1990s. Growing political liberalization in Mexico and
increasing economic integration within North America highlight the political and diplomatic distance between the seat of government in Mexico
City and its neighbors to the south. The PPP, of course, was a Fox initiative to reverse that trend. But it was Brazil, the leader of Mercosur, that
became increasingly wary of Mexican policy, particularly as it appeared
to be more congruent with overall U.S. foreign policy objectives in Latin
America.

It was resented, for example, when Brazilian President Fernando Henrique Cardoso organized the first summit of the heads of state of South
America in 1999, and the Mexican, Central American, and Caribbean
leaders were not invited. Succeeding summits have mentioned common
policy issues, but the meetings have not been opened to include the leaders of North and Central America. Even so, there remains concern within
the Mexican government that obstacles to cooperation need to be reduced,
and that Mexico, in spite of trade and investment flows which link it inexorably to North America, must maintain active diplomacy toward the
South.

To that end, President Fox traveled to South America in July 2002.
Just prior to the trip, it was announced that Brazil and Mexico had completed four years of negotiations on tariff reductions that will ease or eliminate import taxes on more than 800 agricultural and industrial products.
The new accord will not have the force of a full trade agreement, but it
does allow the two countries to restore full trade relations. It replaces an
accord negotiated by the two countries in 1995, an agreement that was
scrapped in 1997 because of a dispute regarding Mexico's membership in
NAFTA. At the time, Brazil was lobbying for tariff preferences from Mex-

ico that were similar to those offered by the Mexican government to
Canada and the United States. Current trade between Brazil and Mexico
amounts to just $2.6 billion; the new agreement is intended to signifi-
cantly boost bilateral trade.[17]

Fox's presidential trip began in Brasília, where the new trade agreement between Mexico and Brazil was signed. Brazil's foreign minister,
Celso Lafer, cast the agreement in the right diplomatic framework when
he commented that the Fox visit "comes at a time when the two countries
are looking to enhance their bilateral relations with an eye toward the
international situation, fundamentally toward Latin American integration."[18] However, other observers noted that Brazil and Mexico have very
different positions on free trade negotiations, and the Mexican government is seen as very supportive of the Bush White House as it presses for
an FTAA. Brazil, on the other hand, is an adamant critic of U.S. protec-
tionism and has publicly voiced apprehension about the absence of a level
playing field for the final round of FTAA negotiations, which Brazil and
the United States are chairing.

President Fox continued his 2002 southern hemisphere visit with meetings in Buenos Aires with the heads of state of other Mercosur countries.
Although he expressed solidarity with the leadership of Argentina, no concrete decisions were taken to deal with the dire economic situation in that
country. The reality of the relationship was expressed in Mexico City after
the president returned home, when it was reported that, "some Mexicans
disapproved [of Fox's efforts to increase trade with the Mercosur coun-
tries], fearing that their country would become more likely to contract the
economic illness afflicting its southern neighbors."[19] While recognizing
cultural and historical affinities, the realities of the marketplace are obvious to most Mexican businessmen and investors. One observer commented
when asked why Fox traveled south that, "the trip was meant to appease
our Latin American friends" who think, "that the natural friends of Mexico
should be its Latin American neighbors."[20]

An important part of the Mexico-Brazil agreement involves the gradual elimination of tariffs on motor vehicle imports. This issue had been a
major stumbling block in the negotiations, given that 40 percent of Brazilian exports to Mexico involve motor vehicles or auto parts. Furthermore,
the agreement cannot go into effect unless all other full members of Mercosur—Argentina, Uruguay, and Paraguay—ratify it. Officials in Mexico
City were quick to point out that the Brazilian accord was a first step
toward negotiating a similar agreement with other members of Mercosur,
but the debt standoff in Argentina, the slow recovery of the Uruguayan
economy, and the sharp economic slowdown in Brazil in 2003 realistically

limited the short-to-medium-term importance for Mexico of any deeper economic relations with the Southern Cone. It is not clear whether or not Mercosur will survive the current turmoil, but the reality is that Mexico's trade balance with South America is surprisingly small. Brazil represents less than 1 percent of Mexico's trade; the entire Mercosur trade bloc represents only 3 percent.[21]

It became increasingly clear in 2002–2003 with the election of new presidents in Brazil and Argentina that there would be a serious difference in opinion between the Southern Cone and North America. As the governments of presidents Lula and Kirchner became stridently opposed to the U.S. position on the FTAA, Mexico found itself caught in the middle. At an FTAA meeting in late 2003 in Miami, the Brazilian-Argentine position made it almost impossible to imagine a successful conclusion of the agreement by 2005, and differences over the regional agreement were reflected in the growing acrimony over the World Trade Organization (WTO) Doha Round talks which broke down in September 2003 at a meeting in Cancún, primarily over the issue of agricultural subsidies imposed by the European Union (EU) and the United States.

There is no doubt that language and culture are important. But the lure of South America in economic and financial terms is negligible in Mexico's future. Trade with North America is the reality and shall remain so in the foreseeable future. The concerns about financial "contagion" from poorly run economies in South America are real to Mexicans. And the fear of a generalized economic crisis in the South having an impact on Mexico preoccupies both political and economic leaders. Mexican presidents will always travel to the South, but it is the sojourns in the North that will drive Mexican diplomacy in the twenty-first century.

Mexican-Cuban Relations

There is no more-dramatic story than the shifting relations between Mexico and the Cuba of Fidel Castro. Since 1959, Mexico had deliberately been sympathetic to the Cuban regime. That played well at home with the vocal but relatively powerless political left. It was also a way of differentiating Mexico City from Washington, D.C., on a foreign policy issue important to the latter. Mexico was the only Latin American country that refused to break relations with the Communist nation after the 1959 revolution, and it remained one of Cuba's most important trading partners outside the Soviet bloc.

As Mexico began to liberalize politically during the presidency of Ernesto Zedillo (1994–2000), relations deteriorated. At a regional summit meeting, Zedillo, one of the architects of the democratic transition in Mexico, criticized the Cuban government for denying basic freedoms. Zedillo's foreign secretary, Rosario Green, infuriated the Castro government in 1999 by meeting a prominent Cuban dissident leader in the Mexican Embassy.

In December 2000, the new Mexican government of Vicente Fox made very clear that it remained deeply committed to supporting democracy throughout the hemisphere. Foreign Secretary Jorge Castañeda, in an appearance before the Mexican Senate Foreign Relations Committee in December 2001, made it clear that the traditional policy of overlooking failures in democratic governance was over. Castañeda underscored Mexico's commitment to strengthening democracy through its support for democratic clauses, as demonstrated by the country's active participation in negotiating the inclusion of a democratic clause in the declaration of the third Summit of the Americas, as well as the formal adoption of the Inter-American Democratic Charter in the Organization of American States (OAS) and the incorporation of a democratic clause into the Puebla-Panama Plan.[22]

After a series of diplomatic incidents that strained the relations between the Fox presidency and more traditional political groups at home, the president announced a visit to Cuba in February 2002. As he prepared to leave, traditional political leaders of the former governing party, the PRI, which continues to hold a majority in the Mexican Congress, urged Fox to mend fences with Castro. But weighing against reconciliation were pressures from the leaders of Fox's pro-business National Action Party (PAN), who urged Fox to meet with Cuban dissidents during the visit. The visit was cordial, but the Mexican delegation made it clear that Mexico wants the relationship to evolve in terms of commerce and regional issues that are important to both governments, and that human rights issues should be openly discussed without rancor or conflict.[23]

The situation for Mexico is more complicated given the pressures from the Bush administration, which has taken a hard line on Castro and his regime. The growing North American relationship is a critical one for President Fox. But he must heed domestic political opinion wherein the Castro government retains a certain nostalgic level of support. The February 2002 visit appeared to have calmed the waters, but the issue of Castro and the United States, and Mexico's role in working with both, was put to the test shortly after the visit.

At a widely publicized March 2002 United Nations International Conference on Financing for Development in Monterrey, Mexico, another incident indicated the difficulty of restructuring the Mexico-Cuba relationship. The conference had been driven by the Bush administration's effort to offset its image as being uninterested in developing-country problems. The purpose of the meeting was to encourage greater economic aid for the poorest countries in order to meet the United Nations' millennium development goals. The meeting was also to be a showcase for President George W. Bush, who planned to continue from Mexico to visit Peru and El Salvador as a sign that the White House had not forgotten the hemisphere after the events of September 11.

Upon his arrival in Monterrey, President Fidel Castro, who was invited to the conference given Cuba's membership in the UN, denounced current aid levels as "genocide" and as "crumbs tossed by the masters of the world." Castro went on to characterize the world economy as a "big casino" and to denounce the Monterrey Consensus as "humiliating." The U.S. delegation, led by U.S. Ambassador to the UN John Negroponte, walked out during Castro's speech. After completing his remarks, Castro dramatically stormed out of the plenary session and flew back to Cuba, accompanied by Venezuelan President Hugo Chávez. Shortly after their arrival in Havana, Cuban officials suggested that White House National Security Advisor Condoleezza Rice had threatened to cancel Bush's appearance if Castro remained in Monterrey. President Fox and his foreign secretary Jorge Castañeda were deeply embarrassed by the incident. The White House denied any complicity in the events, and the conference concluded without further difficulties.

As it appeared that the Cuban issue would escalate, President Fox made the unexpected and surprising decision to replace his foreign secretary in January of 2003. Jorge Castañeda, the architect of Fox's foreign policy during the first two years of the *sexenio*, was removed—and the major international initiatives he set in motion were abruptly interrupted. The new foreign secretary, Luis Ernesto Derbez, an economist by trade, immediately downplayed the most controversial elements in Mexican foreign policy and began a strong reorientation that focused on trade and investment. That decision reflected the realities on the ground, but for conservatives in Mexico it came too late, while for nationalists it should never have happened. In many respects, for Fox and his government it was a lose-lose situation.

Mexico's Changing International Role

Starting with his presidential campaign in 1999–2000, President Fox began a public discussion of the need for a redefinition of Mexico's international role, in particular with respect to hemispheric defense policy.

This reflected internal politics in Mexico, where the existing defense structure was viewed as an arm of U.S. power in the region. President Fox used his September 2001 state visit to Washington, D.C., to forcefully argue his case. He called for the dismantling of a 54-year-old defense treaty between the United States and Latin America that was aimed at protecting the hemisphere against communism and replacing it with pacts that would combat widespread social ills and organized crime.

Fox argued that the Inter-American Reciprocal Assistance Treaty (known as the Rio Treaty for the city in which it was signed in 1947) had become obsolete with the end of the Cold War, and that his government, after consulting with other Latin American nations, would decide within the next 60 days whether to withdraw from it.[24] The treaty obligates signatories to consider an attack from outside the region against any member nation to be an attack against all, and calls for mutual aid in the event of an attack. Speaking at the OAS on September 8, 2001, President Fox stated that communism was no longer the principal threat to the region, and he urged the organization to begin work on the development of new regional strategies that take on "the real threats that stalk us," including extreme poverty, human rights abuses, environmental degradation, and natural disasters.[25] His speech laid out a broad vision for the economic and social development of the Americas that complemented his innovative Puebla-Panama Plan for regional development in southern Mexico and Central America.

There was a sense in Washington, D.C., that the defense initiative was another signal by the new government in Mexico that it aspired to play a role as intermediary between the United States and the countries of Central and South America. The Rio Treaty was not popular throughout the region, and it was seen as a vehicle for the United States to justify military action in the hemisphere (the treaty had been invoked at the time of the Bay of Pigs in 1961 and during the crisis in the Dominican Republic in 1965). Attacking the treaty was a useful ploy to separate Fox from U.S. defense policy. Although the United States did not react officially, there was some U.S. sympathy for a review of the existing arrangement, if carried out in an orderly fashion.

But the effort to bury the Rio Treaty was overtaken by September 11, when, in a sign of support for the United States, the OAS decided to invoke the treaty. Mexico expressed reservation but supported the motion. The resolution committed the nations of the Western Hemisphere to use "all legally available measures to pursue, capture, extradite and punish" anyone who might have assisted in the September 11 attacks. The collective security commitment of the OAS is nearly identical to that in the

North Atlantic Treaty Organization (NATO) defense agreement that had been invoked in Brussels a week earlier.

More damaging, perhaps, to the relationship between Mexico City and Washington, D.C., than Mexico's reservation over invoking the Rio Treaty was President Fox's statement, issued on the eve of the OAS vote, that the treaty was "not the ideal mechanism" to confront such a threat. The White House expressed shock. Following the vote, the U.S. ambassador to the OAS thanked the members for their solidarity, yet, while he singled out Brazil—which had introduced the treaty resolution and promoted it behind the scenes—for its "bold and visionary leadership," he did not mention Mexico. The U.S. ambassador further stated that "a genuine global power and moral leader demonstrates what it is by what it says."[26] Brazil, of course, is seen as Mexico's only serious rival for hemispheric leadership, including for the position of a permanent seat on the United Nations Security Council, if one is created in the future.

In a move reflecting deep animosity within the Mexican political leadership to the Rio Treaty, as well as opposition to any involvement in military action in the war against terrorism, Mexico unilaterally withdrew from the treaty in September 2002. This decision was not viewed in Washington, D.C., as a confidence-building measure. Clearly, domestic pressures led to the ill-timed decision to follow through with the original goal of modernizing the hemisphere's regional security mechanisms; but, as it turns out, it was a useful idea poorly implemented.

Mexico's position on defense and security issues would return to haunt the Fox administration in early 2003 when, as a member of the UN Security Council, Mexico refused to support the U.S. initiative on Iraq. That decision would deeply offend the Bush White House and forestall any meaningful bilateral dialogue for the remainder of the year. An important turning point came with the November 2003 resignation of the Mexican ambassador to the UN, Adolfo Aguilar Zinser, who, as a defender of Mexico's independent foreign policy, was viewed by the White House as a negative element in relations between Mexico City and Washington, D.C. Zinser's resignation was followed by the transfer of Mexico's ambassador to the U.S. from Washington, D.C., to London, furthering a realignment of Mexico's foreign policy vis-à-vis the United States.

Conclusion

The expression "culturally Latin, financially NAFTA" captures the essence of Mexico's role in the Western Hemisphere. The benefits of the partnership with the United States have been extraordinary. In 2001, Mexico's exports to the United States surpassed $140 billion, and U.S. imports into Mexico were over $113 billion.[27] Billions of foreign investment dollars have poured into Mexico since the inception of NAFTA, and a large part of Mexico's economic stability is a result of NAFTA. Members of the dynamic private sector in Mexico have made it clear that they see the country's future as part of the increasingly stable and growth-oriented North America.[28]

The Mexican economy remained sluggish in 2003 due to the slow recovery of the U.S. economy, but predictions for 2004–2005 improved with the resurgence of the U.S. economy. In early 2004 the Mexican economy appeared to be responding to U.S. growth, as demonstrated by a stronger performance by export manufacturers at the end of 2003, and while there is continued concern over the appreciated real exchange rate, forecasts are generally favorable.

It is clear to Mexican policymakers and to the country's business leaders that what happens on Wall Street and in consumption patterns in the United States is far more significant for Mexico than the crisis in Argentina or uncertainty over electoral outcomes in South America. In this sense, there will always be a psychological dilemma in Mexico's deepening integration with North America, when, culturally, the affinities with South America remain strong.

The desire to be seen as less dependent on the United States will also motivate Mexican leaders to seek expanded diplomatic and trade ties with other world areas. One such area is Europe. Early in his administration, Fox visited Europe in an effort to drum up trade and investment between Mexico and the EU in light of the bilateral free trade agreement signed in 2000.[29] The warm reception he received at that time was geopolitically driven. It was reported that "the sense of urgency underscores what Europe sees as a growing need to bolster economic and political ties with Mexico, partly to counterbalance U.S. influence over Latin America."[30] One diplomatic source stated that "the general theme is to foster a multi-axis world, not a single-axis world dominated by one hyper-power, the United States."[31] However, when President Fox undertook a second visit to six EU countries in October 2001, he was more modest in his expectations, stating that Mexico's trade with Europe is minimal compared with NAFTA; yet, he noted, "things grow and develop when you work on them," as demonstrated by the spectacular increase in U.S.–Mexico trade since NAFTA's inception.[32] The trade data, analyzed in greater detail by Gereffi, Martínez, and Santiso in Chapters 6 and 8, support President Fox's observation: in 2001, nearly 78 percent of Mexico's total trade was with the United States, while trade with the EU accounted for only about 6.6 percent of Mexico's total trade.[33] But it is also significant that Mexico's bilateral trade with the United States has tripled under NAFTA, and while it is still early to assess the longer-term impact of the Mexico–EU free trade agreement, it provides an excellent framework for deepening diplomatic and trade ties, an opportunity that, if pursued, could yield important positive results for both parties.

Mexico's role in the Western Hemisphere is evolving. The democratic elections in 2000 that brought Vicente Fox to power set Mexico on an equal footing with other states in the region. Mexico's impressive economic growth and its financial attractiveness to investment and capital flows are the envy of many of its neighbors. But circumstances have limited the prospects for success for Mexico's innovative foreign policy efforts in the hemisphere. There is little reason, other than cultural and historical ties, to believe that relations with South America will deepen. There are important policy differences—in particular, differing approaches to the FTAA—and there is a strong sense in South America that Mexico's destiny is now tied to that of North America. In turn, that reality is clearly true in economic terms. But it has not yielded Mexico the expected benefits on the social and political agenda. While the first months of the new relationship between Vicente Fox and George W. Bush were warm, the hoped-for negotiations on key border issues were stalled on September 11, 2001. And even if the events of September 11 had not occurred, it was unclear to what degree the U.S. Congress was willing to follow the White House on sharp changes in existing legislation regarding legal status for Mexican workers and immigrants. And the clear reality of Washington's push for homeland security makes it difficult to see how a more open border for Mexican— and other—workers will fit into tightened security schemes over the next few years.

Mexico's two-year appointment as a nonpermanent member of the United Nations Security Council temporarily gave the country a new status in the hemisphere; however, in many ways, the once widely anticipated experience became a diplomatic nightmare for Mexico. Although the UN Security Council never voted on the U.S./U.K. resolution calling for the use of force in Iraq, Mexico's decision to join the European members of the Security Council who opposed it was poorly received in Washington. The White House was particularly incensed when President Fox delivered a national television address stating that Mexico would have voted against the final resolution if it had come to a vote. The thinking in the White House was that Mexico could have—and should have—played a far more sophisticated role in the debate, one more supportive of the United States.

Other diplomatic initiatives set forth by the Fox administration have been welcomed, but have not substantially changed Mexico's role in the hemisphere. The twin challenges of globalization and the political stalemate in Mexico City are the two critical defining conditions for the Fox presidency. Continued weak executive leadership could shift the balance of power to the PRI even more strongly than now, with widespread implications for the 2006 presidential elections. The underlying current of suspicion regarding the United States, as demonstrated in Mexico's congressional reactions to September 11, do not indicate an easy road in identifying joint policy responses to difficult border issues and related matters. And a strong showing of the PRI in the July 2003 midterm elections has further diluted the president's room to maneuver. While it is a welcome sign of a deepening democratic process in Mexico, the congressional stalemate, which appears likely to last until 2006, will make it more difficult for any major foreign policy initiatives to come to fruition.

The probable recovery of the U.S. economy in 2004, and its reflection in Mexico, will probably be insufficient to support institutional and policy changes in the second half of the Fox administration. Electoral cycles will introduce new leaders and new approaches to hemispheric issues. Mexico will always be a prime player in those changes but, ultimately, its weight and influence will reflect its capacity to elicit a response from the United States on questions that are of high priority in Mexico and to the Mexican people and their leadership.

Notes

I would like to thank Ilan Solot for his invaluable research assistance while writing this chapter.

1. Robert S. Leiken, "With a Friend Like Fox," *Foreign Affairs* 80, no. 5 (September–October 2001): 91–104.

2. Felipe A.M. de la Balze, "Finding Allies in the Back Yard: NAFTA and the Southern Cone," *Foreign Affairs* 80, no. 4 (July–August 2001): 7–12.

3. Peter Hakim, "Two Ways to Go Global," *Foreign Affairs* 81, no. 1 (January–February 2002): 148–162.

4. Roxanne Roberts and Ann Gerhart, "The State Dinner That Ended with a Bang: Bush Welcomes Fox with Friendship and Fireworks," *Washington Post*, September 6, 2001, p. C1.

5. David E. Sanger, "Mexico's President Rewrites the Rules," *New York Times*, September 8, 2001, p. A1.

6. Robert A. Pastor, "Bush's North American Agenda," *Washington Post,* September 4, 2001, p. A19.

7. Ginger Thompson, "Mexico President Urges U.S. to Act Soon on Migrants," *New York Times,* September 6, 2001, p. A1.

8. Ibid.

9. Sanger, "Mexico's President."

10. "Terrorist Attacks in U.S. Have Repercussions for Mexico," *SourceMex,* September 26, 2001.

11. Commenting on the situation in Mexico City, former Mexican ambassador to the United States Jorge Montaño stated, "All Fox gets is kisses. We have gotten not even a taco." Kevin Sullivan and Mary Jordan, "Fox Laments 'Stalled' Relations Between U.S., Mexico," *Washington Post,* May 10, 2002, p. A28.

12. Tim Weiner, "Mexico Now Appears to be Developing the Politics of Stalemate," *New York Times,* May 14, 2002, p. A4.

13. International Monetary Fund, Mexico Country Information, available online at www.imf.org (last accessed March 2004).

14. Tim Weiner, "A Grand Plan Meets Skepticism in Mexico's South," *New York Times,* July 2, 2001, p. A3.

15. Ibid.

16. Mary Jordan and Kevin Sullivan, "Mexico Plans a Tighter Grip on Its Border to the South," *Washington Post,* June 18, 2001, p. A1.

17. Tony Smith, "Mexico and Brazil Sign Bilateral Trade Pact," *New York Times,* July 4, 2002, p. W1.

18. Adalid Cabrera Lemuz, "Mexico, Brazil Look to Foster Greater Latin American Integration," *Associated Press,* July 2, 2002.

19. Graham Gori, "Mexico Plays a North-South Divide," *New York Times,* July 16, 2002, p. W1.

20. Ibid.

21. Ibid.

22. Jorge Castañeda, speech given by the Secretary of Foreign Affairs during his appearance before the Senate Foreign Relations Committee, Mexico City, December 11, 2001, available online at www.sre.gob.mx/comunicados/discursos/disc_2001/d-03-01.htm (in Spanish) (last accessed March 2004).

23. Ginger Thompson, "Mexican Leader Visits Castro to Repair Damaged Ties," *New York Times,* February 4, 2002, p. A6.

24. "Fox Calls Defense Pact Obsolete," *Reuters,* September 8, 2001.

25. Sanger, "Mexico's President."

26. Karen DeYoung, "OAS Nations Activate Mutual Defense Treaty," *Washington Post,* September 20, 2001, p. A18.

27. Mexican Secretariat of Economy (Secretaría de Economía), "Mexico's Total Exports" and "Mexico's Total Imports," Subsecretaría de Negociaciones Comerciales Internacionales, Inteligencia Comercial, Estadísticas. Available online at www.economia.gob.mx (last accessed March 2004).

28. Gori, "Mexico Plays a North-South Divide."

29. Henry Tricks, "Mexico's Fox Gets the European Red Carpet," *Financial Times,* September 29, 2000, p. 29.

30. Ibid.

31. Ibid.

32. Andrea Mandel-Campbell, "Fox Urges Business as Usual on Eve of European Tour," *Financial Times,* October 10, 2001, p. 13.

33. Mexican Secretariat of Economy.

8

Mexico's Economic
Ties with Europe:
Business as Unusual?

Javier Santiso

In the early 1990s, Mexico became the darling of financial markets and the shining star of Latin America in the eyes of foreign investors. Its status as the first Latin American country to join the Organization for Economic Cooperation and Development (OECD) and to successfully negotiate a free trade agreement—the North American Free Trade Agreement (NAFTA)—with the world's most powerful economy clearly set it apart from its southern neighbors, even after the 1994 financial meltdown shattered the perception of a Mexican economic miracle. A swift macroeconomic recovery resulting from a combination of deep structural reforms and orthodox stabilization policies helped sustain foreign investor confidence in Mexico.

At the same time, beginning in the 1990s, European foreign direct investment (FDI) grew significantly in Latin America. Despite Mexico's attractiveness as an FDI destination, however, Europe's investments in the region concentrated in the Mercosur[1] countries, most notably Argentina and Brazil. Between 1998 and 2003, Spain—the leading European presence in Latin America—invested nearly $90 billion in the region, but only $8 billion of that went to Mexico.[2] Therefore, Mexico's overall favorable investment climate, concomitant with the attractiveness of the NAFTA market, make the pattern of relatively weak economic ties between Europe and Mexico in the past decade unusual, at a time when Europe has sought deeper economic links with Latin America and Mexico has pursued a strategy of economic liberalization and diversification.

The global economic downturn at the start of the century and a delayed rebound in the United States have provided additional incentives for Mexico and Europe to seek a closer relationship. For Mexico, one of the downsides of a NAFTA-led economy is that it is highly synchronized with the U.S. business cycle, making the country particularly vulnerable to any slowdown of the U.S. economy. For Europe, economic crises in countries with a strong European presence—such as Argentina, which suffered an economic meltdown at the end of 2001—are an incentive to seek greater penetration into other markets in the region with the overall goal of diversifying investments. However, the challenges posed by the post–September 11, 2001, international landscape impacted global trade and investment in 2002, when FDI flows decreased for both developed and developing countries, and in Latin America FDI inflows hit a post-1996 record low of $56 billion.[3] In 2003, concerns over the U.S. economy and other international factors continued to erode investor confidence, and FDI levels continued to decline.

In this context, the free trade agreement (FTA) between Mexico and the European Union (EU) is important as the cornerstone for a closer bilateral relationship in the new millennium. Signed in 2000, the agreement—the first transatlantic FTA for the EU—is designed to provide new incentives for European companies to enter the Mexican market and provide greater competitive opportunities for Mexican products in the European market. The results were positive in the first two years of the agreement's enforcement: in 2001, Mexico–EU trade totaled $21.5 billion, an increase of more than 20 percent from 1999 figures.[4]

This chapter traces Mexico's changing economic ties with Europe since the 1990s and analyzes the prospects for a closer relationship in the new century. The analysis is divided into three parts. First, the chapter provides an overview of the main drivers behind the 1990s surge in European foreign direct investment in Latin America and the main reasons Mexico stood out as a special case of low FDI flows from Europe compared with similar markets in Latin America. Second, it summarizes the main characteristics of the Mexico–EU Free Trade Agreement (EU FTA) and its impact on the bilateral relationship. And, finally, the chapter analyzes the shift in global investment trends in light of the international economic downturn that began in the late 1990s and the possible effects of those trends on Mexico's economic relationship with Europe. What is overwhelmingly clear is that Mexico will need to assess its long-term international economic needs and shape its strategic decisions accordingly. Its relationship with both the United States and Europe will have a major influence on these choices.

European Investment in Latin America in the 1990s

Mexico's profound political and economic transformation that began in the mid-1980s quickly made the country an attractive destination for foreign investment. Mexico also experienced an impressive boom in its export sector during the 1990s, reaching by far the fastest growth rate in share of the world trade market in all of Latin America between 1985 and 1998.[5] Even more striking is the product diversification of Mexico's foreign trade. As Gary Gereffi and Martha Martínez note in Chapter 6, petroleum exports represented almost two-thirds of total exports at the beginning of the 1980s, yet by the start of the new millennium they represented less than 8 percent. In 2001, overall exports represented 28 percent of Mexico's gross domestic product (GDP), compared with less than 11 percent in Argentina and 13 percent in Brazil.[6]

Furthermore, Mexico is in a privileged position to act as a hub for international trade and investment, given its geographic location between the rest of Latin America and the United States and its growing network of free trade agreements (see Table 6.2 in Chapter 6). In addition, Mexico's young population provides an abundant source of increasingly skilled labor. Between 1994 and 2000, Mexico attracted $122 billion in foreign direct investment, which made it one of the highest FDI recipients in emerging-market countries, trailing behind China and Brazil.[7] In 2000, Moody's rating agency granted Mexico investment grade level, becoming the only Latin American country that had defaulted on its international financial obligations during the 1980s to receive that recognition.

These factors played a less prominent role in strengthening Mexican-European economic relations in the 1990s than one would expect, however, even though European presence in Latin America grew considerably in that decade. In fact, the surge in European investment—and in particular from Spain—throughout Latin America was so pronounced that it was dubbed the *reconquista* or recolonization, but Mexico received significantly less of that investment than the largest Mercosur countries—Argentina and Brazil. There are various reasons for this.

On the one hand, as explained by several authors in this volume, Mexico's economic interests have centered on its northern neighbor, the United States, despite pursuing a strategy of overall diversification and economic liberalization. As Gereffi and Martínez note, although Mexico has signed a number of free trade agreements with other countries and regions—including the Mexico–EU FTA in 2000—the internationalization of the Mexican economy could be better described as an *Americanization* or *NAFTAization*.[8] Although Mexico's geographic proximity to one of the world's largest markets is an important FDI driver at the global level, it is also an important reason why Mexico's economy is largely NAFTA-led. In fact, since the inception of NAFTA in 1994, Mexico has become the second-largest trading partner of the United States.

On the other hand, the major European industrial investors in Latin America—such as Telefónica, Endesa, and Repsol—have found greater obstacles and fewer opportunities in their sectors (telecommunications, electric utilities, and petroleum, respectively) in Mexico (as explained later, the banking sector is a case apart). By the end of the 1990s, Brazil absorbed nearly 47 percent of the consolidated sales of the largest European transnational corporations in Latin America, and Argentina nearly 25 percent; at the same time Mexico, although ranked third, absorbed just 17 percent of such sales.[9]

Spanish Investment in Latin America

For Spanish corporations during the 1990s, Latin America was by far the major strategic area of investment in emerging countries. Spanish investment in Latin America reached an estimated one-third ($18 billion) of total FDI received by the region in 2000, and in their internationalization process Spanish corporations have been, in fact, heavily *Latin-Americanized*.[10] In the same year, the overall investment made in Latin America by the five major Spanish corporations (Telefónica, Endesa, Repsol, Banco Bilbao Vizcaya Argentaria [BBVA], and Banco Santander Central Hispano [BSCH]) represented more than $80 billion, and the stocks of these five companies represented nearly 70 percent of the Spanish stock exchange (Indice Bursátil, IBEX).[11] This transformed the Spanish stock exchange into a de facto Latin American one.

As unique case studies, Spanish corporations offer the perfect example of an internationalization process via Latin America. Conducted through either horizontal or vertical foreign direct investment, the internationalization strategy of Spanish firms placed an explicit bet on Latin America's potential as a vehicle to become global players by developing a strong regional presence. The Spanish electric utility Unión Fenosa, for example, concentrated more than 60 percent of its major international investments in Latin America.

For the five major Spanish investors in the region—Endesa, Telefónica, Repsol, BBVA, and BSCH—Latin America represented between 40 and 60 percent of their total revenues in 2000.[12] Endesa, the leading Spanish electric utility, became the largest private utility company in Latin America through its subsidiary Enersis, acquired in 1999. In 2000, Latin American operations contributed to more than 42 percent of Endesa's operating income and 29 percent of the company's total net income. Although present in six Latin American countries (Chile, Argentina, Colombia, Peru, Brazil, and Dominican Republic), Endesa's main investments are in Chile—the location for 50 percent of the company's total Latin American assets. Argentina and Brazil are also significant in terms of Endesa's investments— 8.7 and 7.7 percent of total 2000 sales, respectively—but Mexico is altogether absent from the equation.[13]

Telefónica has also invested heavily in Latin America—a total of $36 billion to date—and has become the largest telecommunications company in the region.[14] By 2001, South America was home to half of its 130,000 employees. Telefónica's strategy, like that of Endesa's, has been to become a global player through a strong regional presence, and that presence is concentrated in Argentina, Brazil, Chile, and Peru.[15] It is clear that the driving factors of Telefónica's investment strategy—market size and opportunities created during the 1990s—made South America, not Mexico, the best platform for expansion of this Spanish telecommunications firm.

Repsol, the Spanish oil operator that was privatized in 1997, has also focused its investments in Latin America, though not Mexico, with operations in Trinidad and Tobago, Venezuela, Ecuador, Peru, Bolivia, Brazil, and Argentina. By the end of 2000, 86 percent of Repsol-YPF-identified hydrocarbon reserves were located in Latin America.[16] YPF not only provided complementary skills and assets to Repsol, but transformed, through Latin America, the formerly state-run Spanish oil company into a world-class company. By 2000, Argentina alone represented more than 46 percent of Repsol-YPF total assets and approximately 45 percent of operating revenues. The rest of Latin America accounted for merely 10.5 percent.[17] Without investment opportunities in Mexico (the oil and gas markets there remain closed to foreigners, for reasons explained by Russell Crandall in Chapter 4), the profile of Repsol-YPF's Latin American presence, like that of many other Spanish operators, has a clear Southern Cone bias.

The Banking Sector as a Special Case

Banking has been a particularly appealing area for Spanish investors in Latin America because the sector is relatively standardized, making it a more understood and thus safer financial investment. Because European banks became increasingly aggressive in the Western Hemisphere during the 1990s, they contributed along with other foreign banks in the positive transformation of the region's banking systems. A comparison of the performance of foreign-owned versus domestic banks in Latin America from 1995 to 2000 reveals that foreign banks had a more robust loan growth, a more aggressive and efficient response to asset quality deterioration, and a greater ability to absorb losses.[18]

The two leading Spanish banks, Banco Bilboa Vizcaya Argentaria (BBVA) and Banco Santander Central Hispano (BSCH), have made major acquisitions in Latin America, and, with their U.S. counterparts, significantly contributed to the internationalization of the banking sector in Latin America. In 2001, both banks became the leading franchises in Latin America, and, in terms of asset exposure, BBVA and BSCH are now the two biggest foreign players in the region, with 38 and 33 percent, respectively, of asset exposure in Latin America by the end of 2000 (compared with 3.3 percent for BankBoston and 2.5 percent for Citigroup).[19]

With more than 27 percent of its total sales concentrated in Mexico, BBVA's geographic exposure to Latin America is heavily biased toward Mexico, making it a special case in Spanish investment trends in the region, whereas BSCH has a greater balance between Mexico and Mercosur exposure.[20] In 2001, BBVA's total share of the regional banking market was nearly 10 percent. Mexico alone had more than 32 percent of the total Latin American investments made in 2001 by BBVA (compared with 20 percent in Argentina, 11.5 percent in Brazil, 11 percent in Chile, and 10 percent in Colombia).[21] BSCH also has a 10 percent market share in Latin America, but assets are more evenly spread among Mexico and the Mercosur countries of Argentina, Brazil, and Chile. In the case of BSCH, the biggest investments were made in the Southern Cone countries, a pattern similar to that of other European banks. Brazil received 40 percent of investments made by BSCH in Latin America, followed by Mexico, Argentina, and Chile (17, 15.5, and 12 percent, respectively).[22]

In sum, with the privatization and opening of Latin American banking systems to foreign investment during the 1980s and 1990s, Spanish banks led the charge, investing in more than 12 countries in the region. With its risks and rewards, the banks' Latin American strategy transformed Spanish banks into global players with regionwide franchises; furthermore, the rush to Latin America's investment "El Dorado" propelled BBVA and BSCH into the top tier of Europe's banks in market capitalization—at present they rank just behind HSBC, ING, Lloyds, and Deutsche Bank and ahead of other European counterparts like BNP Paribas, Société Générale, ABN AMRO, or Dresdner Bank.[23] The activity of foreign banks in Latin America also transformed the region's banking sector, particularly that of Mexico. After the takeover of Banacci-Banamex by Citigroup in

2001 (for $12.5 billion, equivalent to all the FDI received by Mexico in 2000), Mexico now has the most internationalized banking sector in the region. Nearly 70 percent of the Mexican banks are now controlled by foreigners, and BBVA and Citigroup each represent 26 percent of total Mexican market share.[24]

The rise in European investment in Latin America throughout the 1990s and the successful negotiation of the Mexico–EU free trade agreement signal the start of a new era in the relations between Mexico and Europe. To be sure, after NAFTA, the Mexico–EU FTA is Mexico's most important free trade initiative in the context of the country's economic diversification strategy. But the key question is to what extent the Mexico–EU FTA provides new incentives and opportunities for closer bilateral economic ties.

The Mexico–EU Free Trade Agreement

The first summit ever between the European Union, Latin America, and the Caribbean, which took place in June 1999 and included 48 countries, marked a formal commitment to deepen economic and political ties between the two regions. The summit was followed in 2000 by the Mexico–EU FTA, the first transatlantic FTA for the EU. The agreement is comprehensive; it covers goods, services, procurement, competition, intellectual property, and investment, and it establishes a rapid tariff dismantling process—as of 2003, all Mexican exports enter duty-free to the EU, and Mexican tariffs on EU exports will be eliminated by 2007.

In the first two years since the agreement's enactment in 2000, bilateral trade grew significantly. However, the global economy has suffered a slowdown since 2001, effectively reducing trade and investment flows worldwide. During the third bilateral Joint Council meeting held in Athens in March 2003, both Mexico and the EU expressed their hopes that an imminent global economic recovery, concomitant with the market access provided by the bilateral agreement, would accelerate the process of strengthening economic ties between the two regions.[25] In assessing the prospects for such an outcome, it is first important to review the main characteristics of the Mexico–EU free trade agreement.

The Mexico–EU Free Trade Agreement: An Overview

The Mexico–EU free trade agreement is part of a broader bilateral framework, the Economic Partnership, Political Coordination and Cooperation

Agreement—known as the Global Agreement—which promotes political dialogue, reinforces bilateral cooperation, and liberalizes trade and investment.[26] The agreement is divided into three main sections: economic and trade relations, political relations, and cooperation. The latter two sections provide a mechanism for institutionalized high-level dialogue between the governments of Mexico and those of the EU members to promote cooperation and joint initiatives in various areas, including regional development, security, and peacekeeping. The economic section of the agreement focuses on bilateral trade and culminated in the signing of the Mexico–EU FTA.

The FTA comprises five main areas: (1) trade in industrial goods; (2) trade in agricultural and fishery products; (3) services; (4) investment; and (5) intellectual property, competition, and dispute resolution. As stipulated in the agreement, Mexico liberalized 47 percent of its industrial products at the outset, and an additional 5 percent in 2003. The remaining 48 percent will be liberalized in 2005 and 2007, depending on the sector.[27] Mexico successfully negotiated gradual liberalization in the automobile and apparel sectors, for example, to allow for Mexican producers to become competitive with EU standards. The EU liberalized 82 percent of its industrial products when the agreement came into force on July 1, 2000, and the remaining 18 percent on January 1, 2003.[28]

In the agricultural sector, which represents 7 percent of total bilateral trade, 62 percent of tradable commodities were liberalized, and tariffs on the most sensitive products will be eliminated over a 10-year period. The agreement also liberalizes 99 percent of fishery products.[29] In the area of services, the agreement stipulates progressive liberalization over a period not to exceed 10 years and includes all sectors except audiovisual services, coastal management, and air transportation. Among the most important of the services liberalized under the agreement are financial services, telecommunications, distribution, energy, tourism, and environmental services. Investment liberalization began three years after the agreement came into force, while the payments related to investments began a progressive liberalization from the start. The agreement also protects intellectual property—including patents, brands, and copyrights—and committees were set up to ensure a level playing field for economic actors and proper implementation of the rules on both sides, in addition to the management of dispute resolution.

The Mexico–EU agreement is important for several reasons. For Europe, it is the first transatlantic FTA, and it symbolizes the EU's commitment to strengthening ties with Latin America. For Mexico, it is an important vehicle for diversification in its external economic relations, and it offers the potential to reduce the country's dependence on the U.S. market. With arrangements on services, public procurement, and investment, the agreement guarantees predictability for exporters and investors, as well as access substantially equivalent to that established under NAFTA. Furthermore, the institutional mechanisms for dialogue—the Joint Council at the ministerial level, and the Joint Committee and technical Special Committees—provide the basis for deepening the bilateral relationship and for effective dispute settlement.[30]

The Mexico–EU Free Trade Agreement: Preliminary Results

The first two years following the mid-2000 ratification of the agreement saw trade between Mexico and the EU grow significantly—by 28.3 percent—yet the current global economic downturn led to a 1.7 percent decrease in bilateral trade in 2002–2003.[31] There is optimism, however, in the prospects for a return to increased bilateral economic activity once the global economic situation improves, based on positive initial results as well as confidence in the institutional framework of the agreement.

Figures exchanged in the third Mexico–EU Joint Council meeting in March 2003 show there are currently more than 5,000 businesses in Mexico with capital originating from the EU (more than 80 percent of them with a majority EU participation), representing 23 percent of the total companies with foreign investment in Mexico.[32] The majority of these businesses are in the services sector, 24 percent of them in trade-related activities, and 39 percent in other service sectors.

Mexican businesses are also increasingly investing in Europe. Several success stories that predate the Mexico–EU FTA have become an important reference to those interested in the European market. The Mexican cement producer Cemex, for example, considered among the leading export-oriented success stories in Latin America, was one of the first Mexican companies to expand into Europe. With investments spread throughout the American continent as well as in some parts of Asia, Cemex is more profitable than its two principal European rivals, France's Lafarge and Switzerland's Holcim, both with significant presence in Latin America. Cemex led the way in Mexican investment in Europe when it purchased two Spanish cement producers in 1992. By 2000, Cemex's European operations represented 13 percent of its revenues, compared with 21 percent from the United States.[33]

Two other Mexican companies have made significant strides in entering the European market. Grupo Modelo, the leading Mexican brewer, has recently engaged in a strategy of diversification and international expansion into markets outside North America, namely Latin America and Europe. The food company Grupo Bimbo followed similar steps. In an effort to diversify its geographic exposure (nearly two-thirds of its sales abroad are in the United States), Grupo Bimbo acquired companies in Germany, Austria, and Eastern Europe. An increasing number of companies are following this trend.

At the macroeconomic level, the early postagreement figures are positive. The inflows of Mexican foreign direct investment to the EU jumped from approximately $179 million in 1999 to about $329 million in 2001; in the same period, European FDI outflows to Mexico jumped from about $2.2 billion to about $6.7 billion.[34] Trade figures are also encouraging. Trade growth accelerated rapidly in 2000, with EU exports rising by more than 30 percent and imports by nearly 50 percent.[35] In 2001, despite an unfavorable international economic climate, EU–Mexico trade still managed to increase, although by 2002–2003, in step with global trends, bilateral trade suffered a decline.

According to the EU trade commissioner, Pascal Lamy, the Mexico–EU FTA is good for Europe because it reestablishes the "proper" weight of Europe's trade relationship with Mexico by neutralizing the distorting impact of NAFTA. It is good for Mexico, he states, because now Mexico has consolidated its position as a bridge between north and south, between the Atlantic and the Pacific, and between Europe and Asia. Moreover, it is good for both Mexico and Europe because it reestablishes a pattern of trade in line with the relative weights and interests of the two parties' economies. It is good for the international trading system, he adds, because it is an interregional agreement that is fully compatible with the World Trade Organization (WTO) rules. Finally, Lamy considers the bilateral trade agreement good for the rest of Latin America because it has proved to be a pathfinder for others in the region.[36] So, as Lamy puts it, whether Mexico and the European Union are married partners, lovers, or just good friends, the potential benefits of the bilateral free trade agreement are many and far-reaching.

Changing Global Investment Trends

Global investment has been on a downward trend since 2000. Not only have FDI flows to developing regions—Latin America, Africa, and Asia—fallen, but FDI levels in developed countries have diminished as well. The United States, for example, the top FDI recipient from 1978 to 2001, plunged to a 10-year low, with its FDI levels falling from $144 billion in 2001 to $30 billion in 2002.[37] According to the United Nations Conference on Trade and Development (UNCTAD), FDI flows to Latin America fell in 2002 for the third consecutive year, declining by one-third to $56 billion, the lowest level since 1996.[38] Argentina, Brazil, and Chile were the most affected by this downturn, especially in services, because economic devaluations had an adverse impact on market-seeking FDI. Outward FDI from Latin America also fell in 2002—by 28 percent—to $6 billion.[39]

Most countries in Latin America have implemented policies intended to attract FDI. Most free trade agreements, for example, now include coverage of investment issues, as is the case with the Mexico–EU agreement. The impact of regional trade and investment agreements on FDI flows is difficult to assess, because countries have unilaterally changed their regulatory frameworks in favor of increased FDI flows. In Mexico, for example, deregulation in sectors that attract FDI—such as petroleum, oil, gas, electricity—would likely increase European interest in the Mexican market, but significant reform in these sectors has been lagging for some time now.

A useful tool to examine foreign investor confidence in the world's main FDI destinations is the yearly survey conducted by the U.S. firm A.T. Kearney, the *FDI Confidence Index*, which measures the degree of attractiveness of the world's main FDI destinations. The index uses a qualitative questionnaire addressed to chief executive officers (CEOs) and chief financial officers (CFOs) of the world's largest companies, which represent all regions and sectors and are responsible for about 70 percent of the world's FDI flows. In the 2001, 2002, and 2003 surveys, nearly 50 percent of the respondents were European executives and about 25 percent were from U.S. companies.

The respondents of the 2001 survey identified the following areas as important drivers of FDI in Mexico: the stability of the peso, privatization issues, and political reform (64, 48, and 46 percent, respectively).[40] Geography was also relevant: respondents mentioned the U.S. growth dynamic and further integration with NAFTA (44 and 37 percent, respectively) as crucial factors for investing in Mexico. The comparison with Brazil is instructive. The study underscores that, contrary to Brazil, one of the major drivers of FDI in Mexico was low production costs, which 43 percent of the interviewed executives cited as one of the major reasons to invest in Mexico, compared with only 26 percent citing the same reason for investing in Brazil. For European companies, Mexico's market size was less important than proximity to the United States as a motivating factor for investing in Mexico; in contrast, Brazil's FDI was markedly more market-seeking, directing transnational investments mainly at local or regional markets. The comparison is illustrative: 45 percent of survey respondents thought market size was important in Mexico, whereas 68 percent thought it was important when referring to Brazil. Finally, the Mexico–EU FTA was identified as an FDI driver, and it ranked sixth in importance. Interestingly, for most European corporations, Mexico was the most attractive emerging-market destination for investment in 2001, overtaking other emerging countries like China or Brazil.[41]

According to the 2002 survey, Mexico's investment attractiveness declined for the first time in five years. Having ranked the fifth most attractive FDI destination worldwide in 1999, Mexico dropped to ninth place in 2002, with European investors and other investors worldwide in the nonfinancial services, telecommunications, and utilities sectors leading in expressions of diminishing interest in the Mexican market. However, when compared with other large emerging economies—China, Brazil, India, and Poland—and considering the worldwide downturn in FDI flows, Mexico's position in the FDI confidence index surpassed Brazil's and it rose from third place among the five countries in 2001 to second in 2002.[42]

In the 2003 FDI Confidence Index, Mexico's ranking jumped from ninth to third place, its highest ranking ever, and Mexican FDI inflows rose to $13.6 billion during 2002, roughly a 6 percent increase from the previous year (excluding the $12.5 billion Banacci-Citigroup merger, which nearly doubled FDI inflows for 2001). The manufacturing sector accounted for 42 percent of total FDI in 2002, and financial services was the second largest investment flow to Mexico. Following the Banacci-Citigroup deal, Bank of America and HSBC Holdings of the United Kingdom made investments of over $1 billion each in Mexico. But as indicated in the survey, European investors were more bullish on Mexico, ranking it the 11th most attractive market; this, however, is a noticeable improvement from the previous year's European ranking of 22nd place. The Mexico–EU FTA has to some degree encouraged European investors to pursue more opportunities offered by Mexico's low production costs and strategic location as an export platform to the United States. For example, Volkswagen recently announced its decision to produce the Bora model for export in Puebla, a move that is expected to raise production by 30 percent, create 1,500 jobs by 2005, and yield $2 billion in new purchases from domestic suppliers.[43]

As noted in several chapters in this volume, however, Mexico's competitiveness in some areas vis-à-vis other emerging economies is declining. Although U.S. investors continue to favor the Mexican market, most global executives prefer other emerging market destinations; Europeans, for example, expressed a preference in 2003 for China, Poland, Russia, and India over Mexico. One of the main concerns for investors is the lack of infrastructure investment in Mexico. A case in point is the electricity sector: industries can expect more frequent power outages if the government fails to invest over the next 10 years the estimated $74 billion needed to meet the Mexico's growing electricity demand.[44]

Conclusion

During the 1990s, European presence in Latin America grew comparable with, if not larger than, that of the United States in terms of FDI; yet European presence in Mexico lagged significantly behind the Mercosur countries, particularly Argentina and Brazil. European interest in Mexico, as well as bilateral economic activity, increased with the signing of the Mexico–EU FTA in 2000, but the current downturn in the world economy has slowed economic activity in and between developed and developing countries, and FDI flows continued on a downward trend in 2003.

President Fox's innovative foreign policy approach has been overall favorable for a closer Mexico–EU relationship, but his administration must do more to stimulate Mexico's competitiveness and infrastructure development, which is what will ultimately drive European and other foreign investment. President Fox has proposed a set of initiatives to expand Mexico's international economic relations through a Trade and Investment Promotion Program, with the central goals of diversifying Mexico's external markets, deepening and widening the benefits of free trade, and improving the legal framework in Mexico to facilitate investment. Although the medium- to long-term prospects for closer Mexico–EU economic relations are encouraging, in the short term it is more likely that a rebalancing in the bilateral relationship will take place, rather than a radical change, as Mexico's geographic proximity to the United States will continue to dominate the country's external economic relations. However, as noted in other chapters in this volume, the growth in trade between the United States and Mexico increased enormously after NAFTA's enactment, and perhaps by 2010 the same may be true for the Mexico–EU economic relationship. What is clear is that both Mexico and Europe could benefit enormously from a closer relationship, and what is encouraging is that the political will and institutional framework to move forward in building closer political and economic ties are already in place.

Notes

1. Mercosur is a customs union formed by Argentina, Brazil, Paraguay, and Uruguay, plus associate members Bolivia and Chile.

2. Joel Millman and Carlta Vitzthum, "Mexico's Familial Toehold in Europe," *Wall Street Journal,* August 6, 2003, p. A11.

3. United Nations Conference on Trade and Development (UNCTAD), "FDI Policies for Development: National and International Perspectives," *World Investment Report 2003*, Chapter 2 (New York and Geneva: United Nations, 2003), p. 52.

4. Mexican Secretariat of Economy (Secretaría de Economía), "Mexico's Total Exports" and "Mexico's Total Imports," Subsecretaría de Negociaciones Comerciales Internacionales, Inteligencia Comercial, Estadísticas. Available online at www.economia.gob.mx (last accessed March 2004).

5. Between 1985 and 1998, the Mexican share of world trade rose from 1.55 percent of total world trade to 2.24 percent. That increase of almost 0.7 percentage points is the biggest in Latin America for that period, well above emerging economies like Argentina and global trade players like Chile. See Michael Mortimor and Wilson Peres, "La competitividad empresarial en América Latina," *Revista de la CEPAL,* no. 74 (August 2001): 37–59; and Jorge Katz and Giovanni Stumpo, "Regímenes competitivos sectoriales, productividad y competitividad internacional," Economic Commission for Latin America and the Caribbean (ECLAC), Santiago, Chile, March 8, 2001 (unpublished).

6. World Bank. World Development Indicators (WDI), Data Query, Argentina, Brazil, and Mexico, Exports of Goods and Services (% GDP), 2001, available online at: www.worldbank.org/data/dataquery.html (last accessed March 2004).

7. All dollar figures are in U.S. dollars unless otherwise noted. Banco de México, "Inversión Extranjera Directa, Cuadro A52: Principales Indicadores del Sector Externo," *Apéndice Estadístico—Informe Anual 2002* (Mexico City), p. 193; and Raymond Colitt, "Multinationals Shifting Strategies: Direct Foreign Investment in Brazil," *Financial Times,* March 8, 2002, p. 4.

8. Although the growth of Mexican exports to the United States preceded NAFTA—as Gereffi and Martínez point out in Chapter 6—the agreement played an important role in consolidating the United States as Mexico's main export market, with the obvious helping factor of geographic proximity.

9. For a detailed analysis, see John Dunning, "European Foreign Direct Investment in Latin America," in Inter-American Development Bank (IADB), *Foreign Investment in Latin America: The Role of European Investors* (Washington, DC: IADB, 2001), pp. 143–175.

10. Ibid.

11. The Mercosur bias of these companies' presence in Latin America was particularly felt after the 2001 Argentine crisis. See, for example, some of the many reports written at the time by European banks: Cazenove, "Argentina and the Spanish banks," London, *Cazenove & Co. Spain Research,* March 26, 2001; Commerzbank, "Repsol-YPF: Latam field trip report," London, *Commerzbank Securities, Spain Oil & Gas,* May 14, 2001; ING Barings, "Telefónica: Latin America

Increases Group Risk," Madrid, *ING Barings Equity Markets*, May 21, 2001; HSBC, "BSCH: A Time to Consolidate," London, *HSBC Equity Research*, April 3, 2001; Société Générale, "Telefónica: Bring on the Bulls," Paris and London, *SG Equity Research*, May 2001. U.S. investment banks that acquired a Spanish broker in 2000 to cover Spanish stocks also produced relevant reports. See, for example, Morgan Stanley Dean Witter, "Spanish Banking Sector: The Fall and the Rise of the Spanish Empire," Madrid, *Morgan Stanley Dean Witter Europe Equity Research*, March 26, 2001; Morgan Stanley Dean Witter, "Telefónica: Hedging the Latam Risk," Madrid and London, *Morgan Stanley Dean Witter Equity Research*, May 2, 2001.

12. Company annual reports and ING Barings, 2001.

13. Ibid.

14. Ibid.

15. Telefónica began investing in Latin America in the early 1990s with the purchase of a controlling stake in Chile's fixed-line operator, followed by another Southern Cone operator, Telefónica de Argentina. Telefónica now also manages companies in Colombia, Costa Rica, El Salvador, Guatemala, Mexico, Nicaragua, Panama, Puerto Rico, the Dominican Republic, Uruguay, and Venezuela. On the internationalization (i.e., Latin-Americanization) of Telefónica, see: Mariola Mesenguer and Lourdes Casanova, "Telefónica: The Making of a Multinational" (Fontainebleau, France: INSEAD, 1999); and, more generally on Spanish investments in the area, Lourdes Casanova, "Lazos de familia: Las inversiones españolas en Iberoamérica," *Foreign Affairs (en español)* 2, no. 2 (Spring 2002): 67–85.

16. Company annual reports and ING Barings, 2001.

17. Ibid.

18. See Jennifer Crystal, Gerard Dages, and Linda Goldberg, "Has Foreign Bank Entry Led to Sounder Banks in Latin America?" *Federal Reserve Bank of New York Current Issues in Economics and Finance* 8, no. 1 (January 2002); and Jennifer Crystal, Gerard Dages, and Linda Goldberg, "Does Foreign Ownership Contribute to Sounder Banks in Emerging Markets? The Latin American Experience," in *Open Doors: Foreign Participation in Financial Systems in Developing Countries,* edited by Robert E. Litan, Paul Masson, and Michael Pomerleano (Washington, DC: Brookings Institution, 2001), pp. 217–266.

19. Salomon Smith Barney, December 2000.

20. See Deutsche Bank, "Spain's sensitivity to Latin America," Deutsche Bank Europe Equity Research, Madrid, May 24, 2001.

21. Crédit Agricole Indosuez Cheuvreux, "BBVA and BSCH," Crédit Agricole Indosuez Cheuvreux, Madrid, March 30, 2001; and Crédit Agricole Indosuez Cheuvreux, "Spanish Banks Quarterly: Latam Risk Increases, Valuations are Still High," Crédit Agricole Indosuez Cheuvreux, Madrid, May 15, 2001.

22. Ibid.

23. On the international strategy of Spanish banks, see Javier Santiso, "The Quest for El Dorado: Spanish Banks are Betting on Latin America," *Crédit Agricole Perspectives,* Paris, Département des Etudes Economiques et Bancaires, no. 44, April 2001, pp. 5–8; Mauro Guillén and Adrian Tschoegl, "At Last the Internationalization of Retail Banking? The Case of Spanish Banks in Latin America," Wharton Financial Institutions Center Working Paper, no. 99–41, The Wharton

School of Business, University of Pennsylvania, 1999 (unpublished); and Carmen Hernansánz and Miguel Sebastian, "The Spanish Banks' Strategy in Latin America," BBVA Working Paper, no. 3, BBVA Servicio de Estudios, Madrid, October 2000.

24. On the internationalization of the Mexican banking sector, see the study by the Federal Reserve Bank of New York economists, Linda Goldberg, Gerard Dages, and Daniel Kinney, "Foreign and Domestic Bank Participation in Emerging Markets: Lessons from Mexico and Argentina," *Federal Reserve Bank of New York Policy Review* 6, no. 3 (September 2000): 17–36.

25. European Union, "Joint Press Release, Third EU–Mexico Joint Council Meeting, Athens, 27 March 2003," (Brussels: European Union, 2003). The document is available on the European Union's website http://europa.eu.int/comm/external_relations/w13/10.htm (last accessed September 2003).

26. The Global Agreement was signed in 1997 and came into force in 2000.

27. Mexican Secretariat of External Relations, "Relación México–UE," Embassy of Mexico, Brussels, www.sre.gob.mx/belgica-ue/relacion_mexico.htm (last accessed October 2003).

28. Ibid.

29. Ibid.

30. For an overview of these and other elements of the Mexico–EU FTA, visit the European Union's bilateral trade relations website, "Bilateral Trade Relations: Mexico," at http://europa.eu.int/comm/trade/bilateral/mexico/index_en.htm (last accessed September 2003).

31. European Union, "Joint Press Release, Third EU–Mexico Joint Council Meeting."

32. Ibid.; and European Union, "Bilateral Trade Relations: Mexico."

33. The Economist, "E-Strategy Brief: The Cemex Way," *The Economist,* June 16, 2001, pp. 75–76.

34. European Union, "EU Foreign Direct Investment with Mexico," available on the European Union's website, http://europa.eu.int/comm/trade/issues/bilateral/countries/mexico/docs/econo_mexico.xls (last accessed September 2003).

35. Pascal Lamy, "Mexico and the EU: Married Partners, Lovers, or Just Good Friends?" Speech at the Institute of European Integration Studies, Instituto Tecnológico Autónomo de México (ITAM), Mexico City, April 29, 2002.

36. Ibid.

37. UNCTAD, "FDI Policies for Development," p. 33; and A.T. Kearney, "FDI Confidence Index," vol. 6 (September 2003), p. 10.

38. UNCTAD, "FDI Policies," p. 52.

39. Ibid., p. 55.

40. For an analysis on what makes Mexico an attractive foreign investment destination, see Jorge Blázquez and Javier Santiso, "Mexico: Is It an Ex-Emerging Market?" *Journal of Latin American Studies* 36, no. 2 (May 2004): 297–318.

41. See A. T. Kearney, "FDI Confidence Index," vol. 4 (February 2001).

42. A. T. Kearney, "FDI Confidence Index," vol. 5 (September 2002), pp. 2, 25 (Figure 16); ibid. (vol. 4).

43. "FDI Confidence Index," vol. 6, pp. 13–14.

44. Ibid.

PART 4

Conclusion

9

Making Mexico's Democracy Work Effectively

Guadalupe Paz

Mexico has made genuine progress in its political, economic, and social development, yet the challenges ahead are many, and the political response to those challenges will in large part define Mexico's course in the coming decades. The 2000 presidential election was an important milestone, not only because the institutionalization of electoral democracy was fully achieved with Mexico's peaceful democratic transition, but also because this historic transition occurred in the absence of an economic crisis, an indication that short-term economic concerns were not the driving force behind the election. But Mexico's emergence from the status of a developing country is still in many ways incomplete. Mexico has yet to effectively address such problems as widespread unemployment, income inequality, the need for fiscal reform, emerging demographic challenges, the yawning deficit in education and human capital development, and migration. These so-called microissues need to be addressed through "second-phase" political, economic, and social reforms, that is, a set of reforms designed to deliver the benefits of a "first phase" of reforms—broadly defined as political and economic liberalization—to the population at large.

The fact that one can now speak of second-generation reforms in Mexico suggests a successful outcome of the structural reforms implemented in the 1980s and 1990s. Yet from the new democratic context in Mexico arises a whole new set of political challenges in addressing these issues. One central theme in *Mexico's Democracy at Work* is that democracy inherently makes the process of reform more complicated, particularly when the proposed reforms call for painful adjustments. In this sense, as Russell Crandall argues in Chapters 1 and 4, indeed Mexico is managing the paradox of success: democracy and economic stability have prevailed, but in order to move ahead with other much-needed reforms, Mexico's political leadership must also find a way to make democracy work effectively.

Mexico's protracted democratic transition, what in Chapter 2 Andreas Schedler calls a silent political revolution, culminated in the consolidation of electoral democracy through the peaceful alternation of power in 2000. Today, Mexico's democratic institutions are beginning to take root; this is evident, Schedler concludes, by the fact that partisan discontent has shifted its focus from the electoral institutions themselves to the individuals inside them. However, the success of Mexico's democracy hinges on much more than credible electoral institutions and transparent elections.

Politically, Mexico is moving in uncharted waters, where governability is no longer guaranteed by a strong president with a corporatist support structure; instead, the new government finds itself struggling to deliver on ambitious political goals in the context of a divided government, of which the former ruling party is an important member. Gridlock between the executive and legislative branches, and the ensuing public disappointment with the failure to achieve many of the goals set forth in 2000, have come to characterize President Vicente Fox's administration (2000–2006). Although some argue that Fox has been unable or unwilling to demonstrate strong leadership and to build the necessary governing coalitions to push forward his agenda, achieving success in the current political landscape is no easy task.[1] The main political parties are internally fragmented and rely heavily on charismatic figures to win at the ballot box, a trend that over time will undermine the party system. A weak executive has little chance of passing legislation without majority-building alliances, yet achieving governing majorities in a divided congress with little democratic experience is a veritable challenge. This political reality will confront Fox's successor as well. It is thus essential that Mexico's leadership make continued political reform a priority. In Delal Baer's words, without reform, Mexico "may end up in a peculiar state of institutional limbo and semi-permanent gridlock: a constitutionally mandated presidential system that operates more like a majority-less parliamentary system."[2]

On the political front, campaign finance reform is one area where some progress is being made, and there are other potentially useful reform initiatives that have been the subject of political debate for some time— for example, reexamining proportional representation and the ban on congressional reelection. The political parties also need to work in tandem to address the critical policy issues at hand, all the while setting aside narrow political interests and personal differences that hinder effective policy-making. What is clear is that Mexico's democracy is far from perfect. As Schedler notes in Chapter 2, the main task ahead is democratizing democracy, a process that could, and perhaps should, last indefinitely.

The course of Mexico's political evolution will be largely determined by a rapidly changing society. Federico Reyes-Heroles explains in Chapter 3 how democratization, urbanization, demographic changes, and economic liberalization have led to a shift in political demands and priorities. The central challenge for current and future leaders is to find the means to successfully address the country's most pressing social needs—alleviating poverty and inequality, investing in infrastructure and human capital, developing Mexico's agricultural sector, among others—through a second phase of economic and social reforms. This will require keen awareness of the new and changing realities of Mexican society, and, most challenging of all, to translate that awareness into political action.

To meet Mexico's changing needs and to make the necessary social investments, policymakers must also focus on generating significant economic growth. As several authors in this volume note, Mexico's growth rate, a disappointing 1.3 percent in 2003, has to exceed 5 percent in order to generate the one million jobs per year needed to absorb the growing labor force. The slowdown of the U.S. economy in 2001 sharply affected Mexico's export-led growth, as U.S. demand for Mexican exports diminished. Although President Fox's success in maintaining inflationary and monetary stability is no small accomplishment, a greater effort to create jobs outside the U.S.-dependent maquiladora sector is imperative, especially as Mexico increasingly loses competitiveness vis-à-vis Asia and Central America, and, as a result, loses jobs in the maquiladora sector at an alarming rate.

What is troublesome, as Russell Crandall indicates in Chapter 4, is that Mexico's declining competitiveness is due not only to a loss of comparative advantage in labor costs—which ultimately benefits Mexican workers if higher labor costs translate into higher wages—but also to structural barriers such as lack of reform in the energy and telecommunications sectors, high manufacturing taxes, rigid labor laws, and poor infrastructure, all of which increase production costs and divert investment and jobs away from Mexico, despite its proximity to the world's largest market, the United States. Although Mexico's export-oriented development strategy under the framework of the North American Free Trade Agreement (NAFTA) has produced many positive results, Gary Gereffi and Martha Martínez argue in Chapter 6 that free trade is not a mechanism that will automatically correct disparities among industries, firms, and individuals. Without proper institutional mechanisms and policy measures, they argue, the benefits of a NAFTA-led economy will continue to fall short of their potential, and new vulnerabilities and grievances will continue to surface.

NAFTA supporters and critics alike agree that Mexico's economic health is precariously tied to the U.S. economy, as events since 2001 have shown. The free trade agreement (FTA) between Mexico and the European Union (EU) signed in 2000 could be an important vehicle to diversify Mexico's export markets and reduce its dependence on the United States. However, as Javier Santiso points out in Chapter 8, the "NAF-TAization" of Mexico's economy has kept the country primarily focused to the north, while at the same time Mexico's attractiveness as a foreign direct investment destination has been limited by lagging reforms in some important sectors where European firms have penetrated elsewhere in Latin America, chief among them energy and telecommunications. But Santiso cautions that even if the Mexico–EU FTA provides a useful institutional framework for deepening economic and diplomatic ties between the two transatlantic partners, a radical change in the bilateral relationship is not likely to take place because Mexico cannot escape its fate: Geographic proximity to the United States will, for the foreseeable future, continue to drive Mexico's external economic relations. Nevertheless, the fact that an institutional framework is already in place will facilitate moving in the right direction.

Whether the issue is NAFTA or free trade agreements in general, one thing is clear: substantial microeconomic reforms in certain key areas are needed in order to broaden the benefits of economic liberalization. In Chapter 5, Manuel Pastor and Carol Wise underscore the need to improve credit market access to help small enterprises better compete in an open economy, as well as the need to promote stronger backward linkages from exporters to domestic suppliers. Fiscal reform is another area where Mexican policymakers must make significant inroads to meet social spending needs and increase human capital investment. As Pastor and Wise point out, although the Mexican Congress did pass a tax reform in late 2001—one that fell far short of the fiscal revenue targets originally set by the Fox administration—the political opposition ultimately succeeded in driving down Fox's approval ratings through the highly publicized battle over some of his more controversial fiscal reform proposals. To be sure, public dissatisfaction with the outcome on fiscal reform and other political initiatives translated into losses for Fox's National Action Party (Partido Acción Nacional, PAN) in the 2003 midterm elections, making the challenge for Fox's success even greater as he entered the second half of his administration.

In the international arena, Mexico's role and regional priorities are evolving as the country increasingly modernizes and integrates into the global economy. When Fox assumed the presidency in 2000, his foreign policy goals centered on deepening Mexico's partnership with the United States, playing an active role in the Free Trade Area of the Americas (FTAA) negotiations, and lifting Mexico's international profile by playing a bolder role in global and regional affairs. But international events and the domestic political climate have limited Fox's ability to achieve these goals.

The terrorist attacks of September 11, 2001, abruptly shifted U.S. priorities, and the central focus of the United States became the war on terrorism; at the same time, the U.S.–Mexico bilateral agenda, which got off to a promising start, lost its momentum. Additionally, Mexico's role in international organizations, such as the United Nations Security Council during deliberations on Iraq or the Organization of American States (OAS) during the debate on the Rio Treaty, has been complicated by pressure at home to maintain an independent foreign policy stance and concomitant pressure abroad to demonstrate support for the U.S.-led war on terrorism. Overall, as stated by Riordan Roett in Chapter 7, the twin challenges of political stalemate and globalization are the critical defining conditions of Fox's presidency, and the central foreign policy initiatives set forth by his administration, although innovative and generally welcomed, have thus far failed to substantially change Mexico's role in the Western Hemisphere. That said, however, there is much to indicate that the next decade or so will witness greater progress in Mexico's foreign policy efforts to deepen the bilateral relationship with the United States and to bolster the country's international role.

The peaceful transition in 2000 from more than 70 years of single-party authoritarian rule to democracy, and the economic stability that accompanied this historic transition, demonstrate that Mexico's reform process over the past decades has been in many respects successful, yet, as noted in Chapter 1, Mexico is far from the end of history.[3] Rather, Mexico is at a critical juncture marked by the challenges of democratic change. The first years of Mexico's democratic transition have been characterized by political stalemate, and, as a result, by public disappointment with the new regime. And the key question is, will future administrations fare better, or will failure to build on the existing institutions lead to a serious decay of the political system and perhaps even to a gradual unraveling of Mexico's social and economic fabric?

The answer will depend on the political players themselves. The dual challenge is to allow Mexico's democracy to mature and at the same time aggressively tackle the country's most pressing economic and social needs. Much can be learned from Mexico's reform process thus far and from President Fox's shortcomings and successes. There is no doubt that public disillusionment with the Fox administration is due in part to the unreasonably high expectations placed on his government at the start of his term—expectations that he himself did little to assuage. But regardless of whether Fox succeeds in shifting the political tide in his favor, Mexicans must not lose sight of the fact that although democracy is never perfect, it is well worth the effort to tirelessly seek its improvement. As the main political parties prepare for the 2006 presidential elections, it is evident that, regardless of the electoral outcome, successful policymaking will in large part depend on the ability and willingness of political leaders to act pragmatically and to build coalitions within Mexico's new democratic context. It is thus essential to learn from Mexico's recent past as we look to the future, a future filled not only with challenges, but also opportunities.

Notes

1 . For more on the current political and economic landscape in Mexico see M. Delal Baer, "Mexico at an Impasse," *Foreign Affairs* 84, no. 1 (January–February 2004): 101–113.

2. Ibid., p. 106.

3. Francis Fukuyama, "The End of History?" *The National Interest* 16 (Summer 1989): 3–18.

Acronyms

BBVA	Banco Bilbao Vizcaya Argentaria
BIE	Economic Information Bank (Banco de Información Económica
BIS	Bank for International Settlements
BSCH	Banco Santander Central Hispano
CAFTA	Central American Free Trade Agreement
CEOs	chief executive officers
CFOs	chief financial officers
CIPI	Intersecretarial Commission for Industrial Policy (Comisión Intersecretarial de Política Industrial)
CNC	National Peasants Confederation (Confederación Nacional Campesina)
COCOPA	Commission for Peace and Reconciliation (Comisión de Concordia y Pacificación)
COMPITE	National Committee for Productivity and Technological Innovation (Comité Nacional de Productividad e Innovación Tecnológica)
CRECE	Regional Centers for Business Competitiveness (Centros Regionales para la Competitividad Empresarial)
ECLAC	Economic Commission for Latin America and the Caribbean
EPR	People's Revolutionary Army (Ejército Popular Revolucionario)
EU	European Union

EZLN	Zapatista Army for National Liberation (Ejército Zapatista de Liberación Nacional)
FARP	Revolutionary Armed Forces of the People (Fuerzas Armadas Revolucionarias del Pueblo)
FDI	foreign direct investment
Fobaproa	Savings Protection Banking Fund (Fondo Bancario de Protección al Ahorro)
FTA	free trade agreement
FTAA	Free Trade Area of the Americas
GATT	General Agreement on Tariffs and Trade
GDP	gross domestic product
IADB	Inter-American Development Bank
IBEX	Indice Bursátil
IFE	Federal Electoral Institute (Instituto Federal Electoral)
IMF	International Monetary Fund
INEGI	National Institute of Statistics, Geography, and Informatics (Instituto Nacional de Estadística, Geografía e Informática)
IPAB	Institute for the Protection of Bank Savings (Instituto para la Protección al Ahorro Bancario)
ISI	import-substitution industrialization
NAFTA	North American Free Trade Agreement
NATO	North Atlantic Treaty Organization
OAS	Organization of American States
OBM	original brand-name manufacturing
ODM	original design manufacturing
OECD	Organization for Economic Cooperation and Development
OEM	original equipment manufacturing
PAN	National Action Party (Partido Acción Nacional)
PPP	Puebla-Panama Plan
PRD	Party of the Democratic Revolution (Partido de la Revolución Democrática)
PRI	Institutional Revolutionary Party (Partido Revolucionario Institucional)
PROGRESA	National Education, Health, and Nutrition Program (Programa Nacional de Educación, Salud y Alimentación)
PRONASOL	National Solidarity Program (Programa Nacional de Solidaridad)

PROPICE	Industrial Policy and Foreign Trade Program (Programa de Política Industrial y Comercio Exterior)
PSUM	Unified Socialist Party of Mexico (Partido Socialista Unificado de México)
SECODAM	Secretariat of the Comptroller and Administrative Development (Secretaría de la Contraloría y Desarrollo Administrativo)
SECOFI	Secretariat of Commerce and Industrial Development (Secretaría de Comercio y Fomento Industrial)
SEDESOL	Ministry of Social Development (Secretaría de Desarrollo Social)
SFP	Government Audit Office (Secretaría de la Función Pública)
SMEs	small and medium-sized firms
SSP	Secretariat of Public Security (Secretaría de Seguridad Pública)
TEPJF	Electoral Tribunal of the Judicial Power of the Federation (Tribunal Electoral del Poder Judicial de la Federación)
TPA	trade promotion authority
UNCTAD	United Nations Conference on Trade and Development
USITC	United States International Trade Commission
VAT	value-added tax
WDI	World Development Indicators
WTO	World Trade Organization

Bibliography

Abrams, Elliott. "Fox Populi: Thanks to NAFTA and Zedillo, Mexico Finally Holds a Democratic Election." *Weekly Standard* 356, no. 8178 (July 2000): 31–32.

Aguilar García, Javier. "El perfil de la política laboral y sindical de Vicente Fox." *Estudios Políticos* (January–April 2001): 153–170.

Alcocer V., Jorge. "Recent Electoral Reforms in Mexico: Prospects for a Real Multiparty Democracy." In *The Challenge of Institutional Reform in Mexico,* edited by Riordan Roett, 57–75. Boulder, CO: Lynne Rienner Publishers, 1995.

Alemán, Marcos. "Central America Joins Mexico in Major Development Plan." *Associated Press,* 16 June 2001.

América Economía. "México prevé crecimiento PIB 1.74 porciento en 2002." 17 October 2001.

Andreas, Peter. *Border Games: Policing the U.S.-Mexico Divide.* Ithaca, NY: Cornell University Press, 2000.

A.T. Kearney. "FDI Confidence Index." A.T. Kearney Global Business Policy Council, vol. 4 (February 2001), Alexandria, VA.

———. "FDI Confidence Index." A.T. Kearney Global Business Policy Council, vol. 5 (September 2002), Alexandria, VA.

———. "FDI Confidence Index." A.T. Kearney Global Business Policy Council, vol. 6 (September 2003), Alexandria, VA.

Authers, John. "U.S. Problems Have an Impact South of the Border." *Financial Times,* 27 June 2002, 29.

———. "Bank of Mexico Acts on Inflation Before Wage Round." *Financial Times,* 21 February 2004, 4.

———. "Mexico Boosts Tax Collection Despite Sluggish Growth." *Financial Times,* 23 February 2004, 3.

Baer, M. Delal. "Mexico at an Impasse." *Foreign Affairs* 84, no. 1 (January–February 2004): 101–113.

Bair, Jennifer, and Gary Gereffi. "Local Clusters in Global Chains: The Causes and Consequences of Export Dynamism in Torreon's Blue Jeans Industry." *World Development* 29, no. 11 (November 2001): 1885–1903.

Banco de México. "Inversión Extranjera Directa, Cuadro A52: Principales Indicadores del Sector Externo." *Apéndice Estadístico–Informe Annual 2002.* Mexico City: Bank of Mexico, 2002, 193.

Basáñez, Miguel, and Alejandro Moreno. *World Values Survey 1990–1993.* Mexico City: MORI de México, 1990.

Bauman, Zygmunt. *Intimations of Postmodernity.* London: Routledge, 1992.

Becerra, Ricardo, Jesús Galindo, Manuel Palma, and José Woldenberg. *Así se vota en la República: Las legislaciones electorales en los estados.* Mexico City: Instituto de Estudios para la Transición Democrática, 1996.

Becerra, Ricardo, Pedro Salazar, and José Woldenberg. *La mecánica del cambio político en México: Elecciones, partidos y reformas.* Mexico City: Cal y Arena, 2000.

Behrman, Jere, Nancy Birdsall, and Miguel Székely. "Economic Reform and Wage Differentials in Latin America." Working Paper 435, Inter-American Development Bank, Washington, DC, 2000.

Bennett, Douglas C., and Kenneth E. Sharpe. *Transnational Corporations Versus the State: The Political Economy of the Mexican Auto Industry.* Princeton, NJ: Princeton University Press, 1985.

Berlanga-Albrecht, Luis A. "Maquiladoras japonesas en Tijuana: Estructura productiva y cadenas mundiales de insumos." *Comercio Exterior* 49, no. 9 (1999): 821–829.

Bislev, Sven. "Introduction." In *Economic Integration in NAFTA and the EU,* edited by Kirsten Appendini and Sven Bislev, 1–16. New York: Palgrave MacMillan, 1999.

Blancarte, Roberto J. "The 1992 Reforms of Mexican Law on Religion: Prospects of Changing State-Church Relations." In *The Challenge of Institutional Reform in Mexico,* edited by Riordan Roett, 95–113. Boulder, CO: Lynne Rienner Publishers, 1995.

Blázquez, Jorge, and Javier Santiso. "Mexico: Is It an Ex-Emerging Market?" *Journal of Latin American Studies,* 36, no. 2 (May 2004): 297–318.

Bloom, David E., David Canning, and Jaypee Sevilla. *The Demographic Dividend: A New Perspective on the Economic Consequences of Population Change.* Santa Monica, CA: RAND, 2002. Available online at www.rand.org, last accessed March 2004.

Brownlee, Jason M. "Double-Edged Institutions: Electoral Authoritarianism in Egypt and Iran." 97th Meeting of the American Political Science Association (APSA), San Francisco, CA, 30 August–2 September 2001.

Buendía, Jorge. "Economic Reform, Public Opinion, and Presidential Approval in Mexico, 1988–1993." *Comparative Political Studies* 29, no. 5 (1996): 575–576.

Business Week. "Mexico's Makeover." 21 December 1998 (International Edition), 50–51.

Cabrera Lemuz, Adalid. "Mexico, Brazil Look to Foster Greater Latin American Integration." *Associated Press,* 2 July 2002.

Cámara de Diputados, H. Congreso de la Unión. "Composición de la Cámara por Partido." Mexican Chamber of Deputies, available online at www.cddhcu. gob.mx, last accessed September 2003.

———. "Integración LVIII Legislatura." Mexican Chamber of Deputies, available online at www.cddhcu.gob.mx, last accessed September 2003.

Cameron, Maxwell A., and Brian W. Tomlin. *The Making of NAFTA: How the Deal Was Done.* Ithaca, NY: Cornell University Press, 2000.

Cameron, Maxwell, and Carol Wise. "The Impact of NAFTA on Mexico." *Canadian Journal of Political Science,* forthcoming.

Camil, Jorge. "Sexenios monotemáticos." *La Jornada,* 7 January 2000, Opinión. Available online at www.jornada.unam.mx/2000/ene00/000107/camil.html, last accessed April 2003.

Campos, José Edgardo, and Hiltion Root. *The Key to the Asian Miracle: Making Shared Growth Credible.* Washington, DC: Brookings Institution Press, 1996.

Camus, Albert. *The Myth of Sisyphus and Other Essays.* New York: Vintage International, 1991 [original 1942].

Cansino, César. *La Transición Mexicana 1977–2000.* Mexico City: Centro de Estudios de Política Comparada, 2000.

Carrillo, Jorge, and Alfredo Hualde. "Third Generation Maquiladoras? The Delphi-General Motors Case." *Journal of Borderlands Studies* 13, no. 1 (Spring 1998): 79–97.

Casanova, Lourdes. "Lazos de familia: Las inversiones españolas en Iberoamérica." *Foreign Affairs en Español* 2, no. 2 (Spring 2002): 67–85.

Case, William F. "Can the 'Halfway House' Stand? Semidemocracy and Elite Theory in Three Southeast Asian Countries." *Comparative Politics* 28, no. 4 (1996): 437–465.

Castañeda, Jorge. Speech given by the secretary of foreign affairs during his appearance before the Senate Foreign Relations Committee, Mexico City, 11 December 2001. Available online at www.sre.gob.mx/comunicados/discursos/ disc_2001/d-03-01.htm.

Cazenove & Co. Spain Research. "Argentina and the Spanish Banks." London, 26 March 2001.

Centeno, Miguel Angel. *Democracy Within Reason: Technocratic Revolution in Mexico.* University Park: Pennsylvania State University Press, 1994.

Chand, Vikram K. *Mexico's Political Awakening.* Notre Dame, IN: University of Notre Dame Press, 2001.

Chávez, María Flor, María Beatriz García, Heliana Monserrat, Josefina Robles, Eunice Taboada, and Leticia Velásquez. *Estudios Sectoriales de las Manufacturas Mexicanas.* Mexico City: Universidad Autónoma Metropolitana, 2000.

Clifford, Richard. "Growth and Competitiveness." In *Mexico—A Comprehensive Development Agenda for the New Era,* edited by Marcelo M. Giugale, Oliver Lafourcade, and Vinh H. Nguyen, 59–83. Washington, DC: World Bank, 2001.

Colburn, Forrest. *Latin America at the End of Politics.* Princeton, NJ: Princeton University Press, 2002.

Colitt, Raymond. "Multinationals Shifting Strategies: Direct Foreign Investment in Brazil." *Financial Times,* 8 March 2002, 4.

Collier, David, and Steven Levitsky. "Democracy with Adjectives: Conceptual Innovation in Comparative Research." *World Politics* 49 (April 1997): 430–451.

Commerzbank. "Repsol-YPF: Latam Field Trip Report." Commerzbank Securities, Spain Oil & Gas, London, 14 May 2001.

Conger, Lucy. "Mexico's Long March to Democracy." *Current History* 100, no. 643 (Fall 2001): 58–64.

Consejo Nacional de la Población (CONAPO). *La situación demográfica de México.* Mexico City: CONAPO, 1999.

———. *Proyecciones de la población de México, 2000–2050.* Mexico City: CONAPO, 2002.

———. "Migración mexicana hacia los Estados Unidos." Migración internacional. Available online at www.conapo.gob.mx, last accessed March 2004.

———. "Tasa global de fecundidad, 1960–2000." Indicadores de salud reproductiva, República Mexicana, Población de México en Cifras. Available online at www.conapo.gob.mx, last accessed March 2004.

Contreras, Oscar. *Empresas Globales, Actores Locales: Producción Flexible y Aprendizaje Industrial en las Maquiladoras.* Mexico City: El Colegio de México-Centro de Estudios Sociológicos, 2000.

Cook, Maria Lorena, Kevin Middlebrook, and Juan Molinar Horcasitas. "The Politics of Economic Restructuring in Mexico: Actors, Sequencing, and Coalition Change." In *The Politics of Economic Restructuring: State-Society Relations and Regime Change in Mexico,* edited by Maria Lorena Cook, Kevin Middlebrook, and Juan Molinar Horcasitas, 3–52. La Jolla: Center for U.S.-Mexican Studies, University of California–San Diego, 1994.

Cornelius, Wayne, Ann L. Craig, and Jonathan Fox, editors. *Transforming State-Society Relations in Mexico: The National Solidarity Strategy.* La Jolla: Center for U.S.-Mexican Studies, University of California–San Diego, 1994.

———. "Death at the Border." *Population and Development Review* 27, no. 4 (2001): 661–685.

Crandall, Russell. "Revolution on Hold?" *SAIS Review* 13, no. 1 (Winter–Spring 2003): 273–277.

———. "Mexico's Changing Domestic and International Dynamics." In *Latin America in a Changing Global Environment,* edited by Riordan Roett and Guadalupe Paz, 171–187. Boulder, CO: Lynne Rienner Publishers, 2003.

Crédit Agricole Indosuez Cheuvreux. "BBVA and BSCH." Crédit Agricole Indosuez Cheuvreux, Madrid, 30 March 2001.

———. "Spanish Banks Quaterly: Latam Risk Increases." Crédit Agricole Indosuez Cheuvreux, Madrid, 15 May 2001.

Crespo, José Antonio. *Votar en los estados: Análisis comparado de las legislaciones electorales estatales.* Mexico City: CIDE, Friedrich Nauman Foundation, and Miguel Angel Porrúa, 1996.

―――. "Balance electoral de 1997." *Metapolítica* 1, no. 4 (October–December 1997): 660.

―――. *Fronteras democráticas en México: Retos, peculiaridades y comparaciones.* Mexico City: Océano, 1999.

―――. "La reforma electoral pendiente." *Política y Gobierno* 7, no. 2 (2000): 445–480.

―――. "Raising the Bar: The Next Generation of Electoral Reforms in Mexico." Policy Papers on the Americas, Center for Strategic and International Studies, Washington, DC, 2000.

Crystal, Jennifer, Gerard Dages, and Linda Goldberg. "Foreign and Domestic Bank Participation in Emerging Markets: Lessons from Mexico and Argentina." *Federal Reserve Bank of New York Policy Review* 6, no. 3 (September 2000): 17–36.

―――. "Does Foreign Ownership Contribute to Sounder Banks in Emerging Markets? The Latin American Experience." In *Open Doors: Foreign Participation in Financial Systems in Developing Countries,* edited by Robert E. Litan, Paul Masson, and Michael Pomerleano, 217–266. Washington, DC: Brookings Institution Press, 2001.

―――. "Has Foreign Bank Entry Led to Sounder Banks in Latin America?" *Federal Reserve Bank of New York Current Issues in Economics and Finance* 8, no. 1 (January 2002).

Dahl, Robert A. *Polyarchy: Participation and Opposition.* New Haven, CT: Yale University Press, 1971.

Damgaard, Bodil. "Labour and Economic Integration: The Case of the Electronic Sector in Mexico." In *Economic Integration in NAFTA and the EU,* edited by Kirsten Appendini and Sven Bislev, 89–105. New York: Palgrave MacMillan, 1999.

Day, Paul. "Gridlocked." *Business Mexico,* November 2001, 26–27.

De Córdoba, José, and Russell Gold. "Pemex to Increase Spending on Energy Exploration." *Wall Street Journal,* 16 September 2003, A3, A8.

De la Balze, Felipe A. M. "Finding Allies in the Back Yard: NAFTA and the Southern Cone." *Foreign Affairs* 80, no. 4 (July–August 2001): 7–12.

De la Garza, Enrique. "The Restructuring of State-Labor Relations in Mexico." In *The Politics of Economic Restructuring: State-Society Relations and Regime Change in Mexico,* edited by Maria Lorena Cook, Kevin J. Middlebrook, and Juan Molinar Horcasitas, 195–219. La Jolla: University of California–San Diego, 1994.

De la Rosa Mendoza, Juan Ramiro. "Relaciones entre apertura y crecimiento económico en México." *Comercio Exterior* 51, no. 5 (May 2001): 438–445.

Deutsche Bank. "Spain's Sensitivity to Latin America." Deutsche Bank Europe Equity Research, Madrid, 24 May 2001.

DeYoung, Karen. "OAS Nations Activate Mutual Defense Treaty." *Washington Post,* 20 September 2001, A18.

Diamond, Larry. *Developing Democracy: Toward Consolidation.* Baltimore: Johns Hopkins University Press, 1999.

―――. "Elections Without Democracy: Thinking About Hybrid Regimes." *Journal of Democracy* 13, no. 2 (April 2002): 21–35.

Dietz, James L. *Latin America's Economic Development: Confronting Crisis,* 2nd ed. Boulder, CO: Lynne Rienner Publishers, 1995.

Di Palma, Giuseppe. *To Craft Democracies: An Essay on Democratic Transitions.* Berkeley: University of California Press, 1990.

Dornbusch, Rudiger. "The Folly, The Crash, and Beyond: Economic Policies and the Crisis." In *Mexico 1994: Anatomy of an Emerging-Market Crash,* edited by Sebastian Edwards and Moisés Naím, 125–140. Washington, DC: Carnegie Endowment for International Peace, 1997.

Dresser, Denise. "Falling from the Tightrope: The Political Economy of the Mexican Crisis." In *Mexico 1994: Anatomy of an Emerging-Market Crash,* edited by Sebastian Edwards and Moisés Naím, 55–79. Washington, DC: Carnegie Endowment for International Peace, 1997.

Dunning, John. "European Foreign Direct Investment in Latin America." In Inter-American Development Bank (IADB), *Foreign Investment in Latin America: The Role of European Investors,* 143–175. Washington, DC: IADB, 2001.

Dussel Peters, Enrique. *Polarizing Mexico: The Impact of Liberalization Strategy.* Boulder, CO: Lynne Rienner Publishers, 2000.

———. "Industrial Policy, Regional Trends, and Structural Change in Mexico's Manufacturing Sector." In *Confronting Development: Assessing Mexico's Economic and Social Policy Challenges,* edited by Kevin Middlebrook and Eduardo Zepeda, 241–274. Palo Alto, CA: Stanford University Press, 2002.

Economic Commission for Latin America and the Caribbean (ECLAC). *Foreign Investment in Latin America and the Caribbean, 2000 Report.* New York: United Nations, 2001.

———. *Foreign Direct Investment in Latin America and the Caribbean, 2001 Report.* New York: United Nations, 2002.

The Economist. "Latin Lessons for Asian Banks." 23 July 1998, 22.

———. "Happy Birthday, Señor Fox." 8 July 2000, 31–32.

———. "PRIde before the Fall." 26 October 2000, Mexico Survey Section, 5–7.

———. "E-Strategy Brief: The Cemex Way." 16 June 2001, 75–76.

———. "Fox's Moment of Truth." 1 September 2001, 31–32.

———. "The Lady Vanishes." 6 December 2002, 33.

———. "Peculiar Practices." 31 May 2003, 36.

———. "The Sucking Sound From the East." 26 July 2003, 35.

———. "Food for Argument." 22 November 2003, 37.

Economist Intelligence Unit. "Country Report: Mexico." *EIU Country Reports.* July 2000–July 2001; January 2002; April 2002.

———. "Mexico Finance: Recovery in Corporate Lending Still Distant." *Country Briefing,* Country ViewsWire Mexico, Economist Intelligence Unit, 19 July 2002.

Edwards, Sebastian. *Crisis and Reform in Latin America: From Despair to Hope.* Washington, DC: World Bank, 1995.

Eisenstadt, Todd A. "Off the Streets and into the Courtrooms: Resolving Postelectoral Conflicts in Mexico." In *The Self-Restraining State: Power and Accountability in New Democracies,* edited by Andreas Schedler, Larry Diamond, and Marc F. Plattner, 83–104. Boulder, CO: Lynne Rienner Publishers, 1999.

————. "Eddies in the Third Wave: Protracted Transitions and Theories of Democratization." *Democratization* 7, no. 3 (2000): 3–24.

————. *Courting Democracy in Mexico: Party Strategies and Electoral Institutions.* Cambridge: Cambridge University Press, 2004.

Elklit, Jørgen, and Palle Svensson. "What Makes Elections Free and Fair?" *Journal of Democracy* 8, no. 3 (1997): 32–46.

European Union. "Joint Press Release, Third EU–Mexico Joint Council Meeting, 27 March 2003." Brussels: European Union, 2003. Available online at http://europa.eu.int/comm/external_relations/w13/10.htm.

————. "Bilateral Trade Relations: Mexico." Brussels: European Union, 2003. Available online: http://europa.eu.int/comm/trade/bilateral/mexico/index _enhtm, last accessed October 2003.

————. "EU Foreign Direct Investment with Mexico." Brussels: European Union, 2003. Available online at: http://europa.eu.int/comm/trade/issues/bilateral/ countries/mexico/docs/econo_mexico.xls, last accessed October 2003.

Ferriss, Susan. "Broken Promises: Mexicans Rely on Dwindling Export Assembly Work." *Cox News Service,* October 30, 2003.

————. "Broken Promises: Mexico's Cash Economy a Symptom of Failed Reforms." *Cox News Service,* December 16, 2003.

Field, Alan M. "Headed South: The Economy and China's Emergence as a Low-Cost Manufacturing Center Are Taking a Toll on U.S.–Mexico Trade." *Journal of Commerce,* 14 April 2003, 19.

Financial Times. "A System That Needs Some Simplifying." *Financial Times,* 14 December 2000, 3.

————. "Central States Dominate the Action." *Financial Times,* 14 December 2000, 4.

————. "Putting 'Missed' Chances Behind." *Financial Times,* 14 December 2000, 5.

Fry, Earl H. "North American Economic Integration: Policy Options." *Policy Papers on the Americas,* July 2003, vol. 14, study 8.

Fukuyama, Francis. "The End of History?" *The National Interest* 16 (Summer 1989): 3–18.

García Barrios, Raúl. "Free Trade and Local Institutions: The Case of Mexican Peasants." In *Economic Integration in NAFTA and the EU,* edited by Kirsten Appendini and Sven Bislev, 34–50. New York: Palgrave MacMillan, 1999.

Gereffi, Gary. *The Pharmaceutical Industry and Dependency in the Third World.* Princeton, NJ: Princeton University Press, 1983.

————. "Global Production Systems and Third World Development." In *Global Change, Regional Response,* edited by Barbara Stallings, 100–142. New York: Cambridge University Press, 1995.

————. "Mexico's 'Old' and 'New' Maquiladora Industries: Contrasting Approaches to North American Integration." In *Neoliberalism Revisited: Economic Restructuring and Mexico's Political Future,* edited by Gerardo Otero, 85–105. Boulder, CO: Westview Press, 1996.

————. "International Trade and Industrial Upgrading in the Apparel Commodity Chain." *Journal of International Economics* 48, no. 1 (June 1999): 37–70.

————. "The Transformation of the North American Apparel Industry: Is NAFTA a Curse or a Blessing?" *Integration and Trade* 4, no. 11 (May–August 2000): 47–95.

————. "Shifting Governance Structures in Global Commodity Chains, with Special Reference to the Internet." *American Behavioral Scientist* 44, no. 10 (June 2001): 1616–1637.

————. "Mexico's Industrial Development: Climbing Ahead or Falling Behind in the World Economy?" In *Confronting Development: Assessing Mexico's Economic and Social Policy Challenges,* edited by Kevin J. Middlebrook and Eduardo Zepeda, 195–240. Stanford: Stanford University Press and Center for U.S.-Mexican Studies, University of California–San Diego, 2003.

————. "The Global Economy: Organization, Governance, and Development." In *Handbook of Economic Sociology,* 2nd ed., edited by Neil Smelser and Richard Swedberg. Princeton, NJ: Princeton University Press, 2004.

Gereffi, Gary, Martha Martínez, and Jennifer Bair. "Torreon: The New Blue Jeans Capital of the World." In *Free Trade and Uneven Development: The North American Apparel Industry after NAFTA,* 203–223. Philadelphia: Temple University Press, 2002.

Gereffi, Gary, David Spener, and Jennifer Bair, eds. *Free Trade and Uneven Development: The North American Apparel Industry after NAFTA.* Philadelphia: Temple University Press, 2002.

Gereffi, Gary, and Donald L. Wyman, eds. *Manufacturing Miracles: Paths of Industrialization in Latin America and East Asia.* Princeton, NJ: Princeton University Press, 1990.

Gill, Manohar Singh. "India: Running the World's Biggest Elections." *Journal of Democracy* 9, no. 1 (January 1998): 164–168.

Gilomee, Hermann, and Charles Simkins, eds. *The Awkward Embrace: One-Party Domination and Democracy.* Amsterdam: Harwood Academic Publishers, 1999.

Giugale, Marcelo M. "A Comprehensive Development Agenda for the New Era—Synthesis." In *Mexico: A Comprehensive Development Agenda for the New Era,* edited by Marcelo M. Giugale, Olivier Lafourcade, and Vinh H. Nguyen, 1–22. Washington, DC: World Bank, 2001.

Giugale, Marcelo M., Olivier Lafourcade, and Vinh H. Nguyen. *Mexico: A Comprehensive Development Agenda for the New Era.* Washington, DC: World Bank, 2001.

Goldberg, Linda, Gerard Dages, and Daniel Kinney. "Foreign and Domestic Bank Participation in Emerging Markets: Lessons from Mexico and Argentina." *Federal Reserve Bank of New York Policy Review* 6, no. 3 (September 2000): 17–36.

González Souza, Luis. "Entre el TLC y el EZLN." *La Jornada,* 9 January 1999, Opinión. Available online at www.jornada.unam.mx/1999/ene99/990109/souza.html, last accessed April 2003.

————. "¿Alianzas con EU?" *La Jornada,* 25 September 1999, Opinión. Available online at www.jornada.unam.mx/1999/sep99/990925/gonzalez.html, last accessed April 2003.

Gore, Charles. "The Rise and Fall of the Washington Consensus as a Paradigm for Developing Countries." *World Development* 28, no. 5 (May 2000): 789–804.

Gori, Graham. "Mexico Plays a North-South Divide." *New York Times,* 16 July 2002, A1.

Grinspun, Ricardo, and Roberto Kreklewich. "Institutions, Power Relations and Unequal Integration in the Americas: NAFTA as Deficient Institutionality." In *Economic Integration in NAFTA and the EU,* edited by Kirsten Appendini and Sven Bislev, 17–33. New York: Palgrave MacMillan, 1999.

Grupo Financiero Banamex-Accival. *México Social 1996–1998 Estadísticas Seleccionadas.* Mexico City: Banamex, 1998.

Guillén, Mauro, and Adrian Tschoegl. "At Last the Internationalization of Retail Banking? The Case of Spanish Banks in Latin America." Wharton Financial Institutions Center Working Paper, no. 99–41, The Wharton School of Business, University of Pennsylvania, 1999 (unpublished).

Hakim, Peter. "Two Ways to Go Global." *Foreign Affairs* 81, no. 1 (January–February 2002): 148–162.

Hanson, Gordon, and Ann Harrison. "Trade Liberalization and Wage Inequality in Mexico." *Industrial and Labor Relations Review* 52, no. 2 (1999): 271–288.

Heath, Jonathan. "The Impact of Mexico's Trade Liberalization: Jobs, Productivity, and Structural Change." In *The Post-NAFTA Political Economy: Mexico and the Western Hemisphere,* edited by Carol Wise, 171–200. University Park: Pennsylvania State University Press, 1998.

———. *Mexico and the Sexenio Curse: Presidential Successions and Economic Crises in Modern Mexico.* Washington, DC: Center for Strategic and International Studies, 1999.

———. "El voto y la economía." *Reforma,* 8 July 2003, Negocios section.

Hellman, Judith Adler. "Opting for Fox: Why, and How, Mexicans Went for the PAN." *Report on the Americas* 34, no. 2 (September–October 2000): 6–10.

Hernansanz, Carmen, and Miguel Sebastian. "The Spanish Banks' Strategy in Latin America." BBVA Working Paper, no. 3 (October 2000), Madrid.

Hirschman, Albert O. "A Generalized Linkage Approach to Development, with Special Reference to Staples." *Economic Development and Cultural Change* 25, Supplement (1977): 67–98.

———. *A Propensity to Self-Subversion.* Cambridge, MA: Harvard University Press, 1995.

Hof, Robert D., Peter Elstrom, Steve Hamm, Marcia Stepanek, William Echikson, and Peter Burrows. "The Tech Slump." *Business Week,* no. 3712, 18 December 2000, 54–59.

Holmes, Stephen. *Passions and Constraint: On the Theory of Liberal Democracy.* Chicago: University of Chicago Press, 1995.

HSBC. "BSCH: A Time to Consolidate." HSBC Equity Research, London, 3 April 2001.

Huntington, Samuel P. *The Third Wave: Democratization in the Late Twentieth Century.* Norman: University of Oklahoma Press, 1991.

ING Barings. "Telefónica: Latin America Increases Group Risk." ING Barings Equity Markets, Madrid, 21 May 2001.

Inglehart, Ronald, Miguel Basáñez, and Alejandro Moreno. *Human Values and Beliefs: A Cross-Cultural Sourcebook.* Ann Arbor: University of Michigan Press, 1998.

Instituto Mexicano de Opinión Pública (IMOP-Gallup Mexico). *World Values Survey 1981–1984.* Mexico City: IMOP, 1981.

Instituto Nacional de Estadística, Geografía e Informática (INEGI). "Asegurados Permanentes en el IMSS por Sectores de Actividad Económica." Banco de Información Económica (BIE), Empleo y Desempleo. Available online at www.inegi.gob.mx/difusion/espanol/fbie.html, last accessed April 2003.

———. "Exportaciones Petroleras y No Petroleras." Banco de Información Económica (BIE), Sector Externo. Available online at www.inegi.gob.mx/difusion/espanol/fbie.html, last accessed April 2003.

———. "Hogares y su Población por Entidad Federativa y Grupos de Edad del Jefe del Hogar, y su Distribución Según Sexo del Jefe del Hogar." *XII Censo General de la Población y Vivienda 2000.* Mexico City: INEGI, 2000. Available online at www.inegi.gob.mx, last accessed March 2004.

———. "Indicadores Mensuales por Entidad Federativa, Total Nacional." Banco de Información Económica (BIE), Industria Maquiladora de Exportación, INEGI. Available online at www.inegi.gob.mx/difusion/espanol/fbie.html, last accessed April 2003.

———. "Personal Ocupado Remunerado." Banco de Información Económica (BIE), Industria Maquiladora de Exportación. Available online at www.inegi.gob.mx/difusion/espanol/fbie.html, last accessed April 2003.

———. "Porcentaje de población por tamaño de localidad, 1950–2000." *Estadísticas sociodemográficas.* Available online at www.inegi.gob.mx, last accessed March 2004.

———. "Producto Interno Bruto Trimestral a Precios Corrientes por Gran División de Actividad Económica." Banco de Información Económica (BIE), Indicadores Económicos de Coyuntura. Available online at www.inegi.gob.mx/difusion/espanol/fbie.html, last accessed April 2003.

———. "Tasa de crecimiento media anual, 1950–2000." Dinámica de la Población. Available online at www.inegi.gob.mx, last accessed March 2004.

———. "Valor Agregado de Exportación." Banco de Información Económica (BIE), Industria Maquiladora de Exportación. Available online at www.inegi.gob.mx/difusion/espanol/fbie.html, last accessed April 2003.

Inter-American Development Bank. *Facing Up to Inequality in Latin America.* Baltimore: Johns Hopkins University Press, 1998.

JP Morgan, "Emerging Markets Outlook," *JP Morgan,* 2 May 2002.

Jordan, Mary, and Kevin Sullivan. "The New Face of Mexico: Vicente Fox's Mexican Revolution." *Harvard International Review* 23, no. 1 (Spring 2001): 24–28.

———. "Mexico Plans a Tighter Grip on Its Border to the South." *Washington Post,* 18 June 2001, A1.

Karl, Terry Lynn. "The Hybrid Regimes of Latin America." *Journal of Democracy* 6, no. 3 (1995): 72–86.

Katz, Jorge, and Giovanni Stumpo. "Regímenes competitivos sectoriales, productividad y competitividad internacional." Economic Commission on Latin

America and the Caribbean (ECLAC), Santiago, Chile, 8 March 2001 (unpublished).

Kaufman, Robert, and Leo Zuckerman. "Attitudes Toward Economic Reform in Mexico: The Role of Political Orientations." *American Political Science Review* 92, no. 2 (1998): 359–374.

Kessler, Timothy. "The Mexican Peso Crash: Causes, Consequences, Comeback." In *Exchange Rate Politics in Latin America,* edited by Carol Wise and Riordan Roett, 43–69. Washington, DC: Brookings Institution Press, 2000.

Klesner, Joseph. "Electoral Politics and Mexico's New Party System." Paper presented at the American Political Science Association (APSA) Annual Meeting, San Francisco, CA, 4–6 September 2001.

Kousser, J. Morgan. *The Shaping of Southern Politics: Suffrage Restriction and the Establishment of the One-Party South, 1880–1910.* New Haven, CT: Yale University Press, 1974.

Krugman, Paul, and Maurice Obstfeld. *International Economics: Theory and Policy.* New York: Addison Wesley, 2000.

Labastida, Horacio. "Globalización y soberanía nacional." *La Jornada,* 3 March 2002, Opinión. Online www.jornada.unam.mx/2000/mar00/000303/labastida .html, last accessed April 2003.

Lamounier, Bolivar. "Authoritarian Brazil Revisited: The Impact of Elections on the *Abertura.*" In *Democratizing Brazil: Problems of Transition and Consolidation,* edited by Alfred Stepan, 43–79. Oxford: Oxford University Press, 1989.

Lamy, Pascal. "Mexico and the EU: Married Partners, Lovers, or Just Good Friends?" Speech at the Institute of European Integration Studies, Instituto Tecnológico Autónomo de México (ITAM), Mexico City, 29 April 2002.

Lehoucq, Fabrice E. "Can Parties Police Themselves? Electoral Governance and Democratization." *International Political Science Review* 23, no. 1 (2002): 29–46.

Lehoucq, Fabrice E., and Ivan Molina. *Stuffing the Ballot Box: Fraud, Electoral Reform, and Democratization in Costa Rica.* Cambridge: Cambridge University Press, 2002.

Leiken, Robert S. "With a Friend Like Fox." *Foreign Affairs* 80, no. 5 (September–October 2001): 91–104.

Levitsky, Steven, and Lucan A. Way, "Elections Without Democracy: The Rise of Competitive Authoritarianism." *Journal of Democracy* 13, no. 2 (April 2002): 51–65.

Levy, Daniel, and Kathleen Bruhn. *Mexico: The Struggle for Democratic Development.* Berkeley and Los Angeles: University of California Press, 2001.

Levy, Santiago. "Reorienting Mexico's Social Policy." In *Mexico in Transition,* edited by Andrew D. Selee, 27–34. Washington, DC: Woodrow Wilson Center Reports on the Americas, 2001.

Loaeza, Soledad. *El Partido Acción Nacional: la larga marcha 1939–1994— Oposición leal y partido de protesta.* Mexico City: Fondo de Cultura Económica, 1999.

———. "An Unhealthy Distance Between Fox and the National Action Party." *Enfoque* (Fall 2000–Winter 2001): 3.

Luhmann, Niklas. *Legitimation durch Verfahren.* Frankfurt/Main: Suhrkamp, 1983.

Lujambio, Alonso. *Federalismo y congreso en el cambio político de México.* Mexico City: Instituto de Investigaciones Jurídicas, Universidad Nacional Autónoma de México (UNAM), 1995.

———. *El poder compartido: Un ensayo sobre la democratización mexicana.* Mexico City: Editorial Océano, 2000.

Lustig, Nora. *Mexico: The Remaking of an Economy.* 2nd ed. Washington, DC: Brookings Institution Press, 1998.

Lyons, John. "Mexico Seeing Few Advances; In First World Race, Nation Falling Behind." *Houston Chronicle,* 26 November 2003, B1.

MacLachlan, Ian, and Adrián Guillermo Aguilar. "Maquiladora Myths: Locational and Structural Change in Mexico's Export Manufacturing Industry." *Professional Geographer* 50, no. 3 (1998): 315–331.

Malamud, Carlos, ed. *Legitimidad, representación y alternancia en España y América Latina: Las reformas electorales (1880–1930).* Mexico City: Fondo de Cultura Económica, 2000.

Malkin, Elisabeth. "U.S. Economy Recovery Begins to Trickle into Mexico." *New York Times,* 18 February 2004, W1.

Mandel, Michael. "Big Spending on IT Has Made Labor More Vulnerable Than Ever." *Business Week,* no. 3718, 5 February 2001, 42–43.

Mandel-Campbell, Andrea. "Fox Urges Business as Usual on Eve of European Tour." *Financial Times,* 10 October 2001, 13.

Mariña Flores, Abelardo. "Factores Determinantes del Empleo en México." *Comercio Exterior* 51, no. 5 (2001): 410–424.

Massing, Michael. "Seeing Mexico: Twelve Years, Three Leaders, Three Prisms—How We Keep Missing the Big Picture." *Columbia Journalism Review* 40, no. 2 (July–August 2001): 46–50.

Máttar, Jorge, Juan Carlos Moreno-Brid, and Wilson Peres. "Foreign Investment in Mexico after Economic Reform." In *Confronting Development: Assessing Mexico's Economic and Social Policy Challenges,* edited by Kevin Middlebrook and Eduardo Zepeda, 123–160. Palo Alto, CA: Stanford University Press, 2002.

Mayer, Frederick W. *Interpreting NAFTA: The Science and Art of Political Analysis.* New York: Columbia University Press, 1998.

Mazza, Jacqueline. *Don't Disturb the Neighbors: The United States, Democracy, and Mexico.* London: Routledge, 2001.

McCubbins, Matthew D., and Thomas Schwartz. "Congressional Oversight Overlooked: Police Patrols Versus Fire Alarms." *American Journal of Political Science* 28, no. 1 (February 1984): 165–179.

Meave Avila, Cristina. "La Canacar le exige a Fox cerrar la frontera a transportistas de E.U." *Siempre* (Mexico City), no. 2505.

Medina Peña, Luis. "México: Historia de una democracia difícil." In *Elecciones, alternancia y democracia: España-México, una reflexión comparada,* edited by José Varela Ortega and Luis Medina Peña, 195–303. Madrid: Biblioteca Nueva, 2000.

Méndez de Hoyos, Irma. "Electoral Reform and the Rise of Electoral Competitiveness in Mexico, 1977–1997." Ph.D. diss., University of Essex, Colchester, 2000.

Merino, Mauricio. "El Instituto Federal Electoral por dentro: algunas zonas de incertidumbre." In *El Dos de Julio: Reflexiones Posteriores,* edited by Yolanda Meyenberg Leycegui, 39–53. Mexico City: FLACSO, IIS/UNAM, and UAM-Iztapalapa, 2001.

Merrill Lynch. "Fiscal Reform." *Merrill Lynch,* 17 July 2001.

———. "Fiscal Reform." *Merrill Lynch,* 18 July 2001.

Mesenguer, Mariola, and Lourdes Casanova. "Telefónica: The Making of a Multinational." Fontainebleau, France: INSEAD, 1999.

Mexican Secretariat of Economy (Secretaría de Economía). "Mexico's Total Exports." Subsecretaría de Negociaciones Comerciales Internacionales, Inteligencia Comercial, Estadísticas. Available online at www.economia.gob .mx, last accessed March 2004.

———. "Las Negociaciones Comerciales Internacionales en la Nueva Estrategia de Desarrollo de Mexico." Available online at www.economia-snci.gob.mx/sic _php/ls23al.php?s=54&p=1&1=1.

Mexican Secretariat of External Relations. "Relación Mexico–UE." Brussels: Embassy of Mexico. Available online at www.sre.gob.mx/belgica-ue/ relacion_mexico.htm, last accessed October 2003.

Mexican Secretariat of Social Development (Secretaría de Desarrollo Social [SEDESOL]). *¿Está dando buenos resultados Progresa? Informe de los resultados obtenidos de una evaluación realizada por el IFPRI* (International Food Policy Research Institute). Mexico City: SEDESOL, 2000.

México Analytica. "Merrill Lynch espera mayor crecimiento PIB México 2002: de 1.2 a 1.4 porciento." 11 March 2002.

Mexico & NAFTA Report. "President Wields the Veto." 20 March 2001.

———. "The Effects of SARS on Mexico." 16 May 2003.

Millán Bojalil, Julio A., and Antonio Alonso Concheiro, eds. *México 2030, Nuevo siglo, nuevo país.* Mexico City: Fondo de Cultura Económica, 2000.

Millman, Joel, and Carlta Vitzhum. "Mexico's Familial Toehold in Europe." *Wall Street Journal,* 6 August 2002, A11.

Mizrahi, Yemile. *From Martyrdom to Power: The Partido Acción Nacional in Mexico.* Notre Dame, IN: University of Notre Dame Press, 2003.

Molinar Horcasitas, Juan. *El tiempo de la legitimidad.* Mexico City: Cal y Arena, 1991.

Moreno, Alejandro. *World Values Survey 2000.* Mexico City: Reforma, 2000.

Morgan Stanley Dean Witter. "Spanish Banking Sector: The Fall and the Rise of the Spanish Empire." Morgan Stanley Dean Witter Europe Equity Research, Madrid, 26 March 2001.

———. "Telefónica: Hedging the Latam Risk." Morgan Stanley Dean Witter Equity Research, Madrid and London, 2 May 2001.

MORI de México, National Poll (Encuesta Nacional), Mexico City, December 1997.

Mortimor, Michael, and Wilson Peres. "La competitividad empresarial en América Latina." *Revista de la CEPAL,* no. 74 (August 2001): 37–59.

Mozaffar, Shaheen, and Andreas Schedler. "The Comparative Study of Electoral Governance—Introduction." *International Political Science Review* 23, no. 1 (2002): 5–27.

National Democratic Institute. "Lessons Learned and Challenges Facing International Election Monitoring." Washington, DC: NDI, 1999.

National Population Council. *La situación demográfica de México.* Mexico City: National Population Council, 1999.

O'Donnell, Guillermo. *Modernization and Bureaucratic Authoritarianism: Studies in South American Politics.* Berkeley: University of California Press, Institute of International Studies, 1979.

———. "Democracy, Law, and Comparative Politics." *Studies in Comparative International Development* 36, no. 1 (Spring 2001): 7–36.

O'Donnell, Guillermo, and Philippe C. Schmitter. *Transitions from Authoritarian Rule: Tentative Conclusions about Uncertain Democracies.* Baltimore: Johns Hopkins University Press, 1986.

Ortiz, Arturo, Héctor Núñez, and Arturo Bonilla. *Cambios Urgentes de la Política Económica a Partir del Año 2000.* Mexico City: Editorial Paz, 2000.

Pastor, Manuel. "Pesos, Policies, and Predictions: Why the Crisis, Why the Surprise, and Why the Recovery." In *The Post-NAFTA Political Economy: Mexico and the Western Hemisphere,* edited by Carol Wise, 119–147. University Park: Pennsylvania State University Press, 1998.

Pastor, Manuel, and Carol Wise. "The Origins and Sustainability of Mexico's Free Trade Policy." *International Organization* 48, no. 3 (1994): 459–489.

———. "State Policy, Distribution, and Neoliberal Economic Reform in Mexico." *Journal of Latin American Studies* 29 (May 1997): 419–456.

———. "Mexican Style Neoliberalism: State Policy and Distributional Stress." In *The Post-NAFTA Political Economy: Mexico and the Western Hemisphere,* edited by Carol Wise, 41–81. University Park: Pennsylvania State University Press, 1998.

———. "The Politics of Second-Generation Reform." *Journal of Democracy* 10, no. 3 (1999): 34–48.

———. "A Long View on the Mexican Political Economy." In *Mexico's Politics and Society in Transition,* edited by Joseph S. Tulchin and Andrew Selee, 179–213. Boulder, CO: Lynne Rienner Publishers, 2003.

Pastor, Robert A. "Bush's North American Agenda." *Washington Post,* 4 September 2001, A19.

Paz Sánchez, Fernando. "Grave crisis en el sector agropecuario y comercial." *Macroeconomía* (Mexico City), no. 94 (May 15, 2001).

Petroleum Economist. "World Gas: Mexico; Reform or Bust." 19 May 2003, 23.

Polaski, Sandra. "Central America and the U.S. Face Challenge—and Chance for Hispanic Breakthrough—on Workers' Rights." *Issue Brief,* February 2003, Carnegie Endowment for International Peace, Washington, DC. Available online at www.ceip.org/pubs, last accessed April 2003.

"President Wields the Veto." *Mexico & NAFTA Report*, March 20, 2001, p. 9.

Przeworski, Adam. "Democracy as a Contingent Outcome of Conflicts." In *Constitutionalism and Democracy,* edited by Jon Elster and Rune Slagstad, 59–80. Cambridge: Cambridge University Press, 1988.

―――. *Democracy and the Market: Political and Economic Reform in Eastern Europe and Latin America.* New York: Cambridge University Press, 1991.

Przeworski, Adam, Michael E. Alvarez, José Antonio Cheibub, and Fernando Limongi. *Democracy and Development: Political Institutions and Well-Being in the World, 1950–1990.* Cambridge: Cambridge University Press, 2000.

Putnam, Robert D. "Diplomacy and Domestic Politics: The Logic of Two-Level Games." *International Organization* 42, no. 3 (1998): 427–460.

Ramírez Cuevas, Jesús. "El Campo: En el Ojo del Huracán." *La Jornada,* 13 March 2003. Available online at www.jornada.unam.mx/2003/ene03/030112/mas-campo.html, last accessed April 2003.

Ramírez de la O, Rogelio. "The Mexican Peso Crisis and Recession of 1994–1995: Preventable Then, Avoidable in the Future?" In *The Mexican Peso Crisis: International Perspectives,* edited by Riordan Roett, 11–32. Boulder, CO: Lynne Rienner Publishers, 1996.

Remmer, Karen. "Elections and Economics in Contemporary Latin America." In *Post-Stabilization Politics in Latin America: Competition, Transition, Collapse,* edited by Carol Wise and Riordan Roett, with Guadalupe Paz, 31–55. Washington, DC: Brookings Institution Press, 2003.

Reséndiz, Julián. "Sin apoyo de la Federación saldrían 50 porciento de maquiladoras." *El Diario,* 17 July 2002.

Reuters. "Fox Calls Defense Pact Obsolete." 8 September 2001.

Reynoso, Diego. "Federalismo y democracia: Las dos dinámicas de la transición mexicana." *Revista Mexicana de Sociología* 63, no. 1 (2002): 3–30.

Roberts, Roxanne, and Ann Gerhart. "The State Dinner That Ended with a Bang: Bush Welcomes Fox with Friendship and Fireworks." *Washington Post,* 6 September 2001, C1.

Robinson, William I. "Latin American and Global Capitalism." *Race & Class* 40, no. 2/3 (1998/1999): 111–131.

Rodríguez Padilla, Víctor. "La política de precios desangra a la planta productiva." *Petróleo y Electricidad,* 6 February 2001.

Roett, Riordan, and Russell Crandall. "The Global Economic Crisis, Contagion, and Institutions: New Realities in Asia and Latin America." *International Political Science Review* 20 (July 1999): 271–283.

Rubio, Luis. "El TLC en el desarrollo de México." *Tres Ensayos: Fobaproa, privatización y TLC.* Mexico City: Cal y Arena, 1999.

Ruiz de la Peña, Alberto. "La quiebra del sector agropecuario, tempestad sobre el campo." *Macroeconomía* (Mexico City), no. 97 (August 15, 2001).

Sanger, David E. "Mexico's President Rewrites the Rules." *New York Times,* 8 September 2001, A1.

Santiso, Javier. "The Quest for El Dorado: Spanish Banks Are Betting on Latin America." *Crédit Agricole Perspectives,* no. 44 (April 2001): 5–8.

Sartori, Giovanni. *Parties and Party Systems: A Framework for Analysis.* Cambridge: Cambridge University Press, 1976.

Schedler, Andreas. "What Is Democratic Consolidation?" *Journal of Democracy* 9, no. 2 (April 1998): 91–107.

———. "Democracy by Delegation: The Path-Dependent Logic of Electoral Reform in Mexico." Paper presented at the 95th Annual Meeting, American Political Science Association (APSA), Atlanta, September 2–5, 1999.

———. "Incertidumbre institucional e inferencias de imparcialidad: El caso del IFE." *Política y Gobierno* 7, no. 2 (2000): 383–421.

———. "Measuring Democratic Consolidation." *Studies in International and Comparative Development* 36, no. 1 (Spring 2001): 61–87.

———. "Elections Without Democracy: The Menu of Manipulation." *Journal of Democracy* 13, no. 2 (2002): 36–50.

———. "The Nested Game of Democratization by Elections." *International Political Science Review* 23, no. 1 (2002): 103–122.

Schurman, Rachel. "Chile's New Entrepreneurs and the 'Economic Miracle': Invisible Hand or a Hand from the State?" *Studies in Comparative International Development* 31, no. 2 (1996): 83–109.

Shapiro, Martin. *Courts: A Comparative and Political Analysis.* Chicago: University of Chicago Press, 1981.

Sheinbaum Pardo, Claudia. "¿Petróleo para México o para EU?" *La Jornada,* 22 February 2000, Opinión. Available online at www.jornada.unam.mx/2000/feb00/000222/pardo.html, last accessed April 2003.

Shepsle, Kenneth A., and Barry R. Weingast. "Structure-Induced Equilibrium and Legislative Choices." *Public Choice* 37 (1981): 503–519.

Shinal, John. "Dead Dot-Coms Can Still Cause Havoc." *Business Week,* no. 3723, 12 March 2001, 50.

Smith, Tony. "Mexico and Brazil Sign Bilateral Trade Pact." *New York Times,* 4 July 2002, W1.

Société Générale. "Telefónica: Bring on the Bulls." SG Equity Research, Paris and London, May 2001.

Solinger, Dorothy J. "Ending One-Party Dominance: Korea, Taiwan, Mexico." *Journal of Democracy* 12, no. 1 (2001): 30–42.

SourceMex. "Terrorist Attacks in U.S. Have Repercussions for Mexico." 26 September 2001.

Sullivan, Kevin, and Mary Jordan. "Fox Laments 'Stalled' Relations Between U.S., Mexico." *Washington Post,* 10 May 2002, A28.

Tardanico, Richard, and Mark B. Rosenberg, eds. *Poverty or Development: Global Restructuring and Regional Transformations in the U.S. South and the Mexican South.* New York: Routledge, 2000.

Téllez, Luis. *La Modernización del Sector Agropecuario y Forestal.* Mexico City: Fondo de Cultura Económica, 1994.

Thompson, Ginger. "Mexico President Urges U.S. to Act Soon on Migrants." *New York Times,* 6 September 2001, A1.

———. "Mexican Leader Visits Castro to Repair Damaged Ties." *New York Times,* 4 February 2002, A6.

———. "Mexico Is Attracting a Better Class of Factory in the South." *New York Times,* 29 June 2002, A3.

———. "Talks in Mexico Push Regional Growth." *New York Times,* 29 June 2002, A3.

Torres, Blanca. "Environmental Cooperation Before and After NAFTA." In *Economic Integration in NAFTA and the EU,* edited by Kirsten Appendini and Sven Bislev, 106–123. New York: Palgrave MacMillan, 1999.

Tricks, Henry. "Mexico Likely to Make Early IMF Payment." *Financial Times,* 31 August 2000, 11.

———. "Mexico's Fox Gets the European Red Carpet." *Financial Times,* 29 September 2000, 29.

Truett, Dale B., and Lila J. Truett. "Government Policy and the Export Performance of the Mexican Automobile Industry." *Growth and Change* 25 (Summer 1994): 301–324.

Tsebelis, George. *Nested Games: Rational Choice in Comparative Politics.* Berkeley: University of California Press, 1990.

Tulsa World. "Mexico's NAFTA Boom Cools Off." *Tulsa World,* 30 November 2003, E7.

United Nations Conference on Trade and Development (UNCTAD). "FDI Policies for Development: National and International Perspectives." In *World Investment Report 2003,* Chapter 2, 33–80. New York and Geneva: United Nations, 2003.

United States International Trade Commission (USITC). *Production Sharing: Use of U.S. Components and Materials in Foreign Assembly Operations, 1992–1995.* Washington, DC: USITC, 1997.

Urquidi, Víctor L. "The Prospects for Economic Transformation in Latin America: Opportunities and Resistances." *LASA Forum* 22, no. 3 (1991): 1–9.

Villarreal, René, and Rocío Villarreal. *México Competitivo 2020: Un Modelo de Competitividad Sistemática para el Desarrollo.* Mexico City: Océano, 2002.

Villegas Cárdenas, Claudia. "La economía, rehén de la inversión externa." *Proceso,* no. 1327, 6 April 2002.

Wada, Takeshi. "Economic Restructuring, Political Liberalization, and Shifting Patterns of Popular Protest in Mexico." Unpublished paper, Department of Sociology, Columbia University, New York, 2002.

Weiner, Tim. "A Grand Plan Meets Skepticism in Mexico's South." *New York Times,* 2 July 2001, A3.

———. "Mexico Now Appears to be Developing the Politics of Stalemate." *New York Times,* 14 May 2002, A4.

Whitehead, Laurence. "Political Change and Economic Stabilization: The 'Economic Solidarity Pact'." In *Mexico's Alternative Political Futures,* edited by Wayne A. Cornelius, Judith Gentlemen, and Peter H. Smith, 181–214. La Jolla: Center for U.S.-Mexican Studies, University of California–San Diego, 1989.

———. "The Drama of Democratization." *Journal of Democracy* 10, no. 4 (1999): 84–98.

Wise, Carol. "Mexico's Democratic Transition: The Search for New Reform Coalitions." In *Post-Stabilization Politics in Latin America: Competition, Transition, Collapse,* edited by Carol Wise and Riordan Roett, with Guadalupe Paz, 159–198. Washington, DC: Brookings Institution Press, 2003.

————. *Reinventing the State: Economic Strategy and Institutional Change in Peru.* Ann Arbor: University of Michigan Press, 2003.

Wolffe, Richard. "The Harsh Realities of 'Amigo Diplomacy.'" *Financial Times,* 7 September 2001, 19.

Woods, Ngaire. "International Financial Institutions and the Mexican Crisis." In *The Post-NAFTA Political Economy: Mexico and the Western Hemisphere,* edited by Carol Wise, 148–167. University Park: Pennsylvania State University Press, 1998.

World Bank. *The East Asian Miracle.* New York: Oxford University Press, 1993.

————. *World Development Indicators* (WDI). Data Query, Argentina, Brazil, and Mexico, Exports of Goods and Services (% GDP), 2001. Available online at www.worldbank.org/data/dataquery.html, last accessed March 2004.

————. "Mexico Urban Development: A Contribution to a National Urban Strategy." Report No. 22525-ME, Vol. 1: Main Report, July 15, 2002.

————. "Mexico: Country Brief." Available online at www.worldbank.org, last accessed March 2004.

Zapata, Francisco. "NAFTA: Few Gains for Mexico's Workers." *Perspectives on Work* 6, no. 1 (2002): 22–24.

Zavala de Cosío, María Eugenia. *Cambios de fecundidad en México y políticas de población.* Mexico City: Fondo de Cultura Económica, 1992.

The Contributors

Russell Crandall is assistant professor of political science at Davidson College and adjunct professor of Latin American Studies at the Paul H. Nitze School of Advanced International Studies (SAIS) of the Johns Hopkins University.

Gary Gereffi is professor of sociology as well as of markets and management studies at Duke University; he is also adjunct professor at Duke's Center for International Development Research in the Sanford Institute of Public Policy.

Martha A. Martínez is a graduate student in the Department of Sociology at Duke University.

Manuel Pastor is professor of Latin American and Latino studies and director of the Center for Justice, Tolerance and Community at the University of California–Santa Cruz.

Guadalupe Paz is assistant director of the Latin American Studies Program at the Paul H. Nitze School of Advanced International Studies (SAIS) of the Johns Hopkins University.

Federico Reyes-Heroles is a writer and political commentator. He is also a professor at the Facultad de Filosofía y Letras at the Universidad Nacional Autónoma de México (UNAM) in Mexico City.

Riordan Roett is Sarita and Don Johnston Professor and director of the Latin American Studies Program and of Western Hemisphere Studies at the Paul H. Nitze School of Advanced International Studies (SAIS) of the Johns Hopkins University.

Javier Santiso is chief economist for Latin America at the Banco Bilbao Vizcaya Argentaria (BBVA) in Madrid.

Andreas Schedler is professor of political science at the Centro de Investigación y Docencia Económicas (CIDE) in Mexico City.

Carol Wise is associate professor at the School of International Relations at the University of Southern California.

Index

Accountability: institutional transparency, 95; judicial review of electoral institutions, 30–31; oversight of electoral system, 23–24
Administrative capacity, 117(n38)
Age and party support, 43
Agriculture, 135; agrarian reform, 48; decline in, 41, 47–49; EU FTA, 180; FDI in Mexico, 1994–2002, 125(fig.); job losses in, 141; NAFTA's impact on, 132–133; southern dependence on, 46
Aguilar Zinser, Adolfo, 167
Airplane manufacturing, 149(n61)
Albania, 13
Alemán, Miguel, 65
Antidemocratic restrictions, 16
Apparel manufacturing, 78, 129–130, 137
Approval rating, 64, 110
Argentina: Brazil–Mexico bilateral trade agreement, 162–163; capital flight, 75; EU investment, 175–176; export diversification, 128; export statistics, 146(n19); foreign direct investment, 173; GDP statistics, 141; global investment trends, 183; Spanish investment in, 177; world trade share, 186(n5)
Asia, 78, 119, 142, 144(n4), 175
A. T. Kearney, 183
Authoritarianism, electoral, 10–13

Automotive industry, 126, 128, 129–131, 137, 162
Autonomy, 111, 132

Bailouts, banking sector, 71–72, 97, 108–109
Banacci-Banamex, 179, 184
Banco Bilboa Vizcaya Argentaria (BBVA), 176–179
Banco Santander Central Hispano (BSCH), 176–179
Bank for International Settlements (BIS), 70
Bank of America, 184
Banking sector: crisis and bailout, 71–72, 97, 108–109; foreign direct investment, 125(fig.), 135; Mexican population's involvement with, 115(n7); Spanish investment, 177–179, 186(n11)
Bartra, Armando, 160
El Barzón, 71
Bay of Pigs, 166
BBVA. *See* Banco Bilboa Vizcaya Argentaria
Belize, 160
Bilateral trade agreements, 161–162. *See also* EU FTA; NAFTA
Biodiversity, 49
Bolivia: Mexico's free trade agreements, 122(fig.)

221

Border concerns: maquiladora placement, 137, 138; regional integration, 159–161; U.S. refusal to comply with NAFTA terms, 133–134; U.S.–Mexico bilateral agenda, 155–158
Borrón y Cuenta Nueva (New and Clean Account) program, 80
Bracero Program, 76
Brazil: EU investment, 175–176; export diversification, 128; export statistics, 146(n19); foreign direct investment, 173; GDP statistics, 141; global investment trends, 183–184; Mexico's foreign policy, 161–163; Spanish investment in, 177; vying for leadership position, 167
Breweries, 181–182
BSCH. *See* Banco Santander Central Hispano
Bureaucratic authoritarianism, 10
Burgos natural gas field, 82
Bush, George W., 105, 153, 155, 157–158, 165
Business sector, 103–104, 116(n19)

CAFTA (U.S.–Central American Free Trade Agreement), 147(n37)
Cambodia, 147(n37)
Campaign finance reform, 192
Camus, Albert, 32
Canada: automotive exports, 131; bilateral trade agreements, 121–122; energy demand, 145(n6); exports to, 135; GDP statistics, 141; industrial upgrading, 127; Mexico's exports by destination, 1990–2000, 136(fig.); Mexico's free trade agreements, 122(fig.)
Capital flight, 75
Cárdenas, Cuauhtémoc, 43, 44, 100
Cardoso, Fernando Henrique, 161
Caribbean Conference on Maritime Borders, 158
Castañeda, Jorge, 156–157, 164, 165
Castro, Fidel, 165
Cement producers, 181
Cemex, 181
Central America, 147(n37), 159–161. *See also* individual countries
Centrists, 43
Chamber of Deputies, 50–51, 56(n28), 61–62. *See also* Congress, Mexican
Changarros, 104, 116(n24)
Chávez, Hugo, 165

Chiapas rebellion, 47, 111
Chile: export diversification, 128; export statistics, 146(n19); GDP statistics, 141; global investment trends, 183; market reforms, 94–95; Mexico's free trade agreements, 122(fig.); Spanish investment in, 177, 187(n15); world trade share, 186(n5)
China, People's Republic of, 78, 142, 175
Chrétien, Jean, 155
Cinturones de miseria (economic misery belts), 106
Citigroup Bank, 179, 184
Citizen organizations, 51–52, 55(n8)
Clinton, Bill, 70
Clothing industry. *See* Apparel manufacturing
Coalitions: Fox's need to establish, 64, 74; instituting political reform, 112; transition without coalition, 91–92
COCOPA (Commission for Peace and Reconciliation), 111
Colombia: Mexico's free trade agreements, 122(fig.); peace process, 154, 159; Spanish investment in, 187(n15)
Colosio, Luis Donaldo, 68
Comisión de Concordia y Pacificación (COCOPA), 111
Commission for Peace and Reconciliation (COCOPA), 111
Communications industry, 125(fig.), 176–177, 177, 186(n11), 187(n15)
Community services: FDI in Mexico, 1994–2002, 125(fig.)
Competition, cycles of, 15–16
Competitive oligarchy, 34(n18)
Competitiveness, economic, 62–63, 77–79, 193
Conflict resolution, 23–24, 28–31, 47
Congress, Mexican: energy privatization, 82; fiscal reform bills, 108–109; hostility towards Fox, 64; indigenous rights bill, 111; opposition to Fox's economic reforms, 74; PRI-held seats, 91; response to September 11 terrorism, 156–157. *See also* Chamber of Deputies
Congress, U.S., 105, 156, 158
Consumption, 68
Contingent consent of opposition parties, 14, 34(n26)
Corn, 48–49, 133
Corporatism, 51, 55(n8), 80, 110
Corruption, 104–105, 110

Costa Rica: Mexico's free trade agreements, 122(fig.); Spanish investment in, 187(n15)
Credit market access, 194
Crespo, José Antonio, 111
Cuba, 158–159, 163–165
Culture, 52–53
Currency devaluation, 66, 69–71, 120
Current account balance, 67–68, 71, 72

De la Madrid, Miguel, 66, 93, 96, 119–120
Debt: Clinton loan, 70; defalcation, 66; drop under Zedillo, 73; ISI economy, 65–66; from ISI to export expansion, 119–120; prepaying external debt, 76; private, 71
Dedazo, 96
Defense policy, 165–167
Definitive reform, Zedillo's, 36(n36)
Democracy as factor in Cuba-Mexico relations, 164
Democratic consolidation, 25–26, 32(n1), 192
Democratic transition, 192
Democratization: complex nature of reforms under, 191–192; by election, 9–10; electoral manipulation and nested games, 13–14; end of political exceptionalism, 10–11; transition from electoral authoritarianism, 35(n33)
Demographic dividend, 54
Demographics: jobs and labor market dynamics, 141; poverty, 44–45; providing economic and political challenges, 40–42; unemployment, 47
Dependency theory, 134–137
Development: market-based development, 92, 94–95; rural development bill, 110; social development, 65. See also Export-oriented development; Import-substitution industrialization
Díaz, Porfirio, 39, 48
Diminished subtypes of democracy, 12
Dispute resolution, 23(table)
Diversification of foreign investment, 173–174
Doha Round of WTO negotiations, 163
Dollar-pegged exchange rate, 93
Domestic savings, 72
Dominican Republic, 166, 187(n15)
Drug traffic, 160–161

Echeverría, Luis, 36(n36), 65

Economic crisis, 65–66
Economic cycles, 135–136
Economic-exchange-rate stability, 68
Economic growth, 193; under Fox administration, 158; Fox administration policies to spur, 101–105, 102(fig.); Mexico's economic performance, 1990–2001, 121(fig.); U.S. economic downturn, 136–137
Economic integration, 80, 161
Economic landscape, 40; decline in agriculture, 47–49; demographic dynamics, 40–42; impact of September 11 terrorism, 156–157; macro and microeconomics, 92–94; Mexico's economic performance, 1990–2001, 121(fig.); political competition stifling reform efforts, 113–114; 2000 election and, 191; undocumented workers, 155–156
Economic liberalization, 64–73
Economic Partnership, Political Coordination and Cooperation Agreement (Global Agreement), 179–180, 188(n26)
Economic reform and policy: democratic politics and, 98–101; under Fox, 62–64; Fox's structural economic reform, 73–82; micro and macroeconomic tasks, 94; neoliberal reforms, 66–68; political competition stifling reform efforts, 113–114; PRI's economic decline, 90–91; reducing income inequality, 105–110; removing pre-democracy structures, 63; under Salinas, 66–69; social and economic considerations, 95–96; spurring economic growth and employment expansion, 101–105; state- and market-sponsored strategies, 94–95; under Zedillo, 69–73; Zedillo-Fox transition, 62–63
Economics-based policymaking, 92
Education, 191; affecting economic development, 49–51; government spending addressing income inequality, 107; need for investment in, 104
EFTA (European Free Trade Association), 122(fig.)
Ejército Popular Revolucionario (EPR), 47
Ejército Zapatista de Liberación Nacional (EZLN), 47, 110–111, 160
Ejidos (government distributed agricultural land), 48

El Salvador: Mexico's free trade agreements, 122(fig.); Spanish investment in, 187(n15)
Election standoffs, 31
Elections: cycles of reform, 17–24; democratic quality, 26–29; democratization by election, 9–10; end of political exceptionalism, 10–11; managed elections, 11–13; nested games, 13–14; predicting the 2006 results, 112–113; suffrage restrictions, 34(n18); virtuous circles, 14–15; volatile vote, 43–44
Elections, mid-term: mid-term redistribution of seats, 112–113; PRD comeback, 99–100; PRI's mid-term gains, 91; PRI's response to Fox's policies, 61–62; questioning Fox's leadership, 154
Electoral authoritarianism: increasing party competition, 15–16; magnitude and speed of transition from, 35(n33); nested games, 13–14; transition to democratic consolidation, 11–13
Electoral competition, 9
Electoral reform: access to resources, 19(table); access to the party system, 18(table); election management body, 22(table); electoral dispute settlement, 23(table); electoral organization, 21(table); Fox's ignoring, 111; PRI conflict with IFE and TEPJF, 28–31; rules of representation, 20(table); test of alternation of power, 24–26; transition from authoritarianism to democratic consolidation, 9, 17–24; Zedillo's attempt to build durable electoral institutions, 26–29
Electoral Tribunal of the Judicial Power of the Federation (TEPJF). See TEPJF
Electricity industry, 81–82, 109, 158, 176–177, 185
Electronics industry, 137
Elite control, 11–13
Employment, 101–105, 103(fig.), 140–142
Endesa, 176–177
Energy: electricity industry, 81–82, 109, 158, 176–177, 185; energy demand for North America, 145(n6); liberalization of investment flows, 123–124; liberalizing energy sector to increase revenue, 108. See also Petroleum industry

Enersis, 176–177
Environmental issues, 42
Ethiopia, 13
EU FTA (Mexico–EU Free Trade Agreement), 121, 174, 179–182, 194
European Union (EU): EU FTA, 168–169, 174, 179–182, 194; Latin American investment, 175–179; Mexico's free trade agreements, 122(fig.)
Exceptionalism, political, 10–11
Exchange rate: Exchange rate between the Peso and the U.S. Dollar and Mexico's rate of inflation, 69(fig.); exchange-rate stability, 68–69; floating exchange-rate system, 72; Fox's economic policies, 75; pegging to U.S. dollar, 93
Export industry: domestic linkages, 101–102; export-oriented development strategy, 123–124; export promotion, 89; export statistics, 135; Fox's need to consolidate, 63; industrial upgrading of, 124–131; macroeconomic stability under Fox, 74–75; manufactured goods, 146(n20); Mercosur statistics, 146(n19); shift from primary products to manufactured goods, 126–129; trade indicators, 123(fig.). See also NAFTA
Export markets, 49
Export-oriented development: emergence of, 120–124; increasing inequality under, 139–140; from ISI to export expansion to reduce debt, 119–120; jobs and labor market dynamics, 140–142; technological dependence, 134

FDI Confidence Index, 183, 184
Federal Electoral Institute. See Instituto Federal Electoral
Fertility rate, 40
First Past the Post system of voting, 20(table)
Fiscal reform, 107–110, 194–195
Fishery industry, 180
Floating-exchange-rate system, 72
Fobaproa, 72
Fondo Bancario de Protección al Ahorro (Fobaproa). See Fobaproa
Foreign capital investment, 67–68
Foreign direct investment (FDI), 194; 1994–2002 statistics, 125(fig.); banking sector, 177–179; current account balance, 72; dependency theory, 134–135; EU FTA's influence on, 182;

EU investment in Latin America, 173; export-oriented economic model, 123–124; global economic downturn, 89–90; global investment trends, 182–185; impact of maquiladora industry, 78; increasing inequality, 140; inflow statistics, 145(n8); levels at Zedillo-Fox transition, 101; maquiladoras, 138; Mexico's high levels of, 175; regional export profiles, 128–129; under Salinas, 67–69; Spanish investment in Latin America, 176–179
Foreign exchange reserves, 70(fig.)
Foreign investment, 69–71; EU FTA, 181; Foreign investment flows to Mexico, 1990–2002, 90(fig.); petroleum and natural gas, 82; portfolio investment, 67–68, 72, 89, 90(fig.); private and public investment in Mexico, 1980–2000, 102(fig.); Standard & Poor's rating, 75–76; sustaining investor confidence, 173
Foreign investment flows to Mexico, 1990–2002, 90(fig.)
Foreign policy: Cuba, 163–165; Fox's policy initiatives, 195; importance of NAFTA and U.S. to Mexico's economy, 168; increasing Mexico's international involvement and stature, 158–159, 165–167; Mexico–U.S. bilateral agenda, 154–158; regional integration in Central America and southern Mexico, 159–161; South America, 161–163
Foundational elections, 14
Fox, Vicente, 44; alternation of power, 24–26; approval rating, 64, 110; on defense policy, 167; divided political structure, 192; economic growth and employment expansion, 101–105; economic policy and need for reforms, 62–64; EU trade potential, 168–169; fiscal reform, 194–195; G-3 countries, 158–159; Iraq stance, 169–170; macroeconomic stability under, 74–76; microeconomic policies, 93–94; need for strong leadership, 83; overcoming public disapproval over lacklustre performance, 98–101; political compromise, 114; pursuing political reform, 110–113; reducing income inequality, 105–110; South American policy and relations, 161–163; structural economic reform, 73–82; technocrat and político styles, 96–98; U.S.–Mexico bilateral agenda, 156–157
Fraud, electoral, 17–24
Free trade agreements, 122(fig.), 193–194; attracting FDI, 183; EU FTA, 179–182. See also EU FTA; NAFTA
Free Trade Area of the Americas (FTAA), 154, 162, 163, 169, 195
Fuerzas Armadas Revolucionarias del Pueblo (FARP), 47

G-3 countries, 154
Gag rules, 31
General Agreement on Tariffs and Trade (GATT), 121, 145(n8)
General Electric, 149(n61)
Geography as factor for FDI, 183–184
Global Agreement, 179–180, 188(n26)
Global economy: Castro on, 165; downturn in, 158; EU FTA, 179, 181; Fox's policy goals, 195; global investment trends, 182–185; radical groups' rejection of Mexican involvement, 47
Globalization, 40, 142, 170. See also NAFTA
Gómez García, Manuel, 133–134
Gordillo, Elba Esther, 74
Government Audit Office, 110
Green, Rosario, 164
Greenspan, Alan, 68
Gross domestic product (GDP): economic growth, 102(fig.), 140–141; exports, 123–124, 126; financing deficit, 72; ISI years, 65; Mexico's economic performance, 1990–2001, 121(fig.); peso devaluation and, 120; petroleum exports, 175
Gross national product (GNP), 93
Grupo Bimbo, 182
Grupo Modelo, 181–182
Guatemala, 122(fig.), 160, 187(n15)
Guerrilla groups, 47, 159

Health spending, 107
Hegemonic party system, 10–11
Hispanic Americans, 158
Honduras: Mexico's free trade agreements, 122(fig.)
HSBC Holdings, 184
Human capital, 94, 105–110, 191

Illiteracy, 45

Immigration, 191; proposals for U.S.-Mexico policy, 116(n32); U.S.–Mexico immigration reform, 155–158. *See also* Border concerns

Import-substitution industrialization (ISI): economic boom and bust, 65–66; from ISI to export expansion to reduce debt, 119–120; Latin American trends away from, 127–128; microeconomic nature of, 92–93; social roots of, 95

Import tariffs, 65, 161–163

Imports, 123(fig.); expansion of, 123–124; maquiladora materials inputs, 138

Income distribution, 141

Income inequality, 99(fig.), 105–110, 107(fig.), 137, 139–140

Independent election body, 23–24

Indigenous population, 45–46, 56(n21), 160

Indigenous rights bill, 110–111

Industrial goods, 180

Industrial upgrading of export industries, 124–131

Industrialization, 39–40, 41–42, 64–66

Inequality. *See* Income inequality

Infant mortality, 45

Inflation, 69–70, 69(fig.), 72, 124

Infrastructure, 42, 45, 47, 77

Institute for the Protection of Bank Savings (IPAB), 108

Institutional reform, 17–24

Institutional revolution, 9, 10–11

Institutional Revolutionary Party (PRI). *See* PRI

Instituto Federal Electoral (IFE), 24; Electoral Reforms in Mexico, 1973–1996: Electoral Dispute Settlement, 23(table); Electoral Reforms in Mexico: Access to Resources, 19(table); Electoral Reforms in Mexico: Access to the Party System, 18(table); independence from the government, 24; PRI conflict with TEPJF and IFE, 28–31

Instituto para la Protección al Ahorro Bancario (IPAB), 108

Intellectual property rights, 128, 180

Inter-American Democratic Charter, 164

Inter-American Reciprocal Assistance Treaty (Rio Treaty), 166–167

Interest rates, 71, 76, 76(fig.)

International Monetary Fund (IMF), 70, 73, 95

Intersecretarial Commission for Industrial Policy, 103

Intersectoral shifts in industry, 126–129

Intrasectoral shifts in industry, 129–131

Investment. *See* Foreign direct investment; Foreign investment

Investment liberalization, 180

Iraq, U.S. invasion of, 167, 169–170

Israel: Mexico's free trade agreements, 122(fig.)

J-curve, 71

Jordan, 147(n37)

Judicial review of electoral institutions, 30–31

Judicialization of conflict resolution, 23–24, 28–31

Labor force: corporatism, 55(n8), 80; domestic labor market reform, 104–105; maquiladora demographics, 137–138; modernization, 39–40; need for economic growth, 193; undocumented workers in the U.S., 155–158; union labor, 41, 104–105, 112, 158; youth as source of skilled labor, 175. *See also* Maquiladora sector

Lafer, Celso, 162

Lamy, Pascal, 182

Land demands and distribution, 41, 48, 160

Language, 53

Law of People's Savings and Credit, 110

Leadership, need for, 63–64, 158, 170

Leftists, 43

Ley de Ahorro y Crédito Popular, 110

Liberalization, 119–120

Loans, 70

Local government, 44, 50–51

López Obrador, Andrés Manuel, 44, 100, 113

López Portillo, José, 66

Macroeconomics: EU FTA, 182; Fox administration policies, 62, 63, 74–76, 101; income distribution, 106; shifting from microeconomics and back, 92–94

Madero, Francisco I., 39

Madrazo, Roberto, 99

Managed elections, 12, 13–14

Manufacturing industry: apparel and automotive industries, 129–131; export categories, 146(n20); FDI distribution, 125(fig.), 135; increasing jobs, 141–142; industrial upgrading from primary products to manufactured goods, 126–129; primary products and manufactured goods, 126–129. *See also* Maquiladora sector

Maquiladora sector, 149(n57); dependence on U.S. economy, 75; description of, 145(n10); domestic linkages, 101–102; employment statistics, 103(fig.); end of the program, 86(n35); job loss and recession, 124; job statistics, 142; loss of jobs, 193; The Maquiladora Industry in Mexico, 1990–2002, 139(table); NAFTA's impact on, 137–139; success breeding obstacles, 76–79

Marcos, Subcomandante, 160

Market-based development, 92, 94–95

Martens, Ernesto, 82

Maternal mortality, 45

Mayan Institute, 160

Media, 19(table)

Mercosur, 146(n17), 186(n1); Brazil–Mexico bilateral trade agreement, 162–163; EU investment, 175, 178, 186(n11); export diversification, 128; foreign direct investment, 173; NAFTA and, 161

Mestizo population, 56(n21)

Mexican Revolution, 39

Mexico–EU Free Trade Agreement. *See* EU FTA

Mexico's economic performance, 1990–2001, 121(fig.)

Mexico's international trade: main indicators (1991–2002), 123(fig.)

Microcrises, economic, 71

Microeconomic restructuring, 103–104

Microeconomics, 62, 92–94

Mid-term elections. *See* Elections, mid-term

Middle class, 39, 51, 68

Migration. *See* Immigration

Military action, 166

Military control, 15, 160

Ministry of Social Development (SEDESOL), 117(n38)

Ministry of the Interior (SEGOB), 18(table)

Misery belts, 106

Monetary policy, 75–76

Monreal, Ricardo, 100

Montaño, Jorge, 171(n11)

Monterrey Conference, 164–165

Moody's rating, 175

Multiparty competition, 15–16

Muñoz Leos, Raúl, 81

NAFTA (North American Free Trade Agreement), 173, 186(n8); apparel and automotive industries, 129–131; competitiveness of maquiladora industry, 63; criticisms of, 131–132; dependency theory, 134–137; expansion to the Southern Cone countries, 153; FDI statistics, 145(n8); impact on southern agricultural economy, 46; importance to Mexico's economic transformation, 121–123; increasing inequality under, 139–140; influence on Mexico's economy, 175–176; jobs and labor market dynamics, 140–142; liberalization of investment flows, 123–124; maquiladora issues, 137–139; maquiladoras, 145(n10); Mercosur and, 161; Mexico's cultural and economic profile, 167–170; Mexico's need to decrease economic dependence on the U.S., 193; migrant labor and, 105; pulling economy out of recession, 71; Salinas's implementation of, 67; sectoral grievances, 132–134; terms in, 148(n38); U.S. refusal to comply with NAFTA terms, 133–134

National Action Party (PAN). *See* PAN

National Education, Health, and Nutrition Program, 96, 105–106

National Peasants Confederation, 110

National Solidarity Program, 96, 106

Nationalism, 52–53

NATO agreement, 167

Natural gas, 82

Natural resources, 45–46, 81–82, 160. *See also* Petroleum industry

Neoliberal reforms, 66–68

Nested games, 13–14, 35(n27)

New and Clean Account program, 80

New York Times, 158

Nicaragua: Mexico's free trade agreements, 122(fig.); Spanish investment in, 187(n15)

North American Development Bank, 155

North American Free Trade Agreement (NAFTA). *See* NAFTA

North American summit, 155

North/south divide: demographics of poverty, 45–46; education levels, 49; Maquiladora Industry in Mexico, 1990–2002, 139(table); maquiladora relocation, 138–139; maquiladora sector's impact on, 77; Puebla-Panama

Plan, 159–160; south's lack of
infrastructure, 47

One-party hegemony, 10–11
Opposition parties, 44
Organization for Economic Cooperation
and Development (OECD), 97, 173
Organization of American States (OAS),
164, 166–167
Oversight of electoral system, 23–24, 30–31

PAN (Partido Acción Nacional): Cuba-
Mexico relations, 164; mid-term
election losses, 61–62, 91–92, 100,
194–195; PRI's election complaints,
28–29; PRI's electoral fraud, 17; rise of
citizen organizations, 51–52; stalemate
over fiscal reform bills, 108–109;
transition from authoritarianism to
democratic consolidation, 16
Panama, Spanish investment in, 187(n15)
Partido Acción Nacional (PAN). See PAN
Partido Revolucionario Institucional (PRI).
See PRI
Partido Socialista Unificado de México
(PSUM), 43
Passports, 155
Patronage system, 64, 67
Peasant sector: corporatism, 55(n8);
decrease in, 41; land distribution,
47–48; rural development bill, 110;
social condition, 44–45
Pemex, 81–82, 112
People's Revolutionary Army (EPR), 47
Peru, 35(n33), 94–95, 177
Peso crisis, 66, 70(fig.), 93, 96, 120,
134–135
Petroleum industry: export profile, 127;
fraction of total exports, 175; illicit
campaign contributions, 112; ISI
development model, 65, 119; Puebla-
Panama Plan, 160; reforms, 81–82;
revenue base, 107; Spanish investment
in Latin America, 177; Zedillo's
policies, 73
Plan Colombia, 159
Plurinomial deputies, 56(n28)
Poland, 10
Political landscape, 40; competition stifling
reform efforts, 113–114; democratic
politics and economic reform, 98–101;
demographic dividend, 54; economic
shift from politics to technology, 96–98;
education levels, 50; politics guiding

economic reform, 73–74; post-election
challenges, 192; PRI's corporatist
structures, 51; radicalization of political
demand, 46–47; rise of citizen
organizations, 51–52; urbanization
determining political values, 42–44
Political reform, 36(n36), 50–51, 110–113,
192
Popular legitimacy of PRI, 16
Popular sector, 55(n8)
Population. See Demographics
Portfolio investment, 67–68, 72, 89,
90(fig.)
Poverty: defined, 56(n20); demographic
dividend, 54; demographics of, 44–45;
environmental concerns, 42; as political
challenge, 41; reducing income
inequality, 105–110
Power, alternation of, 24–26
PRD (Partido de la Revolución
Democrática): indigenous rights bill,
111; mid-term election gains, 61–62, 91,
99–100; political shifts in the
population, 43; rise of citizen
organizations, 51–52; stalemate over
fiscal reform bills, 108–109
Presidency, 25
PRI (Partido Revolucionario Institucional):
conflict with IFE and TEPJF, 28–31;
Cuba-Mexico relations, 164; democratic
politics and economic reform, 98–19;
demographics and declining support,
42; economic decline, 90–91; electoral
fraud and electoral reform, 17–24,
22(table); increasing party competition
to undermine, 16; indigenous rights bill,
111; inhibiting growth of citizen
organizations through corporatism, 51;
macroeconomic strategies, 93; mid-term
election gains, 61–62, 91–92, 99–100;
opposition to Fox's economic reforms,
74; petroleum industry reforms, 82;
regime change without loss of
government power, 25; rise of citizen
organizations, 51–52; stalemate over
fiscal reform bills, 108–109; transition
from authoritarianism, 9–10; VAT
streamlining, 80
Primary products, 126–129, 132–133
Privatization, 67, 81–82, 108, 179
Programa Nacional de Educación, Salud y
Alimentación. See PROGRESA
Programa Nacional de Solidaridad. See
PRONASOL

PROGRESA (Programa Nacional de Educación, Salud y Alimentación), 96, 105–106
PRONASOL (Programa Nacional de Solidaridad), 96, 106
PSUM (Unified Socialist Party of Mexico), 43
Public services, 45
Puebla-Panama Plan (PPP), 159–160, 164, 166
Puerto Rico, Spanish investment in, 187(n15)

Radical left, 43
Radicalism, 54
Radicalization of political demand, 46–47
Recession, 70–71, 93–94, 101, 124
Reform, economic. See Economic reform and policy
Reform, electoral. See Electoral reform
Reforms: agrarian, 48; campaign finance, 192; electoral, 111; fiscal, 107–110, 194–195; immigration, 155–158; petroleum and electricity, 81–82; political, 36(n36), 50–51, 110–113, 192; second-generation, 191–192; tax reform, 79–80
Regional diplomacy, 154
Regional economies, 77; export diversification, 128
Regional government, 44, 50–51
Regional integration, 159–161
Religious organizations, 52
Repsol, 176–177
Resolution Trust Corporation, 72
Revenue, 79–81, 107–110, 176–177
Revolutionary Armed Forces of the People (FARP), 47
Revolutions and insurgencies: Chiapas rebellion, 47, 111; political myths about Mexico, 39–40; potential rise of guerrilla groups, 47
Rice, Condoleezza, 156, 165
Rightists, 43
Rio Treaty (1947), 166–167
Rural development bill, 110
Russian Federation, 13

Salinas de Gortari, Carlos: dedazo (handpicking of), 96; economic policy, 66–68, 93; from ISI to export expansion to reduce debt, 119–120; social issues under, 106
San Salvador summit, 159

Savings Protection Banking Fund. See Fobaproa
Scandals, political, 68, 80–81
SECODAM (Secretariat of the Comptroller and Administrative Development), 110
SECOFI (Secretaría de Comercio y Fomento Industrial), 103
Second-generation reform, 113, 191–192
Secretaría de Comercio y Fomento Industrial (SECOFI), 103
Secretaría de Desarrollo Social (SEDESOL), 117(n38)
Secretaría de la Contraloría y Desarrollo Administrativo (SECODAM), 110
Secretaría de la Función Pública, 110
Secretaría de Seguridad Pública (SSP), 110
Secretariat of Economy, 103
Secretariat of Public Security (SSP), 110
Secretariat of the Comptroller and Administrative Development (SECODAM), 110
Security, 110
SEDESOL (Secretariat of Social Development), 117(n38)
SEGOB (Secretariat of the Interior), 18(table)
September 11, 2001, 105, 153–157, 166–167, 195
Serbia, 35(n33)
Services sector, 39–40
Silent political revolution, 192
Small and medium-sized firms (SMEs), 103–104, 116(n19)
Social considerations, 95–96, 105–110
Social development, 65
Social investment, 96
Social justice, 95
Social landscape, 40–42, 44–46, 77, 193
Social needs, 193
Social security, 117(n42)
Social spending, 105–110
Socialist Party, 43
Socially motivated policymaking, 92
South America, 161–163. See also Mercosur; individual countries
Southern Cone countries, 153, 162–163
Spain, 173, 176–179, 186(n11)
Stagflation, 65
Stalemate, politics of, 158
Standard & Poor's rating, 75–76
State-sponsored development, 92, 94–95
Steel tariffs, 74
Stock market laws, 110

Structural economic reform, 73–82
Suffrage restrictions, 34(n18)
Supreme Court, Mexican, 82, 104–105
Symbolism, political, 110
Systems integrators, 135, 147(n35)

Tariffs: conditions of EU FTA, 180; GATT,
    121, 145(n8); import, 65, 161–163;
    motor vehicles, 162–163; steel, 74
Taxation, 117(n42); evasion, 79–80;
    exemptions, 109; incentives, 116(n23);
    reform, 79–80, 194; revenue, 79–81,
    81–82, 107–110
Taxi drivers, 51
Technocrats, 96–98
Technological dependence, 134
Technology, 149(n61)
Telecommunications industry, 125(fig.),
    176–177, 177, 186(n11), 187(n15)
Telefónica, 176–177, 186(n11), 187(n15)
Téllez, Luis, 73
TEPJF (Tribunal Electoral del Poder
    Judicial de la Federación): electoral
    dispute resolution, 23(table), 24; PRI
    conflict with TEPJF and IFE, 28–31
Terrorism, 153–154, 166–167, 195
Tesobonos (dollar-denominated debt
    instruments), 68–69, 70
Third wave of democratization, 10–11
TPA. See Trade promotion authority
Trade: FDI in Mexico, 1994–2002,
    125(fig.); trade dependence, 134–137;
    trade growth, 182; trade integration, 89
Trade agreements, 161–162;
    Brazil–Mexico bilateral trade
    agreement, 162–163; CAFTA
    (U.S.–Central American Free Trade
    Agreement), 147(n37); Mexico's free
    trade agreements, 122(fig.). See also EU
    FTA (Mexico–EU Free Trade
    Agreement); NAFTA
Trade promotion authority (TPA), 154
Trade relations, 53, 161–163
Transportation industry, 125(fig.), 133–134
Tribunal Electoral del Poder Judicial de la
    Federación (TEPJF). See TEPJF
Two-level games, 35(n27)

UNCTAD. See United Nations Conference
    on Trade and Development
Undocumented workers, 155–156
Unemployment, 45, 47, 124, 193
Unified Socialist Party of Mexico (PSUM),
    43

Unión Fenosa, 176
Union labor, 41, 104–105, 112, 158
United Nations Conference on Trade and
    Development (UNCTAD), 183
United Nations International Conference
    on Financing for Development,
    164–165
United Nations Security Council (UNSC),
    154, 159, 167
United States: Brazil–Mexico bilateral
    trade agreement, 162; Clinton's loans to
    Mexico, 70; Convergence of Mexican
    and U.S. rates, 76(fig.); Cuba-Mexico
    relations, 164–165; Cuba–U.S.
    relations, 163; defense policy, 165–167;
    energy demand, 145(n6); EU FTA
    reducing Mexican dependence on, 181;
    GDP statistics, 141; global investment
    trends, 182–183; immigration policy,
    116(n32); influence on Mexico's
    economy, 175–176; maquiladora sector,
    75, 76–79; Mexico's bilateral agenda,
    154–158; Mexico's economic
    dependence on, 63; Mexico's exports by
    destination, 1990–2000, 136(fig.);
    Mexico's foreign policy, 153; Mexico's
    free trade agreements, 122(fig.);
    Mexico's need to decrease economic
    dependence on, 193; migration issues,
    105; nationalism and the Westernization
    of Mexican culture, 52–53; raising
    interest rates, 68; recession prompting
    Mexican-EU relations, 174; Salinas's
    economic reform, 67; South American
    hostility towards, 163; trade
    dependence, 135–137. See also NAFTA
United States Exchange Stabilization Fund,
    70
Urban flight, 46
Urbanization, 39–40, 41–42
Uruguay: bilateral trade agreements,
    162–163; Spanish investment in,
    187(n15)
U.S.–Central American Free Trade
    Agreement (CAFTA), 147(n37)

Value-added tax (VAT), 80, 109
Velázquez, Fidel, 80
Venezuela: Colombian peace process, 159;
    Mexico's free trade agreements,
    122(fig.); Spanish investment in,
    187(n15)
Villa, Pancho, 48
Violence, 47

Virtuous circles, 14–15
Volatile vote, 43–44

Wages, 77–78, 124, 137, 138, 142
Washington Consensus, 128
Weintraub, Sidney, 149(n61)
Westernization of Mexican culture, 52–53
Women: demographic dividend, 54; as sole family support, 41
World Bank, 44, 56(n20), 144(n2)
World Trade Organization (WTO), 163

Yucatán, 159

Zapata, Emiliano, 48
Zapatista Army for National Liberation (EZLN), 47
Zapatista rebellion, 67
Zedillo, Ernesto: accidental candidacy, 96–97; approval rating, 64; Cuba–Mexico relations, 163–164; economic policy and reform, 62, 69–73; education spending, 104; electoral reform, 26, 36(n36); Pemex privatization, 82

About the Book

Painting a sober yet hopeful picture of current Mexican politics and economics, *Mexico's Democracy at Work* focuses on the country's still incomplete transformation from an authoritarian system, as well as on the many challenges that exist within the new, more democratic context. The authors pay particular attention to both domestic and international economic dynamics and to Mexico's relations with the United States, with its neighbors in Latin America, and with the European Union.

Russell Crandall is assistant professor of political science at Davidson College and adjunct professor at the School of Advanced International Studies (SAIS), Johns Hopkins University. **Guadalupe Paz** is assistant director of the SAIS Latin American Studies Program. **Riordan Roett** is Sarita and Don Johnston Professor of Political Science and director of the Latin American Studies Program and Western Hemisphere Studies at SAIS.